How to Write for Television

Visit our How To website at **www.howto.co.uk**

At **www.howto.co.uk** you can engage in conversation with our authors –
all of whom have 'been there and done that' in their specialist fields. You
can get access to special offers and additional content but most
importantly you will be able to engage with, and become a part of, a
wide and growing community of people just like yourself.

At **www.howto.co.uk** you'll be able to talk and share tips with people
who have similar interests and are facing similar challenges in their lives.
People who, just like you, have the desire to change their lives for the
better – be it through moving to a new country, starting a new business,
growing their own vegetables, or writing a novel.

At **www.howto.co.uk** you'll find the support and encouragement you
need to help make your aspirations a reality.

You can go direct to www.how-to-write-for-televsion.co.uk which is part
of the main How To site.

How To Books strives to present authentic, inspiring,
practical information in their books. Now, when you buy a
title from **How To Books,** you get even more than just words
on a page.

How to Write for Television

A guide to writing and selling successful TV scripts

William Smethurst

howtobooks

Published by How To Books Ltd,
Spring Hill House, Spring Hill Road,
Begbroke, Oxford OX5 1RX. United Kingdom.
Tel: (01865) 375794. Fax: (01865) 379162.
info@howtobooks.co.uk
www.howtobooks.co.uk

How To Books greatly reduce the carbon footprint of their books by sourcing their
typesetting and printing in the UK.

First published in 2000
Second edition 2002
Third edition 2004
Fourth edition 2005
Fifth edition 2007
Sixth edition 2009

British Library Cataloguing in Publication Data
A catalogue record for this book is available from the British Library

ISBN: 978 1 84528 380 3

Produced for How To Books by Deer Park Productions, Tavistock, Devon
Typeset by PDQ Typesetting, Newcastle-under-Lyme, Staffs.
Printed and bound by Cromwell Press Group, Trowbridge, Wiltshire

NOTE: The material contained in this book is set out in good faith for general guidance
and no liability can be accepted for loss or expense incurred as a result of relying in
particular circumstances on statements made in the book. Laws and regulations are
complex and liable to change, and readers should check the current position with the
relevant authorities before making personal arrangements.

Contents

List of Illustrations

The Opportunities

TELEVISION NEEDS *YOU*!

Television is desperately short of writers. Once there was only BBC One and ITV 1, and the only soap opera was *Coronation Street*, which was broadcast just twice a week. Now there are more than a dozen channels commissioning drama, and the soaps – *Coronation Street*, *EastEnders*, *Emmerdale*, together with *Hollyoaks* for teenagers, *Doctors* in the afternoons, and new internet dramas like *Kate Modern* – are putting out three, four, or five episodes a week and between them giving work to well over a hundred writers.

Then there are the one-long series dramas like *Primeval, New Tricks, Waterloo Road, Law and Order UK*. There are, astonishingly, more than 50 of these series either in production or development, and they all need scriptwriters (vibrant, fresh scriptwriters!), and such writers are in very, very short supply. A good new writer on *Casualty*? Word flies round the industry, and before you know it the writer concerned is doing an episode of *Taggart* and the *Casualty* script editors are bitterly complaining about having their writers pinched.

So acute is the writer shortage on series and soaps that the BBC is now paying promising writers – who may not have a single television credit – £400 a week to train as scriptwriters, with guaranteed commissions on *Holby City, Eastenders*, and *Casualty* if

1

they make the grade. (To apply, see Chapter 18.) Script fees across the industry have risen sharply, with *Hollyoaks* now paying £6,300 for a single script (including the omnibus repeat fee), and experienced writers on *The Bill* being paid around £18,000. Even a new, inexperienced (but clearly talented) writer on *Shameless* or *Blue Murder*, can expect £13,500.

There are simply not enough skilled writers to go round. Every year, as the big drama series limber up for production, script editors are stressed, shouted at, and not infrequently sacked, because they cannot find enough skilled writing talent to script their programmes. It is the same story in comedy. Every year the BBC and Channel 4 actively seek out new writers in the hope of finding the next *Gavin and Stacey* or *The Office*.

And this leads to a great puzzle. A mystery more mysterious than even the most deeply mysterious *Lewis* or *Midsomer Murders*. Why, if there is such a shortage of writers, do thousands of would-be writers constantly have their scripts rejected? Why is writing for television seemingly so difficult?

SKILLS AND TECHNIQUES

The first truth, of course, is that writing any kind of drama – theatre, radio, or television – is a skilled craft. It is something that can encompass genius. It is what Shakespeare did, and Ben Jonson, and Molière and Sheridan. It is an activity that requires not only facility with words and skill with structure, but an acute sensitivity regarding people and the way they behave.

A dramatist is an architect, who uses words and pictures instead of bricks and girders to construct an edifice in which every word has its proper place and serves its proper function. To do this skilfully requires techniques and disciplines that no new writer can be expected to know intuitively. Yet out of the 10,000 scripts sent to the BBC each year, only a minority show evidence that the writer has made any attempt at all to study the craft of scriptwriting.

WHAT THE AUDIENCE WANTS

A second truth is that television drama demands more of its writers than most other mediums. Every writer of fiction, be it books, stage plays, or broadcast, is a storyteller, a weaver of tales. But television dramatists must do more than captivate an audience: they must captivate a mass audience. If you write a novel that explores in frightening detail the morality of beekeeping you might find a publisher somewhere willing to print a few copies. If your subject is utterly incomprehensible you might even win a major literary prize.

But this won't do for television. Television – on whatever level – is about entertainment. It may be entertainment of high ambition and cultural value (consider the small but admirable drama output of BBC Four) or entertainment that seeks only to please for a fleeting moment. But every television drama – however literary or demanding its subject – must aim to satisfy millions of people. 'Drama draws people together with its powerful emotions and irresistible storytelling', says the BBC. For any writer, let alone one inexperienced and new to the media, the task of attracting and holding so wide an audience must be daunting.

HIGH COST = HIGH RISK

The high cost of television drama is another factor working against the new, inexperienced writer. Major BBC film drama 'events' (these days often shown over two nights) can cost up to two million pounds to make. An episode of a series like *Law and Order UK* or *Lark Rise to Candleford* will cost anything between £500,000 ('low' price band drama) and £800,000 ('high' price band drama). Even the cost of a half-hour episode of a low-budget soap opera is well over £100,000. An editor has to be very brave to commission an inexperienced writer, however promising, to script a production that is going to cost half-a-million pounds. Inevitably the editor must ask:

- Will the new writer be able to cope with technical problems?
- Will they be able to act on the notes they are given for a second, or third draft?
- Will they become difficult and emotional when script changes urged by the editor and producer are criticised by the executive producer who demands another huge rewrite?
- Will they be able to come up with further rewrites half-way through shooting when the actor playing the lead has been admitted, overnight, to a clinic for alcoholics?

Huge amounts of money are at stake! The competitive edge of the channel against the opposition is at stake! More importantly, the script editor's job is at stake! The temptation is to go with the tried-and-trusted writer. He might be burnt-out and weary unto death, but he will at least deliver a script that is the right length, with the right number of characters, and the right number of scenes.

WORKING IN YOUR FAVOUR

Despite the obstacles, the opportunities are there waiting to be taken. Look at the factors operating in your favour.

- Television drama and situation comedy is a rapidly expanding market.

- Script editors are expected to find new writers. If they fail they risk being sacked. They are as eager to find you as you are to find them.

- Just one programme, the BBC's *Doctors*, will use up to 30 totally new writers in a series.

- Because there is no formal scriptwriter qualification, no 'script school' or college, all new writers start on the outside, and come from diverse and often unlikely backgrounds. A shop assistant in Barrow-in-Furness is just as likely to succeed as a film school graduate in London.

- Comedy writers are in such demand that the BBC runs regular scriptwriting competitions, with script development help and workshops.

- The turnover in existing writers is high. Apart from the normal loss due to age and mortality, television scriptwriters frequently turn to other areas of writing – novels, stage plays – or start up independent production companies and become producers. Others, sadly, find that their scripts are no longer the kind that is wanted.

- Most scripts by new writers are very poor. They are often handwritten, the dialogue dull, the stories repetitive and the plotting obvious. Spelling can be atrocious, and layout careless, with many crossings-out. The urge to write television drama is at its strongest amongst the socially maladjusted – people who cannot cope very well with real life, and seek to live through a fantasy world of their own making. Semi-literates send in scripts – and all too often, the cynic might say, they are accepted. Ninety per cent of scripts can be – and are – mentally dismissed after reading half a page.

■ Few new writers know the type of script they should be writing, or even what to do with their script when they have written it.

How to succeed

In the first place you must write a script that you can show as an example of your writing skills. This script may never be made into a programme – but that doesn't matter, even though it is made with blood, sweat, and tears, and is the joy and pride of your life. This script is your CV. It is known in various script units as a 'calling card' script. Its purpose is to show script editors, agents, and producers, that you have the talent to write dialogue, invent characters, and construct stories. You might be lucky and sell it for production, but it will have done its job brilliantly if it gets you a commission to write an episode of a series drama like *Spooks*, or a soap like *Emmerdale,* or an invitation to join a sitcom workshop.

To impress and excite your script must be:

■ original in concept;
■ well constructed;
■ confidently plotted;
■ have good dialogue;
■ have good characterization;
■ be professionally presented.

In the second place you must learn how to sell your script – and thus sell yourself as a writer. To do this you will need to know:

- the kind of drama that television script editors are looking for;
- the programmes that are actively looking for new writers;
- how to get your script read by the only people who matter: those with the power to commission you to write.

This book is designed to help you to achieve all of these aims. Its first part gives you professional hints on how to write your script – tips that producers, agents, and script editors would give you themselves if they had the time. Its second part gives you the vital inside information you need to actually sell yourself as a writer.

THE REWARDS

In the coming months there will be many, many writers who receive rejection letters. But somewhere there will be a writer – perhaps on the point of giving up hope – who answers the phone one dull, dreary morning and finds himself or herself being told something on the lines of: 'Brilliant script! We're going ahead with it straight away. Contracts department will be on to you about the fee. Can we have lunch tomorrow to talk about casting? We thought of Keira Knightly for the main role, but we'd like your opinion so I've asked her to lunch as well.'

Perhaps that writer will be you.

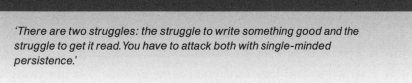

'There are two struggles: the struggle to write something good and the struggle to get it read. You have to attack both with single-minded persistence.'

Christopher McQuarrie, writer of *The Usual Suspects*

1

The Basics

THE CALLING CARD SCRIPT

You are preparing to write a 'calling card' television script that will show your talents as a writer. This script is terribly important: in fact, it's the only thing about you that is important. Nobody in television will care about what you've done in life, or who you are, or who you know, or what your thoughts are about *EastEnders* plotlines these days. All anybody will care about is:

a) can you write?

b) can you write the sort of script I'm looking for?

Your 'calling card' script, as it is known in most script units, is expected to show what you can produce using your own skills, imagination, and judgement. It is the *play that you yourself want to write* and it will be respected as such. That said, and without compromising the script you believe will do justice to your talents, it makes sense to target the market that you ultimately want to write for.

Perhaps you already have a story in your head – some characters – a subject you believe will make a great drama. But how do you know if it is the right sort of script to 'sell' you as a writer? Or how many characters and locations you ought to have? Or how long it ought to be? Before we consider anything else, let us look at the basics:

■ the best length at which to write;

■ the ideal number of characters and locations;

■ the best kind of drama to write.

THE BEST LENGTH AT WHICH TO WRITE

Recognised writing slots are as follows:

■ **Ninety minutes** for major 'event' drama. The advantage of writing a major 90-minute play is that it shows your ability to create characters, to write dialogue, to utilize the camera, and to handle your plot. It also shows that you are capable of sustained writing on a major theme. Major 'event' dramas can be longer than 90 minutes – they can be a two-parter, spread over two consecutive nights' viewing, but it is pointless for a new writer to attempt anything longer than a 90-minute script.

■ **Sixty minutes** for series and serial drama. The advantage of the 60-minute play (only 50 minutes in running time, when advertising breaks and trailers are taken into account) is that it shows the above virtues without requiring script editors to read as much. It also saves you printing and postage costs. And if you are writing to a common theme – e.g. love lost/found/betrayed or the paranormal – it has a faint (but real) chance of being 'packaged' with others in a season of one-hour themed stories.

■ **Thirty minutes** for soap operas and sitcoms. This is not a good length for a calling card drama script. To open, develop, and conclude an original drama in 30 minutes is very difficult.

Other than *Doctors* there are rarely any 30-minute slots for self-contained dramas, and soaps are not interested in reading scripts written for their existing characters/plots. If you are interested in writing a sitcom, however, this is the length to aim for.

- **Ten minutes** for drama 'shorts'. The advantage of writing a 10-minute short is that it is short – and the script editor is therefore more likely to actually read it. It gives a glimpse of your talents without requiring labour and effort. Ten-minute shorts are, though, at the end of the day less convincing than a solid 90 or 60-minute play, they are very difficult to write, and there may not be any 10-minute series in production (and consequently no script editor to read your effort).

THE IDEAL NUMBER OF CHARACTERS AND LOCATIONS

A new writer will generally find it easier to introduce and develop a small group of characters, rather than juggle with a large cast, and it is certainly a kindness to the script reader who is now reading her fourth or fourteenth script of the day. It is also wise for the new writer not to get entangled in location action that involves complex camerawork. That said, there is virtually no market today for plays that involve very few people sitting in a room talking to each other. Today's television audience is blasé and easily bored. Producers who want high viewing figures (i.e. all of them) must try to provide the sort of action and location-shooting common to the cinema and to films made for the video market. Your script (unless it is a sitcom, see Chapter 9) needs to take us out and about, and include visual action. You also stand more chance of success if you give good 'production values' (i.e. provide interesting things to look at) at a relatively low cost. From a budget point of view, a play that has only half-a-dozen principal characters, and takes advantage of, say, the scenic beauty of a nature reserve, a fairground, or perhaps the haunting, sad atmosphere of a seaside resort in winter, is good. A play that requires a cast of thousands, location shooting in Paraguay, and a comet crashing on the Houses of Parliament, is bad. It is true that major drama 'events' have multi-million pound feature-film budgets and can afford global locations, special effects, and large casts, but these films and series are invariably written by experienced writers.

THE BEST KIND OF DRAMA TO WRITE

Some types of drama are more in demand that others. Some are to be avoided by a new writer. Here we look at:

- socially-aware drama;

- human-relationship drama;

- historical drama;

- sci-fi and the paranormal;

- existing series and serials;

- children's drama;

- adaptations;

- comedy drama;

- situation comedy.

Socially-aware drama

The BBC and Channel 4 have traditionally been proud of their reputation for tough, contemporary, socially-aware drama, and there was a time when most one-off television plays had something to tell us about society in Britain. The years of *The Wednesday Play* and *Play for Today* are gone, but a contemporary drama dealing with social issues (e.g. Channel 4's *Sex Traffic* and BBC Two's *White Girl*) is, nevertheless, a good bet. Even if your play is not bought, it will

> *Our drama series need to feel smart and stylish and relevant to the lives and loves of a 25–34-year-old drama audience – 75% of whom have young families and all are asking questions and exploring all areas of adult life.*
>
> BBC Three commissioning brief

most clearly show your ability to write contemporary dialogue and characterization. '*EastEnders, Holby City* and *Casualty* will continue to tackle difficult and sensitive issues' says BBC One. In truth, socially-aware drama does not have to be relentlessly grim and serious: many are written as love stories, comedies (see below), or as thrillers that take us into the world of high finance or environmental disaster. Can you find an area of modern life that has not been exploited by others? Is there something about which you feel strongly? Something you passionately want to write about?

Human relationship drama

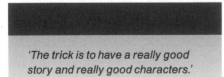

> '*The trick is to have a really good story and really good characters.*'
>
> Writer Lucy Gannon,
> *On Air*, BBC Two

In terms of subject matter you will not go far wrong if you write a story of human relationships: a story of romance, love, sex, and possibly intrigue and betrayal. And if you set it against a background of contemporary life and involve contemporary social issues, your subject matter will have even greater appeal, because you will be combining what the viewers want to see with what the producers and directors want to do. Such a script will show your potential to write for a wide range of soap operas and series dramas. Just as plays about social issues do not have to be relentlessly grim, stories about love do not need to be soft and romantic. Plays in the strand *Love Bites* included a tale of single parents and drug addicts in Glasgow; a searing study of date rape (which included flash-forwards and split screens); and a bitter-sweet comedy about love between a black girl and a white boy. If you're a young writer and want to script programmes like *Skins* or *The Inbetweeners* then human relationships described with wit and humour (dark or otherwise) is what will appeal to script editors. '*The Inbetweeners* delves into the psyche of the British teenage boy and discovers equal amounts of porn, sick and cheap lager', says Channel 4 helpfully.

Historical drama

Avoid unless you have a stunning idea that the programmers cannot resist. Certainly the market is growing, particularly for dramatizations of events in the recent past (e.g. *Einstein and Eddington, Margaret Thatcher: The Long Walk to Finchley* and BBC Two's hugely ambitious *Decades*), and series like *Robin Hood* and *Merlin* have been very successful, whilst *City of Vice* has given us a colourful and sexy cop show in 18th century London. But the expense is great, most historical plays that reach the screen are adaptations (see below), and projects generally originate with programme makers rather than writers. Another problem is that agents and script editors have difficulty assessing your skill with modern dialogue and characterization when you are writing in a period setting.

Sci Fi and the paranormal

Very much in vogue, from a rejuvenated *Dr Who* and its spin off *Torchwood* to *Demons* and *Apparitions*. Subjects and settings can be diverse: BBC One's *Empathy* follows an ex-con whose paranormal visions assist in a murder hunt; *Lifeline* is a supernatural love story. BBC Three's *Being Human* (described by the production company as 'witty, exciting, sexy') is about a werewolf, a vampire, and a ghost sharing a house. If you have a good idea, go for it.

Existing soaps and series

Do not write a script for an existing programme like *Coronation Street*, or *The Bill*, even if you eventually want to write for the programme concerned. Most script editors will not even look at your script – they are interested in your own original talent, not in how well you copy what you see on the screen.

Serials

Most serials are written by one writer. If you have a cracking story that you believe needs telling over several episodes you should write the first episode (60 minutes) and short summaries of the other episodes. Even if the series is not made, it will show your dramatic skills and creativity.

Children's drama

There's quite a lot of it, but the market for new writers is not as great as that for adult series and soaps. If this is your interest, your best bet is to devise a four-part or six-part serial, and write one episode together with synopses of the rest. It might not be accepted, but if your work is liked you will be encouraged and pointed in the direction of children's programmes that use outside writers. Children's drama is almost always low-budget. Independent production companies that do children's programming include Red Kite (*Dennis and Gnasher*), Kudos (*Code 9*), and Dot to Dot Productions.

Adaptations

Although adaptations – particularly of classic novels or detective stories – are frequently made there is no opportunity here for the new writer.

Comedy drama

Very much in demand, but surprisingly little reaches the screen. *At Home with the Braithwaites* scored brilliantly, achieving both a best new drama award and nomination in the British Comedy Awards. ITV's single plays are often comedy drama, and BBC One says it is planning to do more in this area. Writing realistic drama that also makes us laugh is not easy, but if your instincts take you in this direction there is a ready market. A new comedy drama series (e.g. ITV's *Sold)* will have carefully selected writers for its first outing, but if it does well and another series is commissioned there might be oppportunities to join the writing team.

Situation comedy

This is a big market, and the BBC, Channel 4 and ITV are actively looking for new writing talent. See Chapter 9 for specific sitcom writing requirements, and Chapter 13 for information about what programme makers want.

COMMON QUERIES

Is it true that anyone of average ability can learn how to be a scriptwriter?
You must have an aptitude for writing dialogue. Everything else can be learned.

Is it true that you should always write about what you know about?
Generally speaking, yes. But you need to avoid the more obvious situations. Producers get sent a lot of dramas about students living in squalid flats from students living in squalid flats, and about teachers who are sick and tired of teaching from teachers who are sick and tired of teaching. That said, a doctor, nurse, or hospital porter is more likely to write a hospital drama with conviction than a solicitor would. Script editors are impressed – or at the simplest level comforted – if they believe you are writing with inside knowledge. This does not mean that you can't write a drama about life on Saturn unless you've been there; it does mean that you need to know everything there is to know about Saturn and the technology needed to sustain life on it.

The setting and subject do not have to be exotic. Stacking supermarket shelves at night might not be glamorous and exciting, but if your story is well told viewers will be fascinated to know the hidden dramas, rivalries, loves, and routines of supermarket life in the secret hours of the night.

> *BBC Two drama aims to ring true with the big themes in the life of the diverse UK audience. We deliver this through our commitment to the best writing and on-screen talent.*
>
> BBC Two statement of programme policy

How gritty and controversial can I be?
As gritty and controversial as you like. Putting on gritty controversial plays makes BBC and Channel 4 producers feel that they are more than mere hacks in the entertainment business: it makes them feel that they are people of influence in society. In recent years we have seen television dramas about drugs abuse, child abuse, incest, oppression within the family, homosexual oppression, rent boys, transvestites, lesbians, racial tension, prison scandals, mob violence, and corruption. Studies in fidelity, honesty, loyalty, and the happy state of England, however, are only seen on ITV.

So aren't gritty, controversial plays old hat?
Well, possibly. Today's drama heads and commissioning editors are likely to be more concerned with property values in the Ardeche than social values in inner-city Britain, and today's script editors (who are nearly all in their twenties) seem to be apolitical, though healthily interested in sex and money. A play about old-age pensioners dying of hypothermia might make their eyes glaze over, but give them a script called *Lesbian Snogs* and they'll sit up and take an interest right away.

The truth is that they want it all. 'BBC Two drama offers thought-provoking storytelling,' says the BBC. 'We are more than ever committed to drama as entertainment,' says Channel 4.

So make your play thought-provoking *and* entertaining, and everybody will like it.

Are some subjects or settings more likely to be accepted than others?
Yes, but fashions can change very quickly, and all script editors are liable to decide they're sick of buggery plays just as you put the finishing touches to a cracking 90-minutes on the subject. There

might be a leaning towards northern drama series (a successful heart-warming family saga set in the North will be followed by two or three others in similar locations), or there might be a fashion for witty, ironic plays set among young people in London, but by the time you catch the mood of the moment it will have changed, and although it only takes a second on your computer to change 'Iona' to 'Islington' throughout your script, it is unlikely to help you sell it. By the time a drama reaches the screen it might well be three years on from the time when it was proposed, and two years, perhaps, from the time when it was commissioned.

> 'Any series should be based around a bold, provocative idea, covering worlds you have not seen before or from a fresh angle... the target demographic is 16 to 34, but we do not want to make that too exclusive.'
>
> Ben Stephenson, Channel 4 Drama

Both Channel 4 and BBC Three very clearly and openly target younger audiences (after you're 35 you might as well be dead).

The constants, of course, on all channels, are police/detective dramas and medical dramas. Or dramas that cleverly combine both elements.

Is it all right to use 'bad' language if it's realistic and true to character? In moderation, but a surprisingly high percentage of scripts from new writers have characters using crude language, repetitiously, and this doesn't impress script editors, because they are professionals looking for scripts that can be broadcast. (See Chapter 7.)

What if I have a great idea for a series of 30-minute dramas, and don't think the stories will stretch to an hour?
Write to the length you are comfortable with. Script editors would much rather read a good 30-minute script, even if they don't have any 30-minute slots available, than a 60-minute script that rambles about. And there is always the possibility of a 30-minute drama strand being launched in the future (particularly in a low-budget, late-night slot).

Are any drama slots specifically designed for new writing talent?
The BBC provides opportunities for new writers through low-cost drama series like *Doctors* and has an excellent website (*bbc.co.uk/writersroom*) devoted to seeking and nurturing new writing talent. The Writersroom also gives advice on possible markets, current trends in drama, and script opportunities (see Chapter 19). Another good source of information about new writing slots, and indeed about much else, is *twelvepoint.com*. Much of the search for new comedy writing is now done online, and a good source of information and advice is Robin Kelly's Writing for Performance (*writing.org.uk*). Channel 4's excellent website for new comedy-writers, *4laughs,* has disappeared, but there are hopes that it will resurface so it is worth checking the site. For more detailed advice see Chapter 18.

Should my script for the BBC be longer than for ITV or Channel 4, because there will be no advertising breaks?
Nobody is going to be timing your calling card script, and it wouldn't matter if they did, because the BBC makes many programmes to the same length as the commercial channels in order to allow for advertising breaks if they are sold abroad. (This also has the happy effect of allowing the BBC promotions department several minutes every hour to fill with programme trails.)

Should I put commercial breaks in my calling card script?
Yes, in the version you send to ITV or Channel 4 or Channel 5. Not
in the version you send to the BBC. You should not call them
commercial breaks, but 'End of Part One', 'End of Part Two', etc.

SUMMARY

- Sixty minutes is a good length for an original calling-card drama
  script and 30 minutes for a sitcom. Don't worry about accurate
  timing, but using a standard layout (see Chapter 10) your drama
  script should be around 60 pages long, and your sitcom around
  40 pages long, depending on just how fast and funny it is.

- You should write a contemporary play, because this will more
  easily demonstrate your ability with dialogue and characterization.

- It is better to introduce and develop a small group of
  characters than to juggle with a large cast. The critical part
  of your 'calling card' script is the first ten pages. If you succeed
  in writing even one interesting character, in an interesting
  situation, and *leave the script editor wanting to know more*, you
  will have done very well.

- You should give us visual interest (without demanding
  enormous special effects) and show that you can cut between
  interior and exterior scenes.

- It will be an added bonus if you can give us an insight into an
  area of life we would not otherwise know about.

The BBC advises new writers to write the sort of play they
themselves would like to see on the screen, choosing subjects from
their own experience.

2

Story and Theme

This chapter, and the following chapters on style, structure, plotting, visual interest, dialogue, and characterization, are designed to stimulate your creativity and help you to avoid common errors when writing your 'calling-card' script. Here we look at the difference between your superficial story and the underlying subject matter.

WHAT IS YOUR PLAY *REALLY* ABOUT?

You have decided on:

- the length of script you are going to write;

- the story you are going to tell.

But what is the subject of your drama? Will it be about love – love betrayed, love that endures? Or about passion – passion that triumphs over all odds, passion that betrays and destroys? Or will it perhaps be about social justice – justice that triumphs, justice that is blind, justice that is abused?

The underlying subject of a play is sometimes known as '**the theme**' or '**the premise**'. It's what your play is about on a deeper level than the actual story. If an Elizabethan script editor had been asked to sum up *Othello* he might well have said: 'Jealousy.' Or he might have expanded slightly and said: 'The study of a man destroyed by his own unreasoned jealousy.' Alan Plater's play *Belonging*, transmitted on ITV1 in 2004, was a play about a woman whose life was turned upside-down when her dependable husband disappeared, leaving her to care for his three elderly relatives. But it was also, said critic Stephen Pile, 'a moving meditation on selfishness, service and freedom.'

Single plays – particularly those of 60-minute or 90-minute duration – need to contain thoughts and ideas over and above the bricks and mortar of the actual story they tell. Producers and script editors know that *Othello* is more than a bit of chicanery that leads to a nasty domestic crisis. When they read your script they need to be convinced that your play has something to tell us about human nature or about contemporary life.

> *'A theme is an idea ... about life and its meaning, about the human condition. It is the underlying truth signified by the film – universal, enduring, significant, expressive and eloquent. It springs from the writer's view of the way the world is and his sense of morality of the way the world should be.'*
>
> William Miller, American writer and film maker

Consider the following story idea:

SAMMY SLIME is manager of the Hardtimes Residential Home for the Elderly. It is a council home but because of the 'privatization' of social service inspectorate staff (recently and controversially introduced, perhaps, in the real world) he finds that he can claim state money for his residents without accounting for expenditure. Slowly he starves the residents, depriving them of food and heating and comfort until there is a dreary, debilitating reign of terror.

ELSIE, a courageous woman in her nineties, tries to rally opposition to SLIME. But she is frail and catches pneumonia. We know that she will soon die unless SLIME is exposed.

The social services – council workers, overworked doctors – all fail to spot what is happening.

The other old folk long to help ELSIE – but are terrified of SLIME. Surely they will be shamed into helping her? They almost mount a rebellion – but not quite.

ELSIE's daughter is due from America. Will she turn up in time?

She doesn't. ELSIE dies. SLIME covers up evidence of malnutrition and gets a death certificate from a harassed young GP.

It seems that he can get away with everything. Until a dustman finds three dozen empty catfood tins outside the back door...

And the local papers get hold of the story, and investigate.

Shorn of names like Slime and Hardtimes, used here to avoid libel risks inherent in realistic names (see libel, page 199) this is a sound enough, if rather gloomy narrative that would once have had considerable appeal to the BBC or Channel 4. In it we see a man in power ill-treating victims in his care. We see a victim try to oppose him. We wait for the social services or doctors to help the victim – and are horrified when they fail. We see a sudden ray of hope when the daughter is due from America! We see the hope dashed – and the victim die. We then see retribution come from an unexpected but logical quarter.

This is the narrative – the superficial story. But it does not tell us how the play will actually be written, or what the play is actually about.

ANALYSING THE STORY OUTLINE

■ Is it the story of Elsie, a woman who has perhaps been too timid during her life but who finds, when she is in her nineties, the strength to lead a struggle against oppression?

The play will thus be a story of courage in extremity, and the triumph of the human spirit.

■ Is it the story of Sammy Slime? Perhaps as a young man Sam went into his career with high ideals and a genuine desire to help his fellow human beings. Perhaps he makes his first 'profit' by mistake ... then when he is not discovered, and when the old people do not notice, he is tempted to take a 'profit' yet again.

The play will thus be a study of how avarice consumes and destroys a man.

■ Is it the story of the social services, underfunded for decades, with doctors that cannot cope, now inflicted with a form of 'privatization' that leaves the people it ought to protect exposed to sordid profiteers?

Thus it will be a highly partisan political play, a trumpet call to the government to reverse its policies.

The dramatist might say he wants to combine all these elements. The theme or premise might be: 'A searing exposure of neglect in our society, told through the battle of wills between a woman who finds courage she did not know she possessed, and a weak man who falls to temptation.'

Understanding your subject helps you to write your play. Even working it out in your head encourages you to probe deeper into your characters' minds, and understand their motivations. You must always know what you are writing about.

THE DANGERS OF TOO MUCH ANALYSIS

At the same time you have to be careful of this sort of analysis. You can dignify anything if you try hard enough, and the tale of Slime and Elsie (the story of a woman of deep strength and a man of moral weakness) is already sounding like a textual analysis of Macbeth. In his book *The Way to Write for Television* Eric Paice points out that you can make *Little Red Riding Hood* mean anything from

'Wolves should make sure there are no woodcutters around before they dress up in drag' to 'Little girls should have their eyes tested before visiting their grandmothers'.

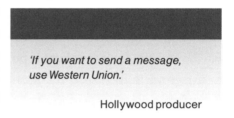

'If you want to send a message, use Western Union.'

Hollywood producer

But a good play, whether it deals with contemporary social issues or not, should always operate on two levels: the story and the idea behind the story. Writing must go deep, and find, beneath the narrative, a thought that will illuminate our view of the world.

SUMMARY

■ Be clear about the underlying theme of your play – the issues it raises, the emotions it explores. This will make it easier to plot your story, develop your characters, and reach an effective and powerful conclusion.

3

Style

WHAT TYPE OF PLAY ARE YOU WRITING?

You know your story, and your characters. You have considered the **theme** of your play – its message, the issues it deals with.

But what **style** should you write in? Will you write a straightforward, realistic, documentary-type of play, with the camera used as an unseen eye to record the scene? Or will you include elements of artifice – people speaking to camera, special effects, flashbacks, fantasy? As the play's narrator, will you allow viewers to know everything that is happening, or will you deliberately keep your audience in the dark about some aspects of the story to encourage their curiosity?

You might call a play 'a love story', but what kind of love story? You may decide to write a comedy, but is it:

- a social comedy, employing wit and irony;

- a farce;

- a black comedy;

- a savage satire?

Viewers will be confused (before them, of course, and more importantly, script readers will be confused) if a much-loved character suddenly develops cancer in the middle of a frothy farce, or if an exposé of homelessness in London is suddenly overrun with bikini-clad girls hiding in wardrobes.

You might argue that drama needs to tear itself free of conventions (Dennis Potter's drama did), but to break the conventions you need first to understand them and to have the ability to write within them. At the very least, you must be breaking them deliberately.

In this chapter we look at:

- plays that show the world as it is (called **narrative realism**);

- plays that utilize fantasy and the imagination (**non-realism**);

- ways to tell your story;

- ways in which the camera can tell your story.

NARRATIVE REALISM

In narrative realism we are out there in real life, in the world of drizzly afternoons, jobcentres and supermarkets. The locations are real, the characters are credible, the stories believable. *Cathy Come Home* is the benchmark, a play that looked back to films like *Saturday Night and Sunday Morning* and *Room at the Top*. Critics say narrative realism is boring and pedestrian, doing something that ought to be done by the straightforward television documentary, and failing to use properly the possibilities of television. Nevertheless, this type of play has many defenders, and is the most accessible form of drama for the new writer. In recent years it has gained a new and controversial lease of life through the drama-documentary – fiction based on real events. Narrative realism plays are invariably filmed on location rather than in the studio. In narrative realism you should maintain the following conventions.

- **Surface accuracy**. In simple terms this means that a fireman's uniform should be a real fireman's uniform. People who ask for drinks in pubs should have to pay for them – and if the price is mentioned it should be believable. The law of the land, as it exists in your script, should conform to the law as we understand it in the real world. If the main character in your crime thriller is a school head teacher, and you find that you want her to interrogate suspects (something that school head teachers do not do), you must not let her do it without providing a logical, believable excuse.

- **Cause and effect**. At its simplest, if somebody is lying in the garden in a swimsuit we should expect it to be summer and the sun shining. If a woman punches a man violently in a restaurant other diners should respond in a believable manner. (This will depend, of course, on where the event is taking place: Cheltenham diners might be expected to respond differently from diners in Rome.)

- **Psychological consistency**. If a character is sensible, they should remain sensible *unless their change in character is part of your story*. If a character suddenly stops being good-natured and becomes spiteful, viewers will try to find a reason, and puzzle over how it fits into the story you are telling.

- **Normal expectations of character and behaviour**. What is portrayed should conform to a common-sense view of what happens in the world. In some ways this is a dodgy rule, a great worry to the politically correct. It means that if the camera strays into a household of Asian immigrants we should expect to find a curry on the table. In the country mansion of Sir Roddy Forescue Bart, we should expect to find roast beef. Reverse the menus without explanation, and viewers will be confused. They will fret over why Sir Roddy is munching curry and the immigrants passing the mustard.

This is a perfectly valid rule, but it does inevitably reinforce stereotypes, and it can make scripts dull and predictable. The writer should try to present a view of the world that is credible but at the same time fresh and different, which is, of course, easier said than done.

NON-REALISTIC DRAMA

This can be simply heightened drama – the characters deliberately larger than life, as seen in many comedies – or it can move into fantasy and use the camera to show us images, ideas, thoughts that might be in the characters' heads. Some dramas combine realism with fantasy, notable examples being *Selling Hitler* and before that *Wingate* and David Rudkin's *Penda's Fen*. In *Trainspotting* the addict swims down the lavatory bowl seeking his lost drugs. Among modern television dramatists Dennis Potter was the most distinguished in carrying the torch for drama of the imagination. In 2004, BBC One acknowledged its debt to Potter with its serial *Blackpool*.

The new writer is often tempted to write fantasy. It frees him from the tedious constraint of believable characterization, logical plots and credible dialogue. But only the most skilled and confident – not to say established – writer can normally break conventions with impunity, and until he is in a position to explain his idea to Channel 4's Head of Drama over lunch, the new writer should stick to the grim business of devising stories that we can believe in.

On the other hand, a major new talent that is exciting and different and revolutionary in its use of the medium, must make – and break – the rules.

WAYS TO TELL YOUR STORY

The way you tell (**narrate**) your story depends on how best you think you can grip your audience and hold its interest.

The omniscient narrator

The narrator knows more than the characters, and lets viewers share the knowledge. In a crime story we see the murder committed. We know the identity of the murderer. We watch the detective stumbling – with many a false trail – towards the truth. This technique can give a valuable element of suspense (will the villain be caught or will the nice chap who has been framed get sent down for ten years by which time his poor widowed Mum will be dead?) but you lose the element of mystery.

The narrator as character

Sometimes the narrator knows only what the principal character knows. We unravel the mystery with the detective, sharing his or her thoughts. This is straight realism, the classic whodunnit.

The narrator as a tease

Sometimes the narrator pretends to know only what the principal characters know, but occasionally reveals other things to us. (Miss Brown stops sobbing and smiles bravely. Detective Inspector Boot takes back his hankie and leaves the room. Miss Brown's expression changes. She picks up the letter. She stares at it, her expression cold. She suddenly rips it into pieces. CUT to the next scene.) Here we cannot be certain that it was Miss Brown whodidit, but we know she is not what she seems – and we thus know more than the detective. This is a very dangerous technique, for if the camera can tell us a bit about what's happening, why can't it tell us everything?

The narrator in the dark

Sometimes the narrator knows less than the characters. Detective Inspector Boot says: 'So that is how he did it – no, don't ask me to tell you, not until my final experiment, but arrange for Madam de Courville and the ticket inspector to be entering this building at precisely 7pm.' This was the basis of the Sherlock Holmes stories, of course. In lesser hands it is a technique that can be infuriating. If Boot knows who did it why doesn't he tell us instead of being smug?

The cheating narrator

The viewer will rapidly, if unconsciously, know which technique you are employing and will expect you to stick to it. If we are solving the crime in company with the detective and suddenly (tempted by the need for a dramatic moment) you show us, the viewers, something that the detective does not know, the play will be in danger of losing dramatic tension.

The real narrator

The real narrator, of course, knows everything. The real narrator (you the writer) has decided which dramatic technique to use.

> *To make a great movie, you need just three things: a great script, a great script, and a great script.*
>
> Alfred Hitchcock

WAYS THE CAMERA CAN NARRATE YOUR STORY

This is a topic that can get fairly esoteric, and is much debated by media course lecturers (is the camera being used in the mode of *histoire* or *discours*?). New writers should avoid getting bogged down in such questions. At its simplest there are two basic narrative modes, as follows.

The impartial narrator

The camera has no viewpoint (although clearly somebody has selected the images and words). We see a succession of things happen as recorded by an impartial eye.

The active narrator

The camera overtly presents us with opinions on what is happening, or on the views that are being expressed (the camera pans along a wall of china ducks while a character is heard saying, 'I've always prided myself on my good taste'); or a character glances to camera and winks as Francis Urquhart did in *House of Cards* or speaks directly to camera (see the opening of Sharon Foster's *Shoot the Messenger* in the BBC Writersroom online script archive).

SUMMARY

■ Most writers use straightforward narrative realism but also employ the camera actively to point up mood, give pace, and emphasise characterization. (See Chapter 6, Visual Interest.) This is an effective method and shows agents and editors that you can think visually and use the camera.

■ Don't get bogged down worrying about who the narrator is. You will almost certainly get it right by instinct. Refer back to this chapter, though, if you get into trouble.

4

Structure

SIMPLER THAN IT LOOKS

Entire books are written about structure. There are those who believe in surface structure and deep structure, who can plot structure on a graph, who can tell you what to do between pages 1 and 5 and between pages 5 and 10 and so on. All this is useful and interesting for students of critical analysis but it can stifle the talents of a writer. Shakespeare, we can be confident, did not have little graphs of character development (set-up and focus point), story development (conflict and confrontation) and climax (moment of truth) on his desk when he penned *King Lear*.

If you take account of the following points you will get your structure right instinctively, without having your freedom to write as your imagination takes you unnecessarily constrained:

■ the basic structure;

■ the opening;

■ classic hooks to keep viewers watching;

■ structuring for commercial breaks;

■ multi-strand structuring.

THE BASIC STRUCTURE

This is the broad shape of any play. Keep to it and you will not go far wrong.

1. **Situation**. You present us with a visual setting, the main characters, and the beginning of a story that interests us and makes us want to go on watching. This invariably involves conflict of some kind (see **conflict in drama**, page 42).

2. **Complication**. The situation you set up in the beginning needs to be complicated, false trails need to be laid, the aims and ambitions of your characters frustrated. At the same time we must be clear about where we are heading, and our interest must not wane.

3. **Reversal**. If things went badly for your hero they should now change and start to go better. Conversely, if your hero has been doing well, things should now go badly (**retardation** of the story).

4. **Climax**. The central issue of your drama must come to a climax – the conflict comes to a head. This can be done through dialogue or through action on the screen. As this is television, a visual climax is preferred. In series drama it is traditionally 'the car chase'. The car chase need not involve cars – it can be a gunman pursuing another through an empty warehouse, or anything else that involves action, movement and pace.

5. **Resolution**. Something must have changed. It may be a purely physical resolution (your hero and heroine united; your villain dragged off to prison) or it may be an alteration in your characters' attitude to life, towards each other. Perhaps your **twist resolution** is that they are not changed at all. If aliens seize a gardener from his allotment and require him to

undergo unbelievable terrors in order to save the galaxy – and the last thing we see is him back in his vegetable plot checking his potatoes and muttering 'The things you have to do in this life, I don't know...' – well, that is a resolution in itself.

Another way of putting it is to say that, however disguised, all plays need to have a beginning, a middle, and an end!

THE OPENING

The first 60 seconds are crucially important. The remote control unit has taught producers that viewers are fickle and disloyal. If they are not hooked in the first minute they are liable to press the button and zap to another channel. One writer, chided by a script editor for having a slow opening, replied: 'I did it deliberately! It's to hook the people who have zapped over after the first minute on something else' – but this cunning excuse is unlikely to be accepted. A strong opening is particularly important for mystery or thriller drama series – *Spooks*, *Midsomer Murders* – where episodes can cost anything up to a million pounds to make, and are designed to anchor the evening's audience to a particular channel and build audiences for future episodes. The way to a good opening is to devise a good hook.

CLASSIC HOOKS TO KEEP VIEWERS WATCHING

Three classic hooks are:

- curiosity;

- mystery;

- suspense.

Curiosity

Curiosity is the basis of all story-telling. If humans were not intractably curious, if they did not by their very nature always want to know *what will happen next*, then novelists and dramatists would have a lean time of it.

> A woman rushes up to a man and says: 'Well, did you do it?' and he looks at her stony-faced, and then nods, and she says: 'O my God.' End of scene. Opening titles.

Hopefully, we are curious to know what the man has done. Murdered his wife? Had the cat put down? Left the bathroom tap running with disastrous consequences?

> A girl watches through the window as the postman approaches. She is clearly excited. The postman turns in at the gate, and the girl runs through to the hall as an expensive-looking white envelope falls to the mat. She picks it up and turns it over, longing to open it and yet frightened...

There is no mystery yet, because we have not been presented with anything mysterious or odd. But such is the human desire to know what other people are up to, and in particular the desire to see inside other people's letters, that even a mildly curious opening will help to keep viewers hooked.

Mystery

A more powerful hook is the use of mystery. Somebody does something strange, something we cannot account for. A dour, sinister man with a mean, cold face slips into a hotel room with a small plastic device that he furtively places behind a vase of flowers. What is it? A bomb? A microphone?

A man visits a private detective and asks that the Mother Superior of a nunnery should be followed night and day. He will not say why, or give an explanation, but he will pay treble the usual rate. What can she be up to?

Sherlock Holmes stories are built around mysteries; on television *The Avengers* always gave us an opening scene in which something totally odd and unaccountable happened. A huge number of plays and serials depend on the use of mystery to a greater or lesser extent, particularly in the first 60 seconds.

Suspense

Suspense is what keeps us on the edge of our seats. If mystery relies on puzzlement, and not knowing what is going on, suspense is when we know perfectly well what might happen, and are fearful in case it does.

> A shadow of a person against a wall in an alleyway, holding a knife. CUT TO: A girl walking along the dark, empty street towards the alley. CUT TO: A police car patrols in a well-lit street nearby. CUT TO: The shadow raises the knife as we hear the girl's footsteps approach. CUT TO: Interior of police car, the driver whistling softly as he turns the car into the dark empty street. CUT TO: The girl reaches the alleyway...

And so on. We are compelled to watch, even if we know that the girl cannot be killed because her engagement to the hero in the next episode is on the cover of *TV Times*.

STRUCTURING FOR COMMERCIAL BREAKS

Like the remote control zapper, commercial breaks give viewers the opportunity to switch to another channel. When structuring a serial or series episode it is vital to lead up to a cliff-hanger before each break. It can involve curiosity, mystery, or suspense. The important thing is that it must make us want to go on watching. When you submit a synopsis or storyline of an episode, the script editor will be looking to see if you have strong commercial breaks.

The one thing you must not do is cheat the viewer. If the dour sinister man with a mean, cold face has slipped furtively into the hotel room, and we have heard edgy ominous music as he carefully placed the plastic device behind the vase of flowers, it is cheating to come back after the commercial break to discover that he is a hotel porter putting air ionisers into the guest rooms.

MULTI-STRAND STRUCTURING

Many plays – and particularly series dramas – have more than one plot. Many have two separate plots and also a comic **sub-plot**. Skilled and experienced writers know how to keep different stories bubbling, but the following tips might be helpful for new writers.

Do not attempt to introduce both stories at once

When you open your play you have to impart a lot of information to the viewers very quickly:

- the visual scene;

- the initial characters, their names, backgrounds, the role they have to play;

- the initial story;

- the 'hook' that will keep people watching.

And you have to do all this in a taut, dramatic and interesting way.

A good Boon *episode? – the girl shows her tits and you end up with a car chase.*

Former producer,
Central TV's *Boon*

It is hard enough to do this with one major story without confusing the viewer with *two* sets of information.

It makes sense to spend the first half-dozen scenes setting up the first story, take it to a point where it can conveniently rest for a moment (preferably with a good 'hook' to keep people interested), and then turn to story number two.

Try to devise stories that are quite different from each other

This helps with **pace**. A story that needs a lot of explaining, a lot of dialogue, a lot of concentration on what is said, needs to be contrasted with a story that is basically simple and has action.

In the *Boon* episode, *Peacemaker*, examined in Chapter 6, page 49, there are three stories, as follows.

1. A pop star due to make his comeback on the Birmingham music scene goes missing. Boon and Margaret have to track him down. This is basically comedy-drama. It is highly visual involving stake-outs and chases through sleazy pubs.

2. A woman wants her husband followed to get proof that he is cheating with his alimony payments. This story is more serious, it is about the consequences of divorce, it has twists as our sympathies are engaged first with one side and then with the other.

3. A comedy sub-story involves Harry entertaining a delegation of Dutch machine tool manufacturers in the Plaza Suite.

In *Peacemaker* the writers are careful to make sure that a comedy-drama sequence from story one is followed by a quieter and more down-to-earth scene from story two; and a scene which imparts a lot of information through dialogue is followed by a scene which is visual.

SUMMARY

- In broad terms the first part of your script (25%) should set up the situation: the second part (50%) should complicate or deepen it; the third part (25%) should resolve it. Ignore these proportions, however, if they do not fit your particular story.

- Hook the reader on page one by creating curiosity, mystery or suspense.

- Always have one of these hooks – curiosity, mystery, suspense – operating on some sort of level.

- If you are running two stories, allow the first to be established before introducing the second.

- Do not overwhelm viewers with verbal information, particularly in the beginning.

5

Plotting

How do you make the plot interesting?

You have a story, you have worked out a broad structure, now take a look at how you can write the script in an interesting way. This chapter deals with the following:

■ the importance of conflict;

■ decision-making by principal characters;

■ consequence of action – cause and effect;

■ creating sympathy;

■ plots to avoid.

Conflict in drama

All drama depends on conflict. That is not the same as saying that drama depends on people shouting at each other. Generally speaking, people shouting at each other should be avoided – most people have enough argument in their lives without watching other people bawling their heads off. At its most basic, conflict means that Character A wants something to happen, and Character B wants something different to happen.

This might mean anything from: A murderer wants to escape – a detective wants to arrest him. A schoolmaster wants promotion –

another wants to sabotage him. A girl wants a bloke – another girl wants him as well. A girl wants a bloke – another bloke wants the girl. A husband wants bacon for breakfast – his wife wants him to have high-fibre muesli.

What does conflict mean?

It can mean:

- a problem to be solved;

- an obstacle to be overcome;

- a threat to be handled;

- a decision to be made;

- a challenge to be met.

Conflict is not the same as aggression. You could write a 50-minute play based on the conflict between a child who wants a kitten, and her family who don't. You could show her manipulations, her relentless purchase of kitten books, her feverish illness caused by not having a kitten, her letters to Father Christmas, finally her finding (or buying) a kitten and bringing it home and hiding it... and the entire play could be gentle and humorous and non-aggressive.

> *There is only one plot in TV drama. There's a guy in Zanzibar with a cork up his arse. The only guy in the world who can get it out lives in Newark, New Jersey. We spend the next 50 minutes watching the second guy fighting overwhelming odds to reach the first guy before he dies of toxic poisoning.*
>
> US film distributor

What does conflict include?

It can include the following.

Man versus elements

Can the mountaineers reach the top of Everest before the storm descends? Will superb seamanship bring the yacht with a hole in it safe to harbour? Can the cork-extracting man from New Jersey (see page 43) fight his way through the Zanzibar swamps?

Man versus time

Can the cork-extracting man from New Jersey fight his way through the Zanzibar swamps in time? Can the rescue squad find the boy lost in the potholes before he dies of hunger? Can the hero struggling on foot through the blizzard (man versus elements) reach the girl in the wooden shack before the rapist arrives in his snowmobile?

Man versus himself

Can Sir Thomas More reconcile his conscience to swearing allegiance to Henry VIII as head of the Church? Can the Old Labour MP accept the British Telecom shares left to him by his aunty? Can the student who cheated at her exam accept the prize scholarship, knowing that she is depriving a fellow-student who is desperately hard-up? Can the newly-divorced man conquer his overwhelming depression?

THE IMPORTANCE OF DECISION-MAKING

Dramatic tension is held if the story develops through decisions made by the main characters. It is not held if the story develops through coincidence and arbitrary accidents. When that happens it ceases to be a story and becomes a succession of incidents.

The viewers need to see a central character faced with a problem. They need to see the options available. They need to see a decision taken – and then to see the result. If a character has to achieve a goal you should put as many obstacles as possible in his path, force him to take as many decisions as possible, and then show how he copes.

Arbitrary accidents can form obstacles – the cork-extractor man from New Jersey might be speeding across Africa in a train that breaks down. But this is a device to offer a new decision to be taken: does he wait for the train to be mended or hitch a ride on a poorly-looking camel owned by a one-eyed bandit with a sharp knife? If he goes on the camel, will it collapse, or will the bandit kill him?

It is important that decisions should be left to your central characters. In this case the bandit must either be innocent of evil intent, or waiting to pounce. It will almost certainly not work if you switch the focus, and have the bandit making a decision: do I kill this cork-extractor man or not? If I do will I escape with his money or get caught?

It will also be profoundly unsatisfactory if the man from New Jersey fails to reach the man with the corked arse because he catches a cold and has to go to bed, where a snake that we knew nothing about bites him and he dies.

CONSEQUENCES OF ACTION: CAUSE AND EFFECT

People who write about, and lecture on, creative writing, often go

> *The King died and then the Queen died. That is a story. The King died and then the Queen died of grief. That is a plot.*
>
> E. M. Forster, *Aspects of the Novel*

on at great length about the difference between plot and story. It really doesn't matter. It's not going to make the slightest different to your script. But at its simplest, the plot is what makes your story happen. It is cause and effect: you set up a situation and then see how your characters react to it, and thus a new situation, and event, is created.

CREATING SYMPATHY

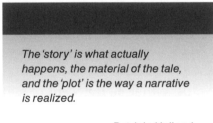

> *The 'story' is what actually happens, the material of the tale, and the 'plot' is the way a narrative is realized.*
>
> Patricia Holland,
> *The Television Handbook*

It is useful to have at least *one* sympathetic character and to introduce him at an early stage. Viewers like to know who to identify with, they like to know who they should be cheering for. You can, of course, show a pleasant character and later reveal a vicious side to his nature – and you can have a vile person who turns out to have all kinds of redeeming features. But at the beginning of a play we need to establish something, or somebody, that viewers can *care about*.

PLOTS TO AVOID

The idiot plot

Script editors hate plots which can only work if basically

intelligent characters behave in a totally stupid way. *Dr Who* was (and indeed still is) a terrible culprit here – the Doctor and his Assistant would be clinging to each other in some noisome underground cave system, we would *all know* they ought to stay together, but sure enough the Doctor would say: 'I'll be back in a minute', and wander off on his own, leaving his assistant to be captured and held prisoner for the next four episodes. In *Dr Who* this was expected, it was part of the formula, but it is basically very lazy plotting.

Story development should stem from character. You should never force characters unnaturally to obey your plot.

Scenes that go nowhere

Every scene should move the story on. It should advance the plot or illuminate the characters – preferably both. Beware of scenes that repeat the plot but in a slightly different way. If you write a scene, and then find you can cut it out of your script without losing anything relevant to the story, then cut it.

Plots that lose tension

We must always want to know what is going to happen next. If a scene satisfies curiosity roused in previous scenes, it should also arouse curiosity about events in the future. Plots often lose tension because:

- you have resolved conflict elements too soon, and there is nothing left for us to anticipate;

- your plot has become bogged down in explanations of past events – viewers are rarely kept on the edge of their seats by verbal explanations of what has gone before;

■ it was a boring idea to start with.

Summary

■ The 'plot' is the order of events in which you choose to tell the 'story'.

■ All drama depends on conflict – but conflict does not have to mean aggression.

■ Do not devise plots that can only work if your characters are stupid. Never force characters unnaturally to obey your plot.

■ Do not let your plot get bogged down in verbal explanations of previous scenes.

6

Visual Interest

You have come up with a brilliant idea, and you have worked out a plot showing how the story will develop. The third thing you need to be able to do is to *tell your story in an interesting way*.

This chapter will look at:

- visual interest on screen;

- using pictures instead of words;

- ways to maintain dramatic tension;

- opening scenes of a *Boon* episode.

HOW TO INCREASE VISUAL INTEREST

Watch any popular drama series on ITV and note how short most scenes are, how quickly we move about, and how few scenes take place in visually boring places like offices or sitting rooms (in other words locations reminiscent of studio plays). In *Peacemaker*, the *Boon* episode looked at in this chapter, there are only three scenes set in the detective agency's office. When a director comes across a wordy, static indoor scene with two people talking to each other, his first instinct is to move the scene to somewhere else: somewhere visually interesting. The longer and more wordy (or delicate and sensitive as you the writer might put it) the scene, the more he will want to break it up with movement, and before you know it your characters will be playing squash or practising on the high trapeze. Even if restrained from his wilder notions, the director would rather have characters walking sedately along a river bank than sitting on opposite sides of a table. This gives him *variety of shots* and allows him to punctuate the dramatic content of the scene with *movement*.

You give the director this:

INT. KITCHEN. DAY.   MARY AND JOHN ARE STILL SITTING AT THE KITCHEN TABLE. HIS HEAD IS SLUMPED.

MARY: John? If you've got something to say then I'd rather you said it.

JOHN LOOKS UP

JOHN: OK. All right. I've been having an affair with Tracy from the catfood factory.

MARY TURNS AWAY SHARPLY. JOHN PAUSES, SHATTERED FOR A MOMENT HAVING FINALLY BROUGHT HIMSELF TO TELL HER. THEN HE CONTINUES WITH NEW CONFIDENCE:

                         We love each other and I want a divorce. I want children and you can't give me children. I know it's not your fault, I know that you desperately want children yourself, but there's no reason for us both to suffer –

MARY: Stop it, stop it, stop it!

And the director gives you back this:

<u>EXT. RIVERBANK. DAY</u>

MARY AND JOHN WALK ON PAST THE WEIR, UNDER THE
FALLING LEAVES OF AUTUMN. THEY ARE STILL SILENT
WITH MISERY. MARY STOPS AND THROWS BREAD TO A
SWAN AND HER CYGNETS.

MARY: John? (HE DOES NOT
RESPOND) If you've got something to say then I'd rather you
said it.

JOHN: OK. All right. I've been having
an affair with Tracy from the catfood factory.

MARY FREEZES. THE MOTHER SWAN AND HER CYGNETS
ARE EATING THE BREAD. JOHN PAUSES SHATTERED FOR
A MOMENT HAVING FINALLY BROUGHT HIMSELF TO
TELL HER. THEN HE CONTINUES WITH NEW CONFI-
DENCE. WE WATCH THE SWAN AND HER CYGNETS FROM
MARY'S POV:

JOHN: (OOV)   We love each other and I want a
divorce. I want children, and you can't give me children. I
know it's not your fault, I know that you desperately want
children yourself, but there's no reason for us both to suffer –

CUT SHARPLY BACK TO MARY WHO TURNS

MARY: Stop it, stop it, stop it!

THE SWAN FLAPS HER WINGS IN ALARM AND HER
CYGNETS SCATTER.

The second version allows the story to progress visually (in this
scene we are at the weir, in a previous scene we would have been
on another part of the river bank); allows us to have a decent
dramatic pause for John and still have something to look at; gives
us a nice bit of symbolism looking at a Mum and her little ones
while John (speaking Out of Vision) cruelly rambles on about
childlessness; and the ominous rumble of the weir in the
background offers a hint that Mary might either drown herself
or, preferably, drown John.

USING PICTURES INSTEAD OF WORDS

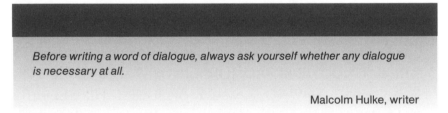

*Before writing a word of dialogue, always ask yourself whether any dialogue
is necessary at all.*

Malcolm Hulke, writer

Picture the following scene:

> A group around a coffin in a country graveyard. The vicar
> intoning from the *Book of Common Prayer*. We see the Range
> Rovers and the BMWs parked on the verges of the country
> lane, the rooks cawing round their nests in the dead elm trees.
> The camera PANS along thoughtful, sober faces, until it finds
> JASPER, who is surreptitiously smiling behind his asthma
> inhaler.

CUT TO: DOLORES, who shoots him a glance of pure hate.

CUT TO: Shovels of earth fall on the coffin. The rooks caw, the vicar intones, and we suddenly become aware of heavy laboured breathing... the breathing of somebody struggling for life.

CUT TO: The rooks wheel round the elms.

CUT TO: JASPER begins to turn blue, his breath wheezing. Somebody screams. JASPER falls into the open grave.

CUT TO: DOLORES turns away. Her hand lightly checks the side pocket of her Burberry, to make sure the zip is fastened. She strolls towards the church gate.

We don't need a competition to see how pictures here can substitute for words in setting the scene (England, C of E, middle-class, rural, springtime because the rooks are nesting, a burial) and also in telling the story (Jasper murdered by Dolores who has the asthma inhaler poison in her Burberry pocket) – and all without a word of dialogue apart from the words of Archbishop Cranmer, who is out of copyright anyway.

Looking at the scenes from *Peacemaker* on pages 57–67 you will see how the scenes with dialogue are punctuated by scenes which move the story along purely with the use of pictures.

DRAMATIC TENSION

You must always have something on screen that holds the interest of the viewer. It might be one of the following.

- **A development of the plot** – our attention is held because we have become involved in the characters and the story, and we want to know what will happen next.

- **Emotion** – happiness, shock, tears. It is distressing but true that people are fascinated by other people's emotional reactions.

- **Humour** – an interlude involving a humorous theme might not move the plot forward or reveal anything new, but providing we laugh all can be forgiven. In *Peacemaker* we have two pop concert promoters who have 'lost' their star – and Boon is trying to find him. We need to cut back to the promoters now and again, simply so that we will not forget their existence. In plot terms the obvious thing would be to show them sitting in their sordid office, waiting – or on the phone to our detectives demanding to know what was happening. Instead the writers run a small sub-theme in which the promoters' sidekick tries to prove his cleverness by suggesting alternative stars. In one scene he is inspired to utter the words 'Gary Glitter', and the promoter opens the window and howls like a soul in torture; in another he modestly suggests his younger brother, and the promoter snarls: 'I've billed this as a comeback. How can your brother come back? He hasn't been anywhere.'

- **Visual interest** – by providing movement, rapid cuts from location to location, interesting locations, people running, vehicles moving at speed. What we see on the screen can help sustain dramatic tension.

Things that lose dramatic tension

■ Scenes or fragments of dialogue that do not go anywhere, and do not relate to the story or plot.

■ Scenes that repeat themselves and fail to move the story on.

■ Characters who fail to react in a logical manner. To a considerable extent viewers look to the reactions of characters in a play in order to work out their own reactions. If a woman hits a man in a restaurant and nobody pays any attention, and the man carries on eating his food, then there will be no dramatic tension. But if the entire restaurant falls silent, and the man stares in cold fury and the woman begins to shake – then there is dramatic tension.

A LOOK AT THE OPENING OF A *BOON* EPISODE

We've looked at some elements that go into telling a story on television. Now take a look at a professional script.

Boon was a Central Television drama series about a private detective, Ken Boon, played by Michael Elphick. It was comedy-drama, but occasionally with a hard edge. Six series were made and the programme moved locations during each series. An outstanding episode was *Peacemaker* written by Diane Culverhouse and Julian Spilsbury for Series Three.

At the time Ken Boon and Margaret Daley were partners in a small Birmingham private detective agency. The agency's office was at the back of the Plaza Suite – a run-down function venue owned by Ken's old friend Harry.

The main story in *Peacemaker* opens with the following situation: A Midland pop star, Bograt, is due to attend a 'comeback' recording session in Birmingham. He loses his nerve and disappears. The promoters hire Boon and Margaret to track him down.

How would you write the first scene, explaining the situation?

The following openings were suggested by students at a television drama seminar.

Suggestion one:
Boon's office. CLOSE UP of a newspaper with a photograph of Bograt and headline 'Comeback for Brum pop star'. PULL BACK to show promoter asking Boon and Margaret to take on the case.

The use of the newspaper picture is good, but otherwise this is a very boring, non-visual opening that does little to whet our curiosity and depends on our absorbing a lot of information through dialogue rather than pictures.

Suggestion two:
Bograt arrives at Birmingham railway station, or airport, and is surrounded by fans. As he leaves the station he is pounced on and pushed into a car that disappears at speed.

Nice and visual and it ought to arouse our curiosity – but Bograt is supposed to disappear in panic, not be kidnapped. All right, he could have set up the kidnap himself, but why come back to Birmingham at all in that case? Is he, perhaps, going into hiding just to seek publicity?

Trying to find a logical motivation for the visually-interesting kidnap is changing the entire storyline – and we are only in scene one!

This opening adds a further complication: the disappearance is now public knowledge, and one area of dramatic tension – only a small group of people aware that he has disappeared has been lost to us.

> *Suggestion three:*
> Bograt on stage at a comeback concert. It's a huge success/ miserable failure. Backstage afterwards the promoter goes to Bograt's dressing room and finds it empty ... and the window open.

This is good and visual. The concert must, presumably, be a success or the promoter is not going to care whether Bograt disappears or not. But if it is a success, then Bograt has already made his comeback – and to some extent at least the story is over. Also, if it is a success, why has he done a bunk?

On a practical level, it is hugely expensive to hire a theatre, put in lighting, stage a pop concert, and fill the theatre with people just to get 30 seconds of material.

Here is how the writers of Peacemaker tackled the opening, and also how they introduced the other stories in the episode.

1. EXT. BIRMINGHAM STREET. NIGHT.
A LARGE HOTEL. THERE IS LOUD, HEAVY METAL MUSIC FROM AN UPPER FLOOR WINDOW. THE MUSIC STOPS ABRUPTLY. THERE IS SHOUTING. A WINDOW BREAKS. A BLACK LEATHERY FIGURE (BOGRAT) EMERGES AND RACES DOWN A FIRE ESCAPE.

WE SEE HIS FACE BRIEFLY BEFORE HE LOPES OFF INTO THE NIGHT.

2. INT. MARGARET'S BEDROOM. NIGHT.
MARGARET IN BED ASLEEP IS WOKEN BY THE PHONE
RINGING. SHE PICKS UP THE RECEIVER, GRUMPILY
LOOKING AT THE CLOCK.

MARGARET: Hello?... Speaking... (WINCES)
What, now? Yes, I know it.... I'll be right round. (SLIGHTLY
INCREDULOUS) What did you say his name was?

3. INT. HOTEL LUXURY SUITE. NIGHT.
PROMOTIONAL MATERIAL ADVERTISES THE 'BOGRAT
AND THE NEKROS' COMEBACK ALBUM. BOGRAT FEA-
TURES PROMINENTLY. THE ROOM IS A SCENE OF
DEVASTATION. THE MINI FRIDGE IS DRY, THE DOOR
HANGS OFF. BOTTLES, CANS, CIGARETTE ENDS LITTER
EVERY SURFACE. BOGRAT'S MANAGER LENNY BRIGHT IS
STUMPING ANGRILY ROUND THE ROOM. GEOFF, HIS
GOPHER, IS JUST FINISHING THE CALL TO MARGARET. A
GIRL, NIKKI, IS SPACED OUT AND SOBBING. THE MEN
IGNORE HER.

GEOFF: She's coming straight over.

LENNY: Nice work, Geoff.

GEOFF: I only turned my back for five
minutes!

LENNY: He didn't need five minutes.
(Thinks) Were you with a bird?

GEOFF: (FOLLOWING HIM AROUND THE ROOM) it was a call of nature. The en-suite was full.

LENNY: (PEERS INTO BATHROOM) Good grief. (TURNS AWAY) It still is.

THE HOTEL MANAGER ENTERS AND LOOKS ROUND IN HORROR AT THE DEVASTATION.

MANAGER: Oh my god!

LENNY: (TO GEOFF) Pay the man.

GEOFF GOES OVER DRAGGING OUT HIS WALLET.

4. EXT. BIRMINGHAM STREET. NIGHT.
A POLICE CAR, SIREN GOING, PULLS UP AT A PUNCH-UP OUTSIDE A SEEDY NIGHT CLUB. THE BLACK LEATHERY FIGURE OF BOGRAT SURVEYS THE SCENE WITH EVIDENT SATISFACTION, THEN TURNS AND WALKS AWAY.

HE LOOKS ROUND HIM AT THE TATTY STREETS, THEN PUNCHES THE AIR AND JUMPS FOR JOY. HE IS HOME, AND HE IS FREE.

5. INT. HOTEL LOBBY. NIGHT.
MARGARET CROSSES FOYER AND ENTERS LIFT.

6. INT. HOTEL SUITE. OUTER ROOM. NIGHT.
GEOFF IS BUYING OFF THE HOTEL MANAGER. THERE IS A PILE OF £20 NOTES BETWEEN THEM TO WHICH GEOFF

KEEPS ADDING. BEHIND THEM SITS NIKKI, STILL SOB-
BING AND IGNORED.

MANAGER: Carpets. Duvets...

MARGARET ENTERS

MARGARET: Mr Bright?

GEOFF: Just follow the wreckage. (TO
MANAGER) Where were we?

MARGARET GOES THROUGH TO THE INNER ROOM.

MANAGER: Carpets.

GEOFF: Two-hundred-and-fifty.

NIKKI: I'm going to be sick!

MANAGER: No you don't!

HE DIVES TOWARDS HER. GEOFF SLIPS A COUPLE OF
NOTES BACK OFF THE PILE.

7. INT. HOTEL LUXURY SUITE. INNER ROOM. NIGHT.

LENNY: Lenny Bright. 'Bright Ideas'.

MARGARET: I understand you're missing a
lead singer.

LENNY: (GESTURES TO A POSTER) You
remember the Nekros?

MARGARET: (TACTFUL) Perhaps you'd
refresh my memory.

LENNY: Split up five years ago, I've got
them back together. Or at least, I had got them back together.

MARGARET: Well done.

LENNY: We're doing a come-back album, but it won't be worth
a fart in a thunderstorm without *him*.

MARGARET: Bograt?

LENNY: You see? You do remember! That's what makes him
special. I found him in Calais.

MARGARET: Calais?

LENNY: (NODS) It'll be engraved on my
heart too.

MARGARET: What was he doing in Calais?

LENNY: On his way to Monte Carlo.
He'd been on his way to Monte Carlo for five years. It was as far
as he got.

MARGARET: And now he's gone again?

LENNY: Has a bust up with his girlfriend and (POINTS TO WINDOW) vroom!

MARGARET: Couldn't he use a door like
anyone else?

LENNY: He isn't like anyone else!

MARGARET: And you want me to find him?

LENNY: And fast! I've got a studio,
session artists, a producer, all standing idle.

MARGARET: (LOOKS AT POSTER) Is this
fairly recent?

LENNY: We've a video in the office
that's better.

MARGARET: I'll send somebody round for it.
(LOOKS AT NIKKI, WHO IS NOW BEING TENDED BY
GEOFF) I take it that's the girlfriend?

LENNY: (NODS) How is she, Geoff?

GEOFF: (WAVES A HAND IN FRONT
OF HER FACE) Nikki? (NO RESPONSE) The lights are on but
there's no one in.

MARGARET: I'll talk to her in the morning.
Mr Bright, this won't be easy. If somebody really wants to hide –

LENNY: I want you on this full time.
Usual rates. Two hundred quid bonus if you get him within
forty-eight hours.

MARGARET: But he could be out of the
country by morning.

LENNY SHAKES HIS HEAD. HE DRAWS HER TO THE
WINDOW. HE TURNS OFF THE LIGHT. THEY LOOK OUT
OVER BIRMINGHAM AT NIGHT, AND WE LOOK WITH
THEM. LENNY'S VOICE CHOKES WITH EMOTION.

LENNY: That's what brought him back.
That city crouched down there like a beast. Those streets, those
subways, they gave him everything. Life, art, inspiration. This is
his city. Bograt's town.

8. INT. PLAZA SUITE. DAY.
HARRY IS IN HIS BEST SUIT. HIS MINIONS ARE PREPARING
A PROMOTION FOR A DUTCH MACHINE TOOL COMPANY.
THERE ARE LITTLE DUTCH FLAGS, BUNCHES OF PLASTIC
TULIPS, AND A DUTCH-STYLE BUFFET BEING LAID OUT
BY LINDA. HARRY CROSSES TO HER, HOLDING A LITTLE
DUTCH PHRASE BOOK.

HARRY: Linda, what do you think 'Ik
geloof dat ik voed-selvergiftiging hab' means?

LINDA: How about 'Go away and let me
finish this buffet in peace?'

HARRY: (LAUGHS) Very close! Actually
it's 'I think I've got food poisoning'.

HARRY SAMPLES SOMETHING FROM A PLATE. LINDA
SNATCHES IT AWAY.

LINDA: Actually that pumpernickel's in
short supply, Mr Crawford.

HARRY: (PULLS FACE) I'm glad to hear
it. (CALLS) Can you put the music on now?

MARGARET HAS WALKED IN. HARRY APPROACHES HER.
SHE LOOKS TIRED.

HARRY: Morning Margaret. Or should I
say 'Goede Morgen'?

MARGARET: Very   good.   Who's   coming,
Queen Beatrix?

HARRY: A   big   machine-tool   company
from Utrecht, here for the week. Quite a coup, actually.

MARGARET: You've   certainly   done   them
proud. All you need now is

THE MUSIC STARTS UP. IT IS MAX BYGRAVES SINGING
'TULIPS FROM AMSTERDAM'.

MARGARET: (FINISHES SENTENCE) Max
Bygraves singing 'Tulips from Amsterdam'.

HARRY WINKS AT HER. HE IS ONE UP.

9. INT. BDI OFFICE. PLAZA SUITE. DAY.
KEN IS TALKING TO A NERVOUS YOUNG WOMAN. WE
CAN STILL HEAR THE MUSIC AND SO CAN THEY. THE
WOMAN TURNS TO LOOK IN THE DIRECTION OF THE
NOISE.

ELAINE: (SMILES SADLY) We went there
on our honeymoon.

KEN: (SMILES   COMFORTINGLY,
REFERS TO HIS NOTES). This business 'Luxor Bathroom
Fittings'. Does he own it?

ELAINE: No. He's the branch manager.

KEN: Still, he's doing all right?

ELAINE: Doing very well by all accounts.
(SIGHS) I sound like a money-grabbing bitch, don't I?

KEN: Course not. The court awarded
you maintenance.

MARGARET ENTERS

MARGARET: Morning Ken, we've got the
most amazing... oh, I beg your pardon.

KEN: Mrs Bache, this is my partner,
Margaret Daley.

ELAINE: How do you do.

MARGARET: Hello. I'll leave you to it.

SHE COLLECTS UP HER POST, SMILES AND EXITS.

ELAINE: (ON VERGE OF TEARS) I've
got bills to pay. And if he's earning more than he says he's
earning, well it's not fair, is it?

KEN: You're sure that's what he's
doing?

ELAINE: Well I can't afford to go gadding
round town all the time.

KEN: And he can?

ELAINE: That's what I've heard.

KEN: Women?

ELAINE: I don't know. Friends don't like
to tell you about other women, do they?

KEN: No, still, it's possible. (LOOKS
AT PHOTOGRAPH) He's not a bad-looking bloke, is he?

ELAINE: Appearances can be very decep-
tive. He's a bastard, Mr Boon. A real bastard.

How does the opening of *Peacemaker* work?

Scene One

The opening is visual and fast moving, from the window
smashing to the darkened figure racing down the fire escape.
The fire escape sequence also allows time for the opening titles.

Scene Two

In one line we establish that the Boon agency is being involved
and that the matter is urgent. Curiosity is roused by the
incredulous: 'What did you say his name was?'

Scene Three

In only eight lines of dialogue we are given two points of conflict
and a second story strand is established:

- Lenny blames Geoff for losing Bograt, Geoff is resentful;

- the hotel manager is horrified by the wreckage: Geoff is told to
  sort him out.

Scene Four

Bograt, enjoying his freedom. It is totally visual but tells us a lot
about his character and the situation he is in.

Scene Five

Again is totally visual, showing Margaret arriving at the hotel.

Scene Six and Scene Seven

The basic situation is explained to Margaret – but note how we have the secondary story of Geoff and the hotel manager to divert us – the manager demanding heavy payment, Geoff doling the money out, Nikki the girlfriend almost being sick, Geoff pinching back some money, Nikki collapsing in a drunken stupor.

Note how future development is set up: Margaret asks if a poster is recent, Lenny says he has a video, Margaret says she'll send somebody round for it.

Scene Eight

A very visual scene with Dutch flags, tulips and buffet in the Plaza Suite sets up the comic subplot and brings Margaret in.

Scene Nine

The mood changes entirely as the second main story is set up. The music 'Tulips from Amsterdam' links the two scenes – but now has sad connotations. This scene has to give solid information, but note how it is given to us through natural dialogue – through the nervousness and distress of Elaine and how the scene ends with an ominous warning for the future: 'He's a bastard, Mr Boon, a real bastard'. Also note that although the scene is only two pages long, it has been broken up by the entry of Margaret.

All three stories have now been introduced – and we have learned as much through the eye of the camera as through dialogue.

SUMMARY

■ Avoid long scenes full of verbal explanation.

■ Avoid long indoor scenes set in one room.

■ Whenever possible use pictures rather than words to tell your story.

■ Moving quickly between short scenes will increase pace and maintain tension.

7

Dialogue

THE THREE FUNCTIONS OF DIALOGUE

Dialogue is traditionally said to have three functions.

1. **To advance the story**. Just as each scene in a play should move the story forward, so each line of dialogue – or sequence of lines – should also move the plot onwards. Dialogue which repeats itself, or tells us things we know already, or gets bogged down in side issues, will destroy the dramatic tension of the scene.

2. **To reveal character**. A good line not only moves the story forward, it also reveals some facet, however minor, of the speaker's personality. See how Anna's character emerges from the two speeches quoted on page 72.

3. **To give us information**. Good dialogue gives us a mass of information – but without us realizing it. If you look at the opening of the *Boon* episode on page 57 you will see how few words have actually been used to set up three stories and introduce half a dozen characters.

HOW TO CREATE CHARACTER THROUGH DIALOGUE

Everyone speaks differently, uses different vocabulary, different speech patterns. The characters in your play should be identifiable by their speech and the expressions they use. A common piece of advice is: after you have written a page of dialogue put a ruler over the names of the characters and then see if you can identify the speakers from their words alone.

Intelligence, class, education, geographical background – all these things contribute to the way people speak. It is a useful dramatic device to give characters expressions of their own: the most famous perhaps being Walter Gabriel's 'Me old pal me old beauty' in *The Archers*, or references to 'She who must be obeyed' in *Rumpole*. Read *The Importance of Being Earnest* and see that for all Wilde's stylization, the languid speech patterns of Lady Bracknell contrast with the down-to-earth speech of Gwendoline.

COLOUR AND TEXTURE

> The barge she sat in, like a burnish'd throne,
> Burn'd on the water. The poop was beaten gold,
> Purple the sails, and so perfumed that
> The winds were love-sick with them, the oars were silver
> Which to the tune of flutes kept stroke, and made
> The water which they beat to follow faster,
> As amorous of their strokes.
>
> (Shakespeare, *Antony and Cleopatra*)

Most television dialogue imitates documentary realism, and you are not expected to be overly lyrical in your average *Casualty* or *EastEnders*. But dialogue needs colour and texture. However naturalistic on the surface, it needs to paint pictures with words. In the script layout example on page 183 a girl desperately in love with a nuclear disarmament supporter tells us that she has been on a protest march. In terms of plot all she needs to say is: 'I went on a march'. But the writer tells us much more than that:

> ANNA: I went on a march – my red slingbacks with four-inch heels all though London, past all the shops and I didn't go in, not even down Sloane Street.

In a single line we are given a picture of Anna on her march, tottering along in red slingbacks with her eyes on the shop windows rather than the protest banners. In an earlier scene in the play Anna admits that she is not actually interested in nuclear disarmament. Her friend Daisy says: 'I'm not convinced your heart's in it' and the simple, flat answer would be: 'No, you're right, it isn't.' In the script, though, we get:

> ANNA: Of course it isn't – the whole thing's totally tedious. I'm not interested in aeroplanes and fighting and wars – that's boys' stuff. American bases and NATO bases and all the bombs have got daft names and numbers. Why hasn't Simon noticed me?

Quality of dialogue, expressed through vocabulary and images, is what stamps your own signature on a script. If you gave Lucy Gannon, Andrew Davies, and Alan Bennett an identical subject on which to write, they would all produce excellent, well-structured, well-characterized plays – but each would be totally different. This would be caused largely by their different views of life, but we would be made most aware of it through each writer's distinctive dialogue.

ECONOMY WITH WORDS

When Oscar Wilde said he had spent all morning deciding to put a comma in a sentence, and all afternoon deciding to take it out, he was probably telling no more than the truth.

In a film or television script every word should count. Every word should have its purpose. Once you have written a scene, go back through it and see how many lines you can lose, how many words you can strike out without losing either plot, atmosphere, or characterization. You must be your own first script editor – and the more ruthless you are the better.

Dramatic dialogue is superficially naturalistic, but in fact is highly artificial. In real life people 'um' and they 'ah', they don't finish their sentences, they employ a surprisingly limited vocabulary, and they generally use ten words where one will do.

The art of television dialogue is to write something that sounds naturalistic, but in which every word has a place and a purpose.

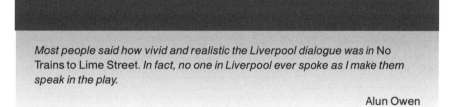

Most people said how vivid and realistic the Liverpool dialogue was in No Trains to Lime Street. *In fact, no one in Liverpool ever spoke as I make them speak in the play.*

Alun Owen

SUBTEXT

Subtext sounds a bit technical and advanced – it's the sort of word (the favourite is **genre**) that script editors like to use. Really it is very simple. The subtext is the meaning that is being conveyed, when the meaning is different from the words actually spoken.

When the lecher sidles up to the girl on a dusky summer's evening and murmurs: 'Why don't we go into the garden and look at the Old English roses?' and she looks him coolly up and down before smiling discreetly and saying: 'Yes, why not?' – we know full well that they are not anticipating a chat about horticulture and ways to combat greenfly.

And when another girl hears the conversation and watches them leave and turns indignantly to another person and says: 'My God, did you see that? What an oily bastard – and what a tart she is!', we know that elements of personal jealousy are bubbling beneath the surface.

The commonly quoted example of subtext through pictures is the scene in the film *Tom Jones* where Tom and Mrs Waters eat a meal with their fingers in an outrageously seductive manner. The pictures show them devouring their food; the subtext tells us that they are devouring each other.

THE THROUGH LINE

The first thing an actor does when he opens a script is to see how big his part is. The next thing he looks for is a 'through line' for his character.

He is looking for a logical progress of thoughts and ideas. He can only memorize his lines if one thought leads to another thought, one exchange of dialogue leads, logically, to another. Actors find lines difficult to learn if the thoughts and expressions are illogical or repetitive.

'BAD LANGUAGE'

Language is extraordinarily powerful; much more powerful than pictures. A BBC survey in 1987 showed that strong disapproval of bad language exceeded strong disapproval of sex on television by a margin of three to one. Television transmits into people's homes, where three generations, from children to grandparents, might be watching at the same time. Television companies therefore have to be careful about the language they use.

There is an evening watershed at nine o'clock. Before then certain words cannot – or should not – be used. Both the BBC and IBA have from time to time graded words according to their offensiveness. In a recent ruling 'bollocks' was not approved before nine o'clock but, curiously, 'bugger' and 'piss off' were all right in small doses. 'Shag' was only allowable before nine if it referred to tobacco or the common cormorant. 'Fuck' could not be said at all.

Times change. Some children's dramas – meaningful, socially relevant ones – now sometimes include phrases like 'piss off' and words like 'arsehole', while 'fuck off' is heard on terrestrial television after nine o'clock. Satellite television now shows feature films that have not been expurgated.

The new writer needs a good story and good dialogue – but providing it is justified, the use of gutsy language will not do any harm. A few 'bollocks' will meet with most script editors' approval; it gives them something to champion, and lets them think they are advancing the cause of television drama. And at the end of the day they can always cut them out.

COMMON FAULTS IN DIALOGUE

Unsayable lines

New writers often write dialogue that looks fine on paper, but is

> *Writing film and TV plays – that is writing dramatic dialogue – absolutely demands that the writer should be alive to the sound of everyday speech.*
>
> Rodney Bennett, director)

actually very difficult to say. Read your lines out loud to see how well they work. Avoid not only tongue twisters like 'the Leith Police dismisseth us', but convoluted lines, repetitive lines, and lines with a great number of very short words: 'I'll just ask if they don't mind us going out to find out what was going on.' (Mind you, if you do write a line as bad as that you might as well give up.)

This is not to say you can't repeat words and phrases:

DICK: OK, all right, that's it then Sunbeam, you've done it this time, this time you are in real trouble, oh yes you are in real trouble...

says our angry policeman moving rapidly across the cell and grabbing his victim by the throat.

Dialogue should be alive, it should sparkle. It has been described as the 'nerve ends of feelings', it is usually based on emotional responses, and if it is well written it gives pace and energy to the script.

Use of dialect

It is risky to get enmeshed in dialect and foreign accents. A play written in dialect is pretty well guaranteed to make a script editor's eyes glaze over. Italians crying 'Mama Mia' and Frenchmen shouting 'Allez mes enfants!' are nearly as off-putting as Yorkshiremen saying 'Ahm gerrin off down't pit but a'l sithi' in't mornin''. Regional clichés ('By gum, it's a bit parky tonight, mother') are also best avoided, and the example of dialogue below not only shows us the awfulness of fake dialect but also demonstrates another fault common in many scripts:

GEORGE: Shall us have our tea now then Martha?

MARTHA: Aye if tha's ready George.

GEORGE: Wilt have an egg wi' bacon for tha's tea Martha?

MARTHA: If that's what tha's having George.

GEORGE: Ah thinks ah'll have a sausage, Martha.

MARTHA: You have what tha' bloody well likes, George.

The additional fault is:

Overuse of character names

A common fault is for characters to call each other by name to an extent that is not credible. In real life we rarely need to tag a person's name on to the end of a sentence, and in conversation most people only use a person's name to create intimacy or to emphasise the importance of what they are saying. A woman might say: 'John, that is not true. I swear to you that I was nowhere near Randy Ron's house last night', or a man might say: 'I'm sorry Michele, I really am.'

Pseudo dialect, badly chosen character names (see page 87) and overuse of character names can ruin dialogue that might otherwise be perfectly acceptable. Look at the dialogue between George and Martha if the dialect is taken out, the characters given different names and the passage put in a dramatic framework.

GILLIAN's nerves are at breaking point. Her father-in-law TOM has been staying in the house since the death of her husband PATRICK in an accident three weeks ago. TOM is a widower in his late eighties, bewildered and lost – GILLIAN tries to be kind, but all she wants is to be alone.

GILLIAN sits staring into the empty fireplace. TOM looks at her once or twice.

TOM: Shall we have some tea?

GILLIAN: If you're ready.

She does not move. TOM says nothing for a moment, then tries to speak brightly.

TOM: Will you have some eggs and
bacon?

GILLIAN: If that's what you're having.

She still does not look up.

TOM: I think I'll have a sausage.

GILLIAN: Have what you bloody well like!

Silence. Slowly, GILLIAN starts to cry.

Summary

■ Every line of dialogue should advance the story, reveal the character of the person speaking, or give us background information. A good line will do all three things.

■ Every word you write should be necessary or should be cut.

■ Dialogue should sound totally natural unless you are writing in a deliberately stylized manner (not recommended: script editors will simply think that you can't write).

■ The more you can make your dialogue fresh, lively and vivid the better.

■ Avoid dialect.

■ Avoid over-using character names.

■ Say lines out loud, or in your head, as you write them.

8

Characterization

GIVING CHARACTERS DEPTH

A common note of dismissal on rejected scripts is: 'characters two dimensional' or 'cardboard characters'. This means that the characters do not 'come off the page' as rounded, interesting, individual personalities. It is not always easy to give characters depth when everything they do, or say, must somehow advance the story. Here are some hints.

■ Avoid stereotypes. For example, do not have retired colonels who cry 'What? What?' in peppery voices and complain about young people today.

■ Give even minor characters more than one aspect to their nature. This does not have to be extreme – you do not have to give a vicar a penchant for roulette – but remember that people are made up of a complex mixture of likes, dislikes, strengths, weaknesses and moral views.

■ At its simplest, if you have a postman who appears two or three times in your script, and whose only function is to deliver letters critical to your plot, decide: is he a happy postman? Or a miserable postman? Does he perhaps whistle, and if so, what sort of tune? A whistling postman is a bit of a cliche, but what if he's a dour, miserable-looking postman who always whistles 'The Sun has got his hat on, hip-hip-hip-hurray?' You will, *without a single line of dialogue*, have given your postman an intriguing feature, a personality.

■ A cunning if weary old ploy used by professional writers is to give the hero a minor failing (a detective hero who can't resist cream buns) and the villain a minor virtue (a gangster with a secret passion for Gilbert and Sullivan operettas). This technique can give the script the appearance, at least, of depth of characterization.

■ You can sometimes rescue a clichéd character late on in a script by adding unexpected humour and self-awareness. Your peppery colonel mutters 'Dear God, young people today! His wife says, 'Why do you *always* have to say that?' He replies musingly, 'I've no idea. Perhaps because it's expected of me', and his wife stares at him in amazement. This technique gives you the advantage of the stereotype (viewers know exactly where they are) with the added virtue of dramatic revelation as a new side to the colonel's character is revealed.

Developing characters

The development of character is an important part of any drama, indeed most dramas are not about action but about reaction, not about car chases and murder but about the effect such events have on the attitudes of the people who survive them.

The important thing is to build the different facets of a person's personality into a coherent

Every single character, even a bastard like Goldberg in The Birthday Party, *I care for.*

Harold Pinter

whole. The actor studying the part will be looking for a **through line** of character development (see page 74). If the character in question is mild and sensible at the beginning of the play, but ends up smashing the furniture and butchering the cat, then the actor will:

■ want to know why his character has changed;

■ want to understand the thought processes that have led to the change;

■ look for the key line, possibly by another character ('People forget George's unpredictable temper, but it's always there, it's not gone away') that will help to understand why he has turned into a cat-murdering fiend;

■ go back to the beginning – and create a performance from the start which allows the character later to reveal hidden emotional depths.

Actors become frustrated when they find in one scene that they are good-natured, and in another scene that they are not – but cannot find any explanation in the script.

ILL-TREATING CHARACTERS

Writers can do terrible things to their characters. They create creatures that live and breathe – and then destroy them, carelessly or ruthlessly, to maintain their plot, or to save a scene that is looking sticky, or because they can't think what to do next and making a character do something highly peculiar will cause a temporary sensation.

There are two forms of character sacrifice to beware of:

- sacrificing character for plot;

- sacrificing character for sensation.

Sacrificing your characters for plot

The most common fault is to make formerly intelligent characters behave stupidly for no reason (see the idiot plot, page 46), or to make characters behave out of character because the plot demands it.

Perhaps your story is that of a 16-year-old girl who is pregnant and who is frightened to tell anyone. You want us to see her attempting to confide in a succession of people, including her mother.

ELVA: The thing is Mum –

MUM: Just look at your father! I don't know what he thinks he's doing!

ELVA: I'm in trouble..real trouble –

MUM: Out there in this wind without his pullover on!

ELVA: I've got to tell you; I'll go mad if I don't tell somebody.

MUM: Just go and give him a shout, Elva – I know I like fresh brussels sprouts but if he gets one of his colds we'll hear about it for weeks.

Mum here is presumably stone deaf and stupid – all very well, but elsewhere in the play we may have found her to be a perfectly normal, reasonably intelligent person. The writer *needs* Elva to fail to communicate so that she can be rejected by the world (and so that the play will run for a full 50 minutes), so in this particular scene Mum's character as a sane human being is sacrificed to make the plot work. A similar occurrence is likely to happen in the doctor's surgery:

ELVA: (Whispers) I'm sorry I've no appointment –

RECEPTIONIST: Twenty past three Wednesday with Dr McClaren.

ELVA: I was hoping this afternoon –

RECEPTIONIST: Sorry, Wednesday's the earliest I can manage. (Phone. She lifts it.) Excuse me. Medical Centre, can I help you?

ELVA turns and goes. The RECEPTIONIST reaches for her appointments book. As ELVA goes out in the dark rainy afternoon we hear:

RECEPTIONIST: (OOV into phone) Can you manage 3.20 on Wednesday with Dr McClaren?

All very well if the intention is to portray the receptionist as unsympathetic but a problem if we have previously found her to be perceptive and warm hearted with a natural affinity for the young.

Sacrificing your character for sensation

Sacrificing a character on the altar of sensation is a major crime, most commonly done in soap operas. Perhaps a happily married woman suddenly goes berserk and starts having an affair with a character she has previously shown no interest in whatsoever. To understand why, we need to go back to a storyline meeting three months previously.

Producer, editors, storyliners and writers are fretting over what to do with Alice, who has not had a decent story for ages. This is a major crisis – not because the actress concerned is complaining night and day (nobody cares about that) but because she has been guaranteed 20 episodes (or at least payment for 20 episodes) and so far she has only been in three. The storyline meeting must find her a story! In the end somebody says: 'We've no story for George, either. Why don't they have an affair?' Everybody of sense at the meeting says it's impossible, Alice is 48 and president of the Mothers' Union, George is a 21-year-old rock singer. It simply would never happen! But the producer is a desperate woman (the bar opens in five minutes) so she says: 'Anything can happen in life, we mustn't be hidebound.' Alice has her pointless affair and her character is irrevocably altered.

It is easy to get a temporary sensation by making somebody behave oddly, but it does not work unless what happens genuinely springs from within the personality of the character concerned.

THE THOUGHT PROCESS

The film *Three Into One Won't Go* opens with a middle-aged man driving his car. He comes across a very attractive girl thumbing a

> *A drama ought to bring out character as a photographer's chemicals bring out the forms latent on the negative.*
>
> William Archer

lift. He stops, some distance beyond her, opens the car door, and waits for her to come and jump in. When he looks back she is standing, hand on hip, waiting for him to back up to her. Unsmiling, he backs the car, and she gets in.

Not a word of dialogue has been spoken, but already we know of his middle-aged sexual frustration, and of her self-assurance and knowledge of the power she has over men of a certain age.

You cannot write for a character unless you know that character and understand what they are thinking at all times. When a character says something you always need to know why, because when an actor plays the part he must have a reason for what he is saying and doing. If you do not supply one, then the actor will have to find his own.

This sounds obvious – of course a writer knows what a character is thinking – but it is far from uncommon for a frustrated and simmering actor to corner a helpless writer after a read-through and say: 'I just cannot understand why I say this line on page 19: "Higgs deserves promotion if anybody does", when on page 5 I nodded in agreement when Jones said that Higgs was a brain-dead idle prat. Am I telling a complete lie? I mean, I can, of course, if that's what you intend.'

'Yes, that's it,' says the desperate writer, his mouth full of chicken vol-au-vent, but the actor continues remorselessly: 'But of course it totally affects the way I say the line, and if I'm lying why do I tell Sarah on page 24 that Higgs is the best thing that ever happened to the school?'

CHARACTER NAMES

A respected series writer had one failing. She could never think up a name for the new characters she had to introduce. She would ponder for hours, but her characters always ended up being called Robinson – usually Jim Robinson or Bill Robinson. A special effort might yield Robertson, and one day she even managed a Roberts. It was always left to the script editor to think up something different.

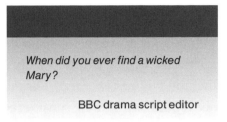

When did you ever find a wicked Mary?

BBC drama script editor

Names are strangely important. Given that in real life our personalities and names are connected in a totally arbitrary fashion, one ought to be able to produce six names for six characters and then shuffle them in a bag. But it does not work like that. See if you agree with the following.

- Hard names go with hard personalities; soft names with good-natured people.

- Working-class characters are called Bert and Maureen, toffs are called Simon and Emma.

- Young working-class characters are called Wayne and Sharon, young toffs are still called Simon and Emma.

- Working classes are surnamed Grice and Leech and Stott, toffs are surnamed Burlington-Smythe and Pomeroy and Beauchamp.

These are the clichés. But in real life, of course, the clichés are often true. You won't find many hereditary peers called Wayne or peeresses called Kylie, and if you shout 'Jeremy' or 'Henrietta' on a Toxteth housing estate you won't hear the patter of many tiny feet.

It is also true that the public has expectations from certain names, and the dramatist can use them as tools of his trade. A psychological study in America revealed that desirable names included Gregory and Craig; unpopular, undesirable names included Elmer, Hubert, Darrell and Horace. In Britain all the above names might be considered unappealing. A British report in the 1980s found that the public regarded:

- John as trustworthy;

- Robin as young;

- Tony as sociable;

- Agnes as old;

- Ann as non-aggressive;

- William as steady.

Names to help portray character

Some of the greatest writers have created names that contain within themselves the essence of the people they describe. David Copperfield's stepfather's sister was Miss Murdstone and the stolid carter was Barkis ('Barkis is willin' ').

Imagine the names changed about, with the hero David Barkis, the horrid stepfather's sister Miss Copperfield, and the carter murmuring 'Murdstone is willin' '.

The trick is to devise names that sound *appropriate* and at the same time avoid the obvious cliché. Jobbing gardeners should not be called Mr Potts – but neither should they be called Fossington-Fawcett (unless there is a deliberate irony, as when you call a pigman Lavender). Dashing, sexy heroes called Raymond Witson or Terry Stott or Kenneth Swindon are facing an uphill struggle, but so are Rik Steele and Jed Tempest.

Names to add colour

Names can be memorable (Dr Strangelove) or likeable and affectionate (Hawkeye and Trapper). The most important thing is that they should stand out (avoid too many characters called Smith and Brown and Tom and Fred) and should roll off the tongue in a satisfying way (Ena Sharples, Annie Walker).

And some to avoid

Avoid names that are similar – a Johnny and a Ronnie, a Mandy and a Sandy – in the same play.

SUMMARY

- Characters must have more than one characteristic.

- Avoid stereotypes.

- Do not force characters to behave stupidly in order to make a creaking plot work.

- Do not allow characters to behave out of character without reason or explanation.

- Remember that everything a character says or does reveals an aspect of their personality.

- Avoid cliché names.

9

Situation Comedy

Situation comedies – sitcoms – are commonly thought to be the hardest scripts of all to write. The problem – as one ITV Head of Comedy put it – is that whilst you can generally get some kind of broad agreement about the merits of a straight drama script, it is virtually impossible to find agreement over what is or is not funny. The first episode of *Jam and Jerusalem* was considered very funny by *Heat* magazine, but another critic said, 'This is like death'. The chemistry of the production is also vital and unpredictable. Sometimes scripts and actors seem brilliant, but the result, after rehearsal and recording, is dull, plodding and deadly. On the other hand a script thought desperately weak might suddenly take off when the cast and director get to work on it. It's a difficult area of writing, but the rewards are high if you can get it right. In this chapter we look at:

- the different types of situation comedy;

- what the programme makers are looking for;

- settings for sitcoms;

- character in sitcoms;

- structure in sitcoms;

- to joke or not to joke?;

- budgets;

- hints for the new sitcom writer;

- hit comedies.

THE DIFFERENT TYPES OF COMEDY

The most common reason for scripts being rejected – apart from them being simply not funny on any sort of level – is that they mix different styles, and thus fail at all of them. As a new writer, you need to be very clear from the beginning about the type of comedy you are writing.

1. Suspended disbelief

In situation comedies like *Blackadder* or *'Allo 'Allo* we happily suspend our disbelief. In other words we don't mind characters doing bizarre, illogical things or reacting to events in a way that would be unbelievable in rational human beings. When Baldrick spends a fortune on a turnip we don't say: 'This is ridiculous, no turnip could cost that much, and if it did surely Mr Blackadder would at least look surprised...' If we do say this sort of thing we are clearly humourless and our spouse will divorce us, and our pets will all seek new homes.

Comedies that incorporate the absurd are the most difficult to get right. All comedy involves a deviation from the norm, and if there are no rules of normal behaviour it is hard to get a laugh out of people deviating from them.

2. Comedy of wit and logic

In a programme like *Yes, Prime Minister* we are presented with a basically unbelievable situation: a not-very-bright prime minister willing to devote hours each day to being outwitted by one obviously manipulative civil servant. But once the unreality of the premise is accepted, the scripts are totally logical and the two characters completely rational and believable. *Fawlty Towers* is the classic: supreme in that every story depends on the remorseless logic of the bizarre situations created.

3. Comedy of Life

From *Absolutely Fabulous* to *Phoenix Nights*, from *Gavin and Stacey* to *The Office*, comedies about believable (if only just) people doing unusual, interesting or just well-observed things have been hugely successful. These comedies may differ in style but all of them are essentially about the way people live, about society today, about ambitions and hopes. We are not required to suspend our disbelief when we watch them – or at least, only a little bit. Most sitcoms fall into this category, and this is the area in which a new writer is most likely to succeed.

4. Broken comedy

This is sketch-type comedy, examples being *That Mitchell and Webb Look* and *Little Britain*.

WHAT THE PROGRAMME MAKERS ARE LOOKING FOR

Comedies that open with the reading of a will, or the winning of the lottery, are said to be clichés – but that doesn't mean you won't see both on screen in 12 months' time. At various times BBC One has asked for 'sophisticated, distinctive comedy which is adult in ambition and tone' for transmission after 9pm, and programmes that have 'inclusiveness and a sense of community' for pre-watershed showing. It is these comedies (e.g. *My Family, Only Fools and Horses, The Vicar of Dibley*), suitable for a family audience spanning three generations, that the BBC says are the hardest to find.

Otherwise, BBC One is not interested in 'laddish' comedies that follow the tradition of *Men Behaving Badly*, but see E4's *The Inbetweeners*. BBC Two says it wants 'quick wit and clever observation to shine a light on favourite obsessions and pastimes' and Channel 4 has shown itself happiest when its comedies have something to say about society – hence *The Wilsons* which featured single parents and social workers – and with experimental shows that incubate writer-actor talent like *Ali G* and the all-female *Smack the Pony.*

> There is a majority of women in charge of commissioning at the BBC these days and all those Janes and Kates and Sophies can't bear a series in which a group of lads sit around, talk about sport and take the piss out of each other... The comedy buzzword at the BBC these days is 'uplifting'.
>
> BBC producer

Both Channel 4 and BBC Three target audiences in their twenties and thirties.

SETTINGS

Good sitcoms often take a very ordinary setting and then let the characters turn it upside down – suburbia in *One Foot in the Grave,* a seaside hotel in *Fawlty Towers.*

Zany, off-beat situations on the other hand are regarded as notoriously hard to make funny. 'A fish running an Internet café set on the dark side of Mars is not original but desperate,' says the BBC scathingly.

At the end of the day the setting is not as important as what you, the writer, do with it. 'Flat sharing' has for long been said to be an overworked and clichéd setting – but that didn't stop the BBC Two hit *Gimme, Gimme, Gimme* or BBC One's *Not Going Out*.

CHARACTERS

Sitcom characters ought not to be too nice, says the BBC, and by nice they mean bland. Characters in comedy engage our interest because of their flaws, not because of their good nature. Captain Mainwaring and Victor Meldrew are likeable, of course, but it is the former's pomposity and the latter's frustration that makes us laugh. Most comedy characters have ordinary characteristics that are heightened. Stupid characters are extra stupid, snobby people are extra snobby. The golden rule is that *characters must be consistent.* In *Blackadder* Baldrick always has a cunning plan, Blackadder is always cynical, and the deeply, if engagingly, stupid character is always deeply and engagingly stupid.

Situation comedy is also very much about the **conflict** of characters within the situation you have set up. Conflict in sitcom can include the following.

- **Opposites** – *Friends* got much of its background comedy from an untidy person sharing a flat with an obsessionally tidy person; and a bloke confident with the opposite sex sharing a flat with a bloke who was insecure with the opposite sex.

- **Role reversal** – in *Absolutely Fabulous* Edina Monsoon is wild and irresponsible, while daughter Saffy is sensible and grown-up.

STRUCTURE

The structure of a sitcom is the same as that for any other kind of drama. (Crisis. Confusion. Resolution.) Typically in a sitcom, however, there will be a final twist to the end.

a) You set up a crisis.

b) The crisis deepens as your principal characters try – hilariously if possible – to resolve it.

c) They believe they have finally succeeded.

d) They suddenly find that they haven't.

The final stage might only last for four seconds – time for the ceiling to collapse, the studio audience to roar, and the signature tune to play loudly as we go chortling into the credits.

TO JOKE OR NOT TO JOKE?

The BBC in particular has an aversion to jokes and 'one-line gags'. You should not try to make every line a laugh, they say, severely, but should create humour out of characters reacting to comic situations with actions and dialogue. In other words, the rules of straight drama also apply to comedy. This does not mean you must avoid comic lines like Hancock's 'A pint? Ave you gone mad? That's very nearly an armful!' in *The Blood Donor*.

At the end of the day all you can do is write what you yourself believe to be funny. 'Do not simply try to match some mediocre show you saw on TV last night,' the BBC warns, probably fearing a thousand proposals based on *My Hero*.

If you can't come up with an idea just stick some kids in it, it never fails. 'My Son the Boss' – you work in a crazy company where your son is the boss, it's insane. 'Castaway Kids' – where you adopt some kids who were left on your doorstep. 'Kids in Space' – where you adopt some kids who were left on your doorstep by aliens.

American writer Andy Kindler

20 TOP TIPS FOR THE NEW SITCOM WRITER

1. Most successful sitcoms have only three or four central characters.

2. Those with a larger cast work best when there is a place where the characters can meet and interact without the need to explain what they are doing there. In *Dad's Army* and *The Vicar of Dibley* the characters meet naturally in the church hall, in *Phoenix Nights* they meet naturally at the Phoenix Club, in *The Office* they are in the office.

3. A high proportion of sitcoms explore aspects of the British character and the British way of life.

4. Most sitcoms are recorded before a live audience, and therefore have only three or four sets.

5. In sitcoms that are recorded before an audience, the action usually happens over a short period of time – this avoids changes in costume that slow down the recording.

6. Give yourself a theme – e.g. the recurrent theme of *Friends* is the nature of friendship; the theme of *Last of the Summer Wine*

is that you don't have to be young to be foolish; the theme of *Men Behaving Badly* is men behaving badly.

7. Make sure that your theme – the premise of your situation – has ongoing comic possibilities.

8. Few comic ideas can sustain half an hour. Consider having two or three stories running at once – they don't necessarily have to interweave, though it is regarded as neat if the outcome of one story alters or shapes the outcome of another.

9. Don't rely on coincidence to make your plot work. The story should unfold the way it does because of the actions and reactions of your characters to a particular situation.

10. As in other forms of drama, don't let your characters tell each other things they already know (and which they know they already know) just to make your story clear.

11. Surprise and outwit your audience. The classic example provided by Charlie Chaplin was: A man walks along a street. The camera cuts to a banana skin on the pavement. The audience expect him to slip on it – but instead he carefully steps over it, looks back at it with a smile, and promptly falls down a manhole.

12. Avoid spending the first dozen pages of your script introducing the characters and setting the scene. For some reason this almost always involves over-acting, feeble jokes, and forced humour. Start your episode with a strong story that gives the actors something to act, and makes us want to know what happens next. Write two or three episodes, and then submit the best. It is surprising how little information is genuinely needed to introduce a situation and set of characters.

13. Humour has to be sustained. American sitcom producers aim to trigger a laugh every 13 seconds.

14. But don't force your humour. It must arise naturally from the situation you have skilfully created (in between your 13-second laughs).

15. Sitcom writing often works well as a joint effort – two writers exchanging ideas and rewriting each others' draft scripts.

16. Do not write for a specific star actor, even if you have an ideal actor in mind. The production companies want to see how you write original comedy for characters of your own creation.

17. Do not write a long explanation of why your idea is funny, and do not write long descriptions of your characters. Give a very brief synopsis (two or three lines if possible) of your story idea, short character notes if you must, then let your script itself do the work.

18. The BBC suggests that when you submit your script you tell them what writing experience you have had. Treat this advice with caution. It's fine to say you are new to television writing (they like to discover a star of tomorrow) but don't say that you have been writing scripts and submitting them without success since *Dad's Army* was the best new sitcom of the year.

19. Go and watch a sitcom being made. For information on BBC sitcom recordings phone 020 8576 1227 or write to:
BBC Audience Services
PO Box 3000
London WI2 7RJ.

20. Take advantage of online comedy workshops. They are run from time to time by the BBC, Channel 4, and even by independent companies (see Chapter 18).

HIT COMEDIES

For what it's worth, and to show what comedy afficionados want – which is not necessarily the same as what programme-makers want – in a 2004 BBC Two poll to find the most popular British sitcoms, over 40% voted for either *Only Fools and Horses* or *Blackadder,* and for every viewer who voted for the critically-acclaimed *One Foot in the Grave* seven viewers voted for *The Vicar of Dibley.* The top ten were:

Only Fools and Horses
Blackadder
The Vicar of Dibley
Dad's Army
Fawlty Towers
Yes Minister
Porridge
Open All Hours
The Good Life
One Foot in the Grave

10

Presentation

How to make the right impression

The all-important moment will come when a script editor or professional reader opens your script at the first page – and instantly forms a judgement. This judgement will be based on the style and presentation of your work. It will be a superficial judgement and a work of quality will shine through the poorest layout. But it makes sense to give a good impression: the impression of a serious writer confident about his work.

Presentation that lets you down

Avoid at all costs sending in scripts that are:

- written carelessly;

- poorly laid out on the page;

- lazily presented;

- tired and travel-stained;

- written for another medium (e.g. radio);

- professionally 'packaged'.

Careless scripts

Script editors are not impressed by scripts that are carelessly typed with obvious mistakes and characters muddled up:

JOHN
I love you now and I have always loved you.

SALLY
Conviction, John, conviction is what I want to hear.

SALLY
I love you and I have alwoys loved you, dammit!

SALLY
Somehow it still doesn't sund right.

As Sally cannot have three speeches one after another, it is, of course, easy to work out that the middle speech belongs to John. Typing errors are easily explained. But working this out slows up the reading of the script, interrupts the flow of the narrative, and reveals that the writer has not bothered to read his work through before posting it.

'I always write fast – once the idea comes to me I just have to get it down on paper, and once I've written it, that's it, I just can't look at it again.' So says the hopeful writer, presumably believing that the script editor will be impressed or at the very least indulgent.

The script editor will not be impressed or indulgent. The script editor will think: 'This is an amateur wasting my time.'

Poor layout on the page

Avoid layout that is confusing or unfamiliar, or makes it hard to separate dialogue from studio directions. Do not write:

John 'Good Morning'
Jane 'Good morning, darling. What do you want for breakfast'
John 'Egg and bacon please.' John pauses then says 'On second
thoughts I'll just have coffee.' Jane shakes her head.
Jane 'You and your silly diet'
John sits down and hides behind his copy of the paper. He is
annoyed by Jane mentioning his weight again. I see the West
Indies are all out for ninety five.
Jane 'You know I never read cricket.'

Scripts do arrive written like this, and the prejudice against them
is considerable. The script editor assumes, reasonably, that if the
writer cannot be bothered to consider the basic principles of script
layout – or even to be consistent in the style he has chosen – then
he has little chance of ever succeeding in the demanding,
professional world of television.

Lazy presentation

A surprisingly large number of new writers use initials for the
names of characters rather than spelling them out each time the
character speaks. The writer tells us on the first page that his
characters are called Henry and June and have two children
called Kylie and Tom. In the script itself he writes:

H: I want everybody in the car in five minutes.
K: I can't find my cosie! Where's my cosie!
J: I haven't the foggiest idea, but I do know I told you to start
looking for it three hours ago.
T: I've got mine. I always know where mine is.

Script editors hate this. They keep having to refer back to the front
page to remind themselves who T is and who K is. This makes it

hard for them to become absorbed in your work.

Tired and travel-stained script

Do not submit scripts that are:

- world-weary, crumpled and yellowing with age;

- have comments on them from a previous submission.

Do not expect wonderful results from scripts that are creased and curly at the corners, decorated with ancient coffee stains, festooned with little messages like 'Ack 27/3/94' and with comments in the margins: 'Does not follow', 'Who is this character?', 'Weak dialogue' or even, showing the ultimate boredom, some previous script reader's shopping list. These are the signs of a well-travelled script that has seen the world and knows what it is to be rejected. It is a script that expects, even as the editor lifts it gingerly from her 'unsolicited' tray, to be rejected again. And it is.

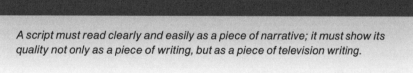

A script must read clearly and easily as a piece of narrative; it must show its quality not only as a piece of writing, but as a piece of television writing.

Arthur Swinson

Scripts written for another medium

If you have had no luck with a radio play and decide to try it on television – fine. But make sure you adapt it first. There is no point in sending a radio play to a television company with the hopeful plea: 'Although this is written for radio, I now think it would be very good on television.' Few editors will bother to read it. You might just as well make a chair and try to sell it to somebody who wants a table.

If you do adapt a radio play, check it carefully before you send it off. All too often, around page six or seven, can be found the tell-tale sound direction: 'Fade up grams FX of storm at sea'.

It is also common for writers to adapt a play from television to radio, and still to leave in directions for cameras to pan, or cut, or zoom. Radio producers loathe this. They feel inferior enough already without people conning them into buying television drama's rejects.

Overkill presentation

Some writers go to endless trouble getting their script typed by a professional agency, often with the title printed via the magic of desktop publishing, and the result bound lavishly like a Hollywood studio script.

It seems heartless to say to a writer so obviously making an effort 'Don't bother' – but it is a mistake to spend too much time concentrating on presentation. Nobody is going to buy a script because it comes in a lavish presentation package. Many script editors will be actively put off.

There is a feeling that the script has already been 'processed' in some way, or that it is being dressed up smartly to cover its inadequacies. The script editor, remember, is sustained by the hope that the next unsolicited script she reaches for will be a work of genius – a first offering by the Dennis Potter or Alan Plater of the future.

Somehow nobody expects genius to come in a glitzy, professional presentation.

> *There is a perverse rule of thumb amongst editors and producers in British television that the more impeccably the script is presented, the duller the contents.*
>
> Eric Paice, writer

PRESENTATION THAT HELPS YOU

Things to think about here are:

- page layout;

- writing for the camera;

- writing for the actor.

Page layout

Some new writers worry endlessly about layout. They know that television scripts wastefully use only half of the page, and that there is a mysterious professional code governing the use of CAPITAL letters for characters' names, and that colons and underlinings feature strangely, and that professional scripts are dotted with terse instructions demanding an MCU or a 2-SHOT or a PAN LEFT. (See Chapter 17, TV Talk.)

In fact, there is no fixed layout even among production scripts, which vary between the BBC and ITV companies and in small details often follow the personal whim of the production secretary. Certainly at the first stage of writing there are no vital formulae, and as you are not typing a studio script it is pointless to imitate one.

That said, it is common sense to conform to a layout that will be familiar to the script editor, and will be easy to read and to understand. Two of the basic rules are:

- always make a clear distinction between dialogue and description;

- always leave a wide margin on the left-hand side of the page.

What you are trying to achieve is a simple, straightforward layout that will allow the reader or script editor to read your play effortlessly, gripped by your story, intrigued by your characters and savouring your excellent dialogue.

There are two basic layouts. They have one thing in common: they are easy to read, and they are familiar to script editors, readers and directors alike. (See Figures 1 and 2 on pages 107 and 108.)

The BBC also provides free script-layout software that you can download from *bbc.co.uk/writersroom.*

Writing for the camera

Should you indicate when you want a medium close up (called an MCU)? or a two-shot? Or when you think the use of a crane shot or dolphin arm might be of artistic use? The answer is no, don't do any of these things unless they are vital to the telling of your story. Script editors find they get in the way, writers get bogged down in technicalities and end up thinking they have written a professional script just because it *looks* like a professional script.

It is not your job to write a camera script, it is your job to write a play.

1. EXT. FRONT GARDEN OF CROSSLEY HOUSE. EARLY MORNING

The front door opens and the family Rottweiler CONAN is let out into the garden.

> BOBBY (OOV)
> Go on, get out!

The front door closes. CONAN trots to the front gate and looks out. A dirty and rather old Ford Escort is parked on the other side of the road.

2. INT. UNMARKED POLICE CAR. EARLY MORNING

DC ROBERTS, the passenger, stares across the road at CONAN.

> ROBERTS
> That's the best looking member of the family I've seen so far.

DC LAWLESS, the driver, peeps from behind his Sun.

> ROBERTS
> It looks almost intelligent, comparatively.

LAWLESS folds his paper and starts the car.

> LAWLESS
> Time for breakfast.

> ROBERTS
> It's the eyes, there's something behind them, that's what makes the difference.

3. INT. BOBBY CROSSLEY'S BEDROOM. EARLY MORNING

BOBBY is watching the car drive down the road.

> BOBBY
> Bastards.

Fig. 1. Script layout: style one.

47. EXT. CROSSLEYS FRONT GARDEN. NIGHT

TWO POLICE OFFICERS WEARING BLACK WITH BLACK
NYLON BALACLAVAS MOVE TOWARDS THE MOTORBIKE. THE
SECOND KEEPS WATCH AS THE FIRST STARTS TO FIX A
BLACK BOX TO THE UNDERSIDE OF THE BIKE.

48. EXT. CROSSLEYS BACK YARD. NIGHT

CONAN GETS UP AND LISTENS.

49. EXT. CROSSLEYS FRONT GARDEN. NIGHT

POLICEMAN ONE IS FIDDLING WITH THE BOX.

50. EXT. CROSSLEYS BACK YARD. NIGHT

CONAN MOVES TOWARDS THE FRONT OF THE HOUSE

51. EXT. CROSSLEYS FRONT GARDEN. NIGHT

CONAN APPEARS FROM THE BACK YARD. HE GROWLS

POLICEMAN TWO: (Whisper) Dog!

POLICEMAN ONE: Sodding hell, I thought
you said it was inside for the night.

CONAN GETS CLOSER AND MORE ANNOYED LOOKING.
POLICEMAN TWO GETS A LUMP OF PIPING FROM INSIDE
HIS LEATHER JACKET. CONAN LOOKS AT HIM.

POLICEMAN ONE: Do something about it.

POLICEMAN TWO CLUMPS CONAN OVER THE HEAD WITH THE
PIPING. CONAN WHIMPERS AND DROPS. POLICEMAN ONE
STARES DOWN.

POLICEMAN TWO: Get on with it,
they'll kill us now if they find us.

POLICEMAN ONE CONTINUES WITH HIS TASK. CONAN IS
BREATHING LIKE A DOG WITH A PROBLEM.

Fig. 2. Script layout: style two.

At the same time you need to write with the camera in mind, and it is quite legitimate for you to indicate a camera move *if it is important to the telling of your story.*

Suppose you are writing a play about a doctor investigating the effect of a sinister new drug on blood cell structure. You want to open a scene with the screen filled with pictures of the drug molecules killing helpless blood cells, while a character tells excitedly of the discovery she has made.

INT. LABORATORY. DAY.

The screen is filled with a computer simulation of ZYX cells attacking ABC cells. We hear DR WARD:

> WARD (OOV)
> They multiply at bloodheat, and within 2.4 seconds they begin to attack. They are deadly and they are irresistible. Your placebo, Professor Smith, is a killer.

CUT TO: WARD and SMITH staring down at the screen. SMITH's face is expressionless.

> WARD
> You understand why I wanted you to come straight away. I'm sorry.

CUT TO: CU of SMITH staring down. From his POV we move slowly in again on the screen. Eerie theme music plays as we go closer and closer.

> WARD (OOV)
> Professor Smith? Are you all right?

In this illustration (OOV) indicates that Ward is speaking 'Out of Vision' and CUT TO indicates, as you would expect, that the camera cuts directly to WARD and SMITH. (We could have written PULL BACK instead of CUT TO, and this would have meant that the camera would slowly pull back from the screen to reveal the two characters staring down.) We then go to a CLOSE UP of SMITH before looking at the screen again from SMITH's POV ('Point of View') before the camera zooms slowly down again to a CLOSE UP of the battling blood cells.

These camera directions are quite acceptable as a way of telling your story. The director is unlikely to follow them: when the programme is made he will regard it as a point of honour to shoot the scene differently, but at least you will have shown your artistic intention. Camera directions commonly used by writers are as follows.

- POV – meaning we see something from a particular character's point of view.

- CLOSE UP (CU) – meaning the camera is close to something, generally somebody's face unless you indicate otherwise.

- PULL BACK – the camera is in close up and you want to pull back to show more.

- ZOOM IN – generally meaning that the camera moves quickly in on an object or person, although you can ask for a SLOW ZOOM.

- CUT TO – the camera cuts from one scene to another, or from one object to another. You can indicate that you want to cut from one person's face to another to show their reactions, but you are getting dangerously into the director's domain.

- OOV – the camera is showing something but we hear the voice of an actor who is speaking at the *same time* in the same scene.

■ VO – the camera is showing a scene but we hear the 'Voice Over' of an actor who is not in the scene but might be narrating a story or recalling something in retrospect.

There are more television terms in Chapter 17 but, generally speaking, experienced writers leave pointing the camera to the person who's paid to point it: the director.

Writing for the actor

Actors have two major hates: not having a through line of thought (much more about this in Chapter 7), and being told how they should feel at any particular moment.

GEORGE
(Playfully)
I thought you said you hadn't bought a new dress.

JOANNA
(Angrily)
I haven't bought a new dress, I've had this for ages.

GEORGE
(Tongue in cheek)
That's impossible, it's the very latest fashion (cunningly devious) or perhaps my love, you would make any dress seem to be the latest fashion.

JOANNA
(Fondly)
Oh George, oh do you really think so?

Some actors will tell you that 'mood directions' kill any chance they might have of building a scene during rehearsals, of developing moods themselves and finding their own moments of dramatic tension. They will tell you that if a script *needs* constant pointers as to mood then there is something wrong with it. They will say there is nothing worse than working on lines, creating a scene with a fellow actor, discovering from the text the thoughts and intentions of the character they are playing, and then suddenly finding that – for no reason they can fathom – they are supposed to say a line 'Whimsically' or 'Laughingly'.

The trouble is that not all actors are intelligent. There is a world of difference between:

JULIAN
(Acidly)
Well done. What a genius you are my dear.

and

JULIAN
(Warmly)
Well done. What a genius you are my dear.

And not every actor can be relied upon to know how you, the writer, intended it to be spoken. See how the above scene reads quite differently if we change the mood indicators.

GEORGE
(Sharply)
I thought you said you hadn't bought a new dress.

JOANNA
(Wearily)
I haven't bought a new dress, I've had this for ages.

GEORGE (Coldly) That's impossible, it's the very latest fashion (cutting) or perhaps, my love, you would make any dress seem to be the latest fashion.

JOANNA (Sarcastic) Oh George, oh do you really think so?

Writers cannot afford to trust actors entirely. Certainly not in soap operas and series where lines are being learned and performed very quickly. Many actors would not spot that a line was meant to be ironic if you hit them over the head with it, and no writer in his right mind trusts a television director to understand his script.

If you feel you need to indicate a mood at a given time, do so. If the script editor disagrees when she reads the script she will cross it out. Otherwise it will go through and, with luck, the actor will do what you want him to do.

11

From Script to Screen

TURNING A SCRIPT INTO A PROGRAMME

Here we look at how a long-running serial drama is made – from the initial idea, through the storyline stage, and through the different script stages and into production.

Jupiter Moon was a co-production made in 1990/1991 by an independent production company, Primetime Andromeda, for British Satellite Broadcasting and Axel Springer of Germany. One hundred and fifty episodes were recorded and are still being shown in over 30 countries worldwide, from the USA and Canada to satellite channels over Asia. Episodes are available on DVD from Amazon (UK) and in 2007 from Amazon (US) for region 1 players.

How writers are contacted for serial dramas

Jupiter Moon used several new writers. The script department worked to the following system which is common to most long-running serial dramas.

1. Script editors contact writers they have worked with in the past, and suggest that they read the programme's Guide for Writers and send in a trial script sample. Writers with a track

record are paid to write a sample script, writers from another medium (i.e. novels, radio) are sometimes expected to write a half-episode without a fee.

2. Agents (see page 185) are approached and told that the programme is looking for writers who can:

   ■ write a strong narrative with good pacy dialogue;

   ■ write humour – not sitcom humour but the humour of human relationships;

   ■ have an interest in the particular programme's background, i.e. science fiction for *Jupiter Moon*.

3. New writers who telephone or write are usually asked to send in an example of their previous work. If this is interesting they will be asked to submit story ideas and/or write half a trial script (without a fee). If this is greeted with enthusiasm they will be commissioned to write a single episode, and invited to their first script meeting.

Writers, therefore, come through personal contact, through agents, or by approaching the programme directly. Over the following pages (Figures 3–20) we see what happens next...

SUMMARY

■ The writer is commissioned.

■ The Guide for Writers describes what the programme is about and includes character breakdowns.

■ Writers new to the programme are given guidance notes.

■ The Storyline is distributed to writers after the storyline meeting.

■ The script comes in from the writer.

■ The script is sent to the specialist adviser – who adds his own notes and comments.

■ The rehearsal script is typed up and distributed.

■ The Props department goes through the script and makes a list of props needed for each scene.

■ A requisition is made for food requirements.

■ Special effects for the studio are ordered – anything from snow or fireworks to cobwebs and explosions.

■ The director orders the graphics he will need.

■ The PA breaks down the scenes and makes a brief note of what happens in each scene.

■ The actors get their call times for wardrobe and make-up.

■ A studio script is marked with camera moves.

■ The PA notes the running time of each scene – from the first rehearsal through to the Producer's Run, the studio, and the edit.

■ After the studio the sound effects are dubbed on to the tape.

■ Transmission details are sent to the broadcasting station.

Contract Number..003.....

AN AGREEMENT made the sixth   day of October 1989 between
PRIMETIME ANDROMEDA LIMITED whose registered office is 401, St. Johns
Street, London EC1V 4LH (hereinafter referred to as "Primetime
Andromeda") of the one part and JULIAN SPILSBURY of
                              Warwickshire hereinafter referred to as "The
Writer") of the other part.

WHEREBY IT IS AGREED as follows:-

Primetime Andromeda hereby commissions The Writer and The Writer accepts
the commission to write and deliver the scripts/script (hereinafter
referred to as "The Work") detailed in the table below in consideration
of the basic fees/fee payable in accordance with the table below and
subject to the attached terms and conditions.

DETAILS OF THE SCRIPTS/SCRIPT COMPRISING THE WORK

DESCRIPTION	PROGRAMME TITLE	APPROXIMATE DURATION	BASIC FEE
To write episodes 3, 6, 11, 12, 16, 23, & 24 for the series	"JUPITER MOON"	25 minute slot time	£ 1650.00 x7 £11550.00

DELIVERY DETAILS			TABLE OF PAYMENTS	
SCRIPT	DATE DUE	No.	WHEN DUE	AMOUNT
First and final drafts	between October and 18th December 1989	1	ON INDIVIDUAL COMMISSION	50%
		2.	ON ACCEPTANCE OF EACH SCRIPT	50%

The rewrite of each script
must be delivered within
SEVEN DAYS of notification
to The Writer by the Programme
Producer/Script Editor of a
requirement for said rewrite

All fees payable to The Writer hereunder shall be payable to Julian
Spilsbury whose receipt thereof shall be a complete and valid discharge
of Primetime Andromeda's liability

Fig. 3. The writer is commissioned – in this case an experienced writer is commissioned for several episodes.

117

Introduction

JUPITER MOON is a serial drama about life in a space college in the year 2050. Although aimed at a young, intelligent audience it is not designed to be a "cult" space/science programme but to be a programme that will appeal to general viewers.

150 half hour episodes are being made between January 1990 and January 1991. Special effects and OB are being filmed at Barrandov Studios, Prague, but the bulk of the programme is being recorded at Central Television Facilities, Birmingham.

JUPITER MOON is made by independent production company Primetime-Andromeda and has been shown on the Galaxy channel of British Satellite Broadcasting since March 26th, 1990.

The Idea

Columbus College in 2050AD is part of the University of Space, housed in the spaceship ILEA. It is used by the children of European scientists, administrators, and mining engineers working on the moons of Jupiter; and by undergraduates from Earth, Mars, SpaceStation and Moonstation.

The ILEA floats in permanent orbit over Callisto, the outermost of the Galilean moons. By the ship are the wharves and nuclear tugs of a vast space harbour.

Below, on the satellite itself, is the colony "Space City", with its liquid hydrogen plant, its hostel, spaceport, hospital, cafe/restaurant, nightclub and seedy bar.

JUPITER MOON is about the loves, passions, jealousies and ambitions of young people growing up in an alien but exciting environment.... how they mature as they learn to live with responsibility and cope with emotional relationships...

About the courage, fortitude, and occasional disillusion of men and women who have chosen to make new lives many million miles away from Earth... in particular the men and women working on "Daedalus 10" - a project to build man's first "starship" for a 12 year journey outside the Solar System.

Fig. 4. The *Guide for Writers* describes what the programme is about and includes character breakdowns.

IMPORTANT RULES FOR WRITERS

If you can stick to the following it helps us enormously at the production end.

Try not to have more than 29 scenes per episode (excluding special effect modelwork sequences)

Use only 12 characters per episode (if you need 13 talk to a script editor.)

Please use the script layout as per the sample at the end of this guide.

Please list the characters used, at the front of the script.

Each script should have between 44 and 47 <u>full</u> pages
- if you like to go to a new page for a new scene make proper allowance for the blank sheets.

DON'T send in a genuine first draft. We need a script that you believe is ready to go into production. It should be properly polished, with tightly written stories, perceptive characterisation, and vivid, lively dialogue.

Please try to balance tense action stories with humorous themes and love/human interest themes.

Fig. 5. Writers new to the programme are also given guidance notes.

VOYAGE OF THE ILEA

STORYLINE 24 (cont)

Episode 149: Part One (Cont)

Sara's Story

It's EVA 1 "space mobility" time for SARA and GABY. SARA has
been desperately putting it off. She's happy to do the theory
and go in the Zero Chamber - but not outside the ship! REBECCA
says: "You've got to do it! What's the point in coming all the
way to Jupiter System and never setting foot outside the
ship?" Now SARA thinks it will have to be put off again
because the Ilea is approaching Jupiter's magnetic field. She
is quite cheery. Then DRUMMOND tracks her down. EVA space
mobility is on!

GABY chats like an old campaigner - she's been out on G33,
she's been to Simpson Base! SARA is terrified. So, too,
really, is GABY.

The Ship

VICTORIA joins DANIEL on the bridge. Petra announces:
"Mercedes Page wishes everyone on the Ilea to know that her
Engagement to Professor Charles Bonapart Brelan is cancelled,
and invites all her friends to a celebration drink in the Club
Galileo at 2100 hrs." DANIEL says: "Is it true about you and
Brelan?". VICTORIA says: "Would you be surprised?" DANIEL:
"You've always been the serious one." VICTORIA says: "I'm the
one who couldn't stand change - I hated my Dad for making me
come to Space, but I couldn't not come with him..."

"But you're the one going to Arial 9 - to swim in that ocean
perhaps...walk a Mediterranian shore with no people, no
pollution.. just sand and sea and sky" - "and little green
men!"

A small surge in magnetic force. "Oi oi, better get them in."
"Funny the forward opic sensors didn't react."

DRUMMOND in. Computer re-routing. The ship now entering the
magnetopshere.... flashing lights.

The dead sentinels spring to life... not flashing amber but
red. PETRA issues warning: Red Alert, Red Alert, override,
override... and the ship heels as it goes to emergency burn.
(Commercial Break)

Fig. 6. The *Storyline* is distributed to writers after the storyline meeting.

JIM reaches for his autosec. ANNA grabs her dressing gown and staggers to the shower.

          JIM
          Petra, Red Spot Radio.

Music blares.

2. COMCEN

DRUMMOND just sitting down. On screen radar sweep with ALL SYSTEMS ON AUTOMATIC over it in green.

          DRUMMOND
          Petra Systems and Met summary.

          PETRA
          Good Morning, Commander.

          DRUMMOND
          Good morning Petra.

          PETRA
          All shipboard systems nominal. We are on course
          to intercept with Hymalia in 17 hours 50.
          Metsat Ayola 9 reports ionised hydrogen and
          sulphur plumes (<u>Doug help!!!</u>)

REBECCA IN

          REBECCA
          Why does my heart sink when metsats go on about
          sulphur plumes.

          DRUMMOND
          Scale four. We won't even notice. What are you
          doing up?

          REBECCA
          Petra what woke me up at 0500 hours?

Fig. 7. The script comes in from the writer – this is the generally accepted layout.

JUPITER MOON — EPISODE 149

6th January 1991

Scene 5 page 12

<u>SARA</u>   The Jovian Magnetosphere is the largest in the Solar System...

OK. But for absolute accuracy, add the word 'planetary'

<u>SARA</u>   The Jovian planetary Magnetosphere is the largest in the Solar System...

— thus implicitly eliminating the Sun from the comparison

Scene 9 page 22

re: Bow shock and magnetosheath. Someone has been reading up! Congrats to Rowena Rumble I presume

---

Scene 9 page 23

<u>DRUMMOND</u>   We didn't pass through Io's flux tube at the same time. 4 million amps, a potential difference of 350,000 volts...

The current is way too high and the voltage would be expressed as a potential difference gradient. But we want high values for what is going to happen in Episode 150. We don't want to use too technical stuff like 'and grad V (∇V) is ...', cos the punters have got to grasp all this. So how about the following?

<u>DRUMMOND</u>   We didn't pass through Io's flux tube at the same time. With the plasma eddies you can get effective local currents of 4 million amps, and potential difference gradients of 350,000 volts per centimetre...

Scene 12 page 30

<u>JIM</u> (SHARP)   six hundred and eighty six days, Anna. ...

It is actually 686.98 so it's a lot closer to 687 as a whole number. Change to 687 if you want to

---

Scene 13 page 31

with regards to the pre-breathing. The figure mentioned is 4 litre. That is nowhere

Fig. 8. The script is sent to the scientific adviser – who adds his own notes and comments.

WEEK 5	DIRECTOR: David Dunn
EPISODE 149	PA: Fiona Napier
	PRODUCER: William Smethurst
STUDIO	ASSOCIATE PRODUCER: Jane Fallon
29TH, 30TH, 31ST JANUARY	WRITER: Rowena Rumble
	POST PRODUCTION EDITOR: Diane Culverhouse
	SCRIPT EDITOR: Jane Fallon

CAST [in order of appearance]

* PROFESSOR BRELAN.......................... RICHARD DERRINGTON
MERCEDES PAGE............................. ANNA CHANCELLOR
PETRA (VO)................................ CHARLOTTE MARTIN
PAUL FITZROY DRUMMOND..................... RICHARD HAINSWORTH
REBECCA HARVEY........................... ALISON DOWLING
ANNA BEGANI.............................. ANNA PERNICCI
DANIEL WETHERBY.......................... DANIEL BEALES
VICTORIA FROBISHER....................... NICOLA WRIGHT
FIONA McBRIDE............................ LUCY BENJAMIN
SARA ROBBINS............................. KAREN MURDEN
GABRIELLA TANZI.......................... FAY MASTERSON
JIM HAWKINS.............................. JIM SHEPLEY

Fig. 9. The rehearsal script is typed up and distributed.

```
          WEEK 5   EPISODE 149   SCENE 2


          SCENE  149.2 INT DAY 2 0730
          SET   COMCEN

          DRUMMOND:                Richard H
          PETRA (VO):              Charlotte
          REBECCA:                 Alison
          ANNA (ON SCREEN):        Anna P
          MERCEDES (ON SCREEN): Anna C


          DRUMMOND JUST SITTING DOWN.  ON
          SCREEN RADAR SWEEP WITH 'ALL SYSTEMS
          ON AUTOMATIC' OVER IT IN GREEN.

          DRUMMOND:       Petra, Systems and Met
          summary.

          PETRA (VO):    Good morning,
          Commander.

          DRUMMOND: (WEARY TOLERANCE)
          Good morning Petra.

          PETRA (VO):    All shipboard systems
          nominal.  We are on course to
          intercept Hymalia in 17 hours 50.
          Metsat Ayola 9 reports ionised
          hydrogen and sulphur plumes scale 4
          zero zero in Io flux tube, intercept
          T minus 8 hours forty.

          REBECCA IN.

          REBECCA:        Why does my heart sink
          when metsats go on about sulphur
          plumes?

          DRUMMOND:       Scale four.  We won't
          even notice.  What are you doing up?


                         4
```

Fig. 10. Layout of the rehearsal script.

M E M O R A N D U M

TO:	ALAN BARRETT	cc:	Setting Office x 2
			Design x 2
FROM:	PETER COTTON		FM & AFM's
			Props Stores
DATE:	7th December 1990		PA
			Director

JUPITER MOON: PROPS REQUIREMENTS: EPISODES 136/137/138

EPISODE 136 (Studio Date): 18th December 1990

SC	SET	PROPS
1	STORAGE ROOM	N/P
2	EXT ILEA	N/P
3	COMCEN	Breakfast ?
4	LONG CORRIDOR	Tim's jacket with food in pockets
5	STORAGE ROOM	Mushroom Quiche ?
6	GANTRY 2 LOBBY	Coffee, Finbow's glasses
7	COMCEN	Finbow's glasses
8	LAB 5	Files, papers etc
9	COMMON ROOM	Breakfast, autosec - Jim
10	LIFT	N/P
11	LECTURE THEATRE	Files, papers etc
12	EXT ILEA	N/P

Fig. 11. The Props department goes through the script and makes a list of props needed for each scene.

125

M E M O R A N D U M

TO: DAVID WRIGHT - CATERING MANAGER   cc: Setting Office x 5
                                              Design x 2
FROM: PETER COTTON   FM + AFM's
                                              P A
DATE: 12 DECEMBER 1990   Director

JUPITER MOON: PROP FOOD REQUIREMENTS: EPISODES 136/137/138

TUESDAY 18 DECEMBER 1990

3 Doz. Canapes (some to be for a vegetarian)
18 Grilled Mock Halibut Steaks (To look like Salmon)
Tarragon + Cream Sauce (Must be separate not on fish)
18 Portions of Braised Fennel
18 Portions of Stuffed Aubergines (Vegetarian Stuffing)
48 Profiteroles (Golf Ball Size) (Orange Sauce Separate- with bits of
orange peel in it)
24 Jam Packs
24 Butter Packs

****

WEDNESDAY 19 DECEMBER 1990

Nothing Required

****

THURSDAY 20 DECEMBER 1990

Ass. Salad for 10 people

****

Many thanks

Fig. 12. A requisition is made for food requirements.

Originator

SPECIAL EFFECTS – SPECIALITY PROPS REQUIREMENTS

CENTRAL

Date Issued 10.12.90	Production a JUPITER MOON	Prod No. 8500/137	Date Req. 19.12.90	P.A. SHAN DUCKETT	Ext. 4006
RAIN [C.M.]	SNOW—Falling —Static [C.M.]	WIND [C.M. S.M.]	FOG [E.S. L.W.]	SMOKE 137.18 – Dome 137.24 – Dome [C.M. E.S. L.W.]	STEAM [C.M.]
COBWEBS [C.M.]	B.P.—Still —Moving [C.M.]	HOUSE APPLIANCES Elec. Prac. [C.M. S.M. Proj.]	HOUSE APPLIANCES Gas—prac. [E.S. S.M. L.W.]	DROP BOXES [C.M. S.M.]	LAMPS—prac. [S.M. E.S. L.W.]
WATER—tanks [S.M. C.M.]	WATER—Baths/ Showers [S.M. C.M.]	WATER—Baths/ Sinks Poss.prac hand basin t.b.c 137.1 & 137.3 [C.M.]	LAB EFFECTS [C.M.]	DRY ICE MACHINE [C.M.]	FIRES—Log [C.M.]
FIRES—Coal [C.M.]	CANDLES—prac. or not [C.M.]	EXPLOSIONS [S.M.]	FLAME EFFECTS [C.M. E.S. L.W.]	MACHINE GUN EFFECTS [C.M. E.S. L.W.]	FIREWORKS [C.M. S.M. L.W.]
ANIMATED PROPS [C.M.]	MAGIC TRICKS/ EFFECTS [C.M. S.M.]	FIRE EXTINGUISHERS —prac. [C.M. S.M.]	GUNS—practical Non-prac. [C.M. S.M.]	BALLOON NETS [C.M. S.M.]	REVOLVES Turntables [E.S. S.M. L.W.]

1. Fill in relevant section giving brief details about effect required.
2. If the effect you require is not specified please use the blank sections.

Fig. 13. Special effects for the studio are ordered – anything from snow or fireworks to cobwebs and explosions.

DIRECTOR   HENRY FOSTER

P.A.

EPISODE: 136

EPISODES   136-138

STUDIO   18 - 20 Dec

EDIT   7 - 9 Jan.

SCENE	PAGE	SPFX DESCRIPTION	NEW/ EXISTS	GRAPHICS ACTION REQUIRED	TAPE NO.	TIMECODE
2	8	EXT: SUNRISE OVER GANYMEDE	EXISTS	no	454	52.50
3	9	COMCEN: General	EXISTS	NO		
7	17	DITTO	------------			
8	19	LAB 5: DRUMMOND WORKING: Oort cloud	NEW	YES		
11	26	LECT. THEATRE: Graphics as per page.	NEW	YES		
12	28	EXT: ILEA IN TRANSIT: DAY	EXISTS	NO	757	01.00 - 01.39
13	29	DOME?				
14	32	COMCEN: Scan of ship especially central storage bay hangar. Then hologram of Tim comes up. *General scan of ship:*	EXISTS?		766	03.25.

Fig. 14. The director orders the graphics he will need.

SCENE	PAGE	ARTISTES	D/N	OB/ STUDIO	NOTES
136.8	22 to 24	INT LAB 5 REBECCA DRUMMOND MERCEDES	DAY 1 0900		Mercedes decides to invite Drummond & Rebecca to the dinner party
136.9	25 to 29	INT COMMON ROOM JIM SARA BRELAN MERCEDES	DAY 1 0905		Brelan asks Jim to the prepare the meal for the party but is surprised when Merc tells him it is for 6 people
136.10	30 to 31	INT LIFT MERCEDES BRELAN	DAY 1 0907		Mercedes asks Brelan if he minds her inviting Drummond & Rebecca to the party
136.11	32 to 34	INT LECTURE THEATRE JIM DANIEL SARA NS STUDENTS 'MODULE ONE STUDENTS	DAY 1 0930		Daniel is not interested in helping with the party & Jim decides not to move into Cabin 3 with him
136.12	35 to 35	EXT EXT ILEA	DAY 1 1029	EXT	
136.13	36 to 39	INT DOME JIM SARA ~~AND PLAYERS OUT~~	DAY 2 1030		Jim decides what to cook for the d. party & Sara decides she will help with the serving
136.14	40 to 41	INT COMCEN NATASHA PETRA (VO) TIM (HOLO)	DAY 1 1045		Tim is discovered in the Central Storage bay hangar - Natasha is annoyed
			End of PART 1		
136.15	42 to 44	INT COMMON ROOM JIM SARA	DAY 1 1930		Jim & Sara start to prepare the meal - Sara is having problems Jim gets annoyed
136.16	45 to 46	INT BRELAN'S SUITE BRELAN MERCEDES	DAY 1 1944		Brelan gets the drinks ready - Mercedes arrives & Brelan sends her away to get changes

Fig. 15. The PA breaks down the scenes and makes a brief note of what happens in each scene.

STUDIO CALL TIMES - "JUPITER MOON"

EPISODES 148/149/150

VTR: TUESDAY 29TH JANUARY, 1991

ARTISTE	CHARACTER	WARDROBE	MAKE UP	ON SET
NICOLA WRIGHT	VICTORIA	0800	0830	0900
RICHARD DERRINGTON	BRELAN	0830	0845	0900
JANNA STRIEBECK	TRANQUILITY	0800	0830	0915
ANNA CHANCELLOR	MERCEDES	0800	0830	0930
ALISON DOWLING	REBECCA	0845	0915	1000
CHRISTOPHER SIMON	CHRISTOPHE	0930	0945	1000
FAY MASTERSON	GABRIELLA	0915	0945	1015
JIM SHEPLEY	JIM	0930	0945	1015
LUCY BENJAMIN	FIONA	1000	1030	1100
KAREN MURDEN	SARA	1000	1030	1100
RICHARD HAINSWORTH	DRUMMOND	1045	1100	1115
DANIEL BEALES	DANIEL	1145	1200	1215
ANNA PERNICCI	ANNA	1415	1445	1530

Fig. 16. The actors get their call times for wardrobe and make up.

WEEK 51   EPISODE 136   BLUE   SCENE 136.1

TIM: Oh....

TRANQUILITY: I didn't even
leave the Transit Lounge, and I
didn't give them a chance to get
their claws into me/I just
slipped off the end of one queue
and onto the end of another.

TIM: But where are you
going to go?/

TRANQUILITY: Pasiphae, Mars,
Earth. Can you hide me
somewhere?/

TIM: But we're going to
Ganymede and Hymalia before
Pasiphae! We won't get to
Pasiphae for weeks.

TRANQUILITY: (PAUSE, THEN)
How'd you like to hi-jack a
space ship, Timmy?

END OF SCENE

5
4
MCU TIM

6
1
MCU TRANQUILITY

7
4
TIGHT 2 SHOT DEVELOP TO
MCU TIM

Fig. 17. A studio script marked with camera moves.

131

CENTRAL
TELEVISION FACILITIES

MEMORANDUM

from   J.H.Parker.

to   H.Foster,S.Duckett,Sound Dubbing.

date   20/12/90

<u>JUPITER MOON DUBBING NOTES EPISODES 136-138.</u>

Episode 136.

Sc 5   Door open.

Sc 8   Door open and close.

Sc 10   Lift arrive,stop and depart.

Sc 16   Door open and close.

Sc 18   Door open and close.

Sc 20   Composed of different passes and pickups.
            Start of sequence   Roll 203/28-19
            WT trolley   Roll 203/44-16
            WT crockery breaking Roll 203/44-38

Sc 22   Composed of different passes and pickups.
            Start of sequence Roll 203/37-48

Sc 26   Doors open and close.

Sc 29A   Door open and close X 2.

Sc 31   Door open and close X 2.
            Door buzz on light cue.
            WT Daniel's "Lights."   Roll 204/45-04

Episode 137.

Sc 1   Door open and close.
            Music "Africa".

Sc 2   Add FX of two cups of coffee being poured.

Sc 3   Door open and close.
            Music "Africa".

Sc 10   Lift arrive.

                                    (Continued)

Fig. 18. The PA notes the running time of each scene – from the first rehearsal through to the Producer's Run, the studio, and the edit.

JUPITER MOON:	EPISODE 137	PN:	TR:			EDIT

SCENE	READ	FRI	SAT Rod Run	MON	MTR	EDIT
✓ REPRISE	0025 0025	0025 0025	0025 0025	0025 0025	0058 0058	
✓ OPENING TITLES	0035 0100	0035 0100	0035 0100	0035 0035	0036 0134	
1 CABIN 3	0050 0150	0040 0140	0035 0135	0040 0040	0027 0201	
2 COMCEN	0035 0225	0040 0220	0040 0215	0035 0035	0036 0237	
3 CABIN 3	0030 0255	0030 0250	0030 0245	0025 0240	0030 0307	
4 COMCEN	0125 0420	0120 0410	0120 0405	0130 0410	0026 0333	
5 GANTRY & LOBBY	0045 0505	0035 0445	0035 0440	0035 0445	0037 0410	
6 COMMON ROOM	0050 0555	0045 0530	0045 0525	0045 0530	0045 0455	
7 COMCEN R	0055 0650	0100 0630	0025 0625	0020 0550	0020 0515	
8 CABIN 3	0115 0805	0100 0730	0100 0725	0115 0705	0053 0608	
9 CABIN 1	0010 0815	0010 0740	0010 0735	0010 0715	0010 0618	
10 GYM	0135 0950	0135 0915	0130 0905	0140 0855	OUT →	
11 CABIN 1	0055 1045	0115 1030	0125 1030	0110 1005	0040 0405	
12 CABIN CORRIDOR	0035 1120	0030 1100	0030 1100	0030 1035	0036 0741	
13 CABIN 1	0035 1155	0035 1135	0040 1140	0045 1120	0048 0829	
14 CABIN 3	0105 1300	0140 1315	0135 1315	0135 1255	0131 1001	
15 COMCEN	0045 1345	0045 1400	0055 1410	0120 1415	0105 1126	
16 CABIN 1	0040 1425	0040 1440	0040 1450	0100 1515	0102 1228	
END PART ONE	0005 1430	0005 1445	0005 1455	0005 1520	0003 1231	

	PT1 1430	PT1 1445	PT1 1455	Part 1 1520	Part 1 1231
7057	PT2 1027	PT2 1117	PT2 1100	Part 2 1110	Part 2 1154
	TOTAL 2457	TOTAL 2602	TOTAL 2555	TOTAL 2630	TOTAL 2425

Fig. 19. After the studio the sound effects are dubbed onto the tape.

TRANSMISSION INFORMATION   ◆ BSB

IF PROGRAMME IS DELIVERED ON DAY OF TRANSMISSION **PLEASE**

FAX TOP SHEET (THIS PAGE (1)) TO PRESENTATION DEPT. FAX. NO.: 627 6565

FAX PAGES 2 AND 3 (COMMERCIAL REFERENCES TO AIR TIME SALES Fax. NO.: 627 6256

HARD COPY OF PAGES 1-12 TO PROGRAMME SERVICES DEPT. FAX NO.: 627 6556

PROGRAMME TITLE: _JUPITER MOON._

BSB PROG. NO.: _00012580_

SERIES TITLE: _JUPITER MOON_   EP_136_ OF____

FIRST TX DATE/TIME:_____ CHANNEL:_____

IS PROGRAMME CONTINUOUS OR DISCONTINUOUS? _DISCONTINUOUS_

ARE THERE END/BEGINNING OF PART CAPTIONS? _YES_

PLEASE INDICATE BELOW ACTUAL OR ADVISORY BREAK POINTS.

Pt 1.   TC   IN: _00:03:00:00_   TC OUT: _00:14:13:06_   DURATION: _11' 13"_

     CUE   IN:_____

     CUE OUT:_____

Pt 2.   TC   IN: _00:16:00:00_   TC OUT: _00 28 51 00_   DURATION: _12' 51_

     CUE   IN:_____

     CUE OUT:_____   _TOTAL_

Pt 3.   TC   IN: ___:___:___:___   TC OUT: ___:___:___:___   DURATION: _24' 04"_

     CUE   IN:_____

     CUE OUT:_____

(PLEASE CONTINUE MORE PARTS ON SEPARATE SHEET)

TOTAL PROGRAMME DURATION (min:sec): _24:04._

FIRST END CREDIT: _TIMOTHY SHAW (ANDREW READ)_   AT TC: _00:28:02:15_

LAST END CREDIT: _PRIMETIME ANDROMEDA_   AT TC: _00:28:51:00_

DOES PROG CONTINUE AFTER LAST END CREDIT? _No_

ATTACH ANY CONTACT NUMBERS OR ADDRESSES MENTIONED IN PROGRAMME. PLEASE ADVISE OF ANY FACTORS AFFECTING TRANSMISSION OF PROG., (eg. Mute sections, Periods of black, Contrived breakdowns, Deliberate distortion of sound or vision)

PRODUCTION COMPANY:_____ TEL:_____

ADDRESS:_____ FAX:_____

PRODUCER/DIRECTOR_____ HOME TEL:_____

ADDRESS:_____

PRODUCTION COMPANY'S TAPE NO.: _7195P30_

PLEASE RETURN ALL THESE COPIES TO B.S.B., THE MARCOPOLO BUILDING, QUEENSTOWN ROAD, LONDON SW8 4NQ.

Fig. 20. Transmission details are sent to the broadcasting station.

The Difficult Markets

WHICH ARE THE MOST DIFFICULT AREAS TO GET INTO?

The hardest markets for new writers are:

- single plays;

- serials;

- adaptations.

SINGLE PLAYS

These are the prestige dramas that aspire to say something significant about the world in which we live. Through the single television play some of the best writers in Britain have been discovered and nurtured. Playwrights like David Edgar, David Hare, David Rudkin (David is clearly a helpful name in television drama) have written some of their most important work for the single television slot.

Today, sadly, few writers are discovered and nurtured through one-off drama, and this has become one of the most difficult slots for the beginner. There are two reasons for this. Firstly, broadcasters have moved more and more to long-running series dramas that can build a mass audience. Secondly, the cost of making the single play has risen sharply because of the visual expectations of viewers.

What viewers look for

When Sydney Newman was producing *Armchair Theatre* on ITV the single drama was both popular viewing and cheap to make. Writers nurtured on the theatrical tradition wrote intelligent plays in which the action was contained in one or two studio sets, and which had few characters.

Today viewers expect more. They expect single plays to be shot on film, they expect gloss and colour and excitement on the screen, they expect to be visually as well as mentally entertained. The cost of the single-play drama shot on film is now well over a million pounds per hour. This is the most expensive television there is.

> *Our focus on TWO ... is to create drama events of immense scale and impact. Broad in cultural and geographical appeal, we are looking for 1 or 2 very big ideas a year, that will take audiences to places that drama has never taken them before.*
>
> BBC Commissioning Guide

The BBC and Channel 4 now call single plays, or plays shown over two nights, 'event drama', by which they mean drama that will be sensational enough, either in its subject matter (e.g. Channel 4's *Sex Traffic*, a multi-strand story about the sex industry filmed in five different countries) or in its star casting, to be widely noticed and commented on by newspapers and magazines. These 'event dramas' will certainly be international co-productions. Well-crafted single plays, dealing with domestic British issues, are still made by ITV. But there are fewer slots than in the past, and it is increasingly rare for these precious, prestigious, incredibly expensive dramas to be given over to the new writer. BBC Two's hugely ambitious *Decades* was entirely commissioned before it was even announced.

Single plays are normally written by:

■ television writers with a track record. A writer puts forward an idea to a producer or independent production company, and is then commissioned to write a script;

■ writers from other media – journalism, literature – who already have a high (or at least interesting) reputation.

Even among prestigious writers more scripts are commissioned (such is the power of a good lunch and a persuasive top literary agent in a Charlotte Street restaurant) than there are slots available. When a new writer sends in an unsolicited script, therefore, he is likely to be competing for the sole remaining slot of the year against a script by an established writer that has already cost the BBC or Channel 4 several thousands of pounds.

So should a new writer bother writing a one-off play?

The answer is most definitely YES – and for the following reasons.

1. As was said in **How to Succeed** on page 6 a single play of your own devising is your *curriculum vitae* – your claim to be taken seriously. In the one-off 60-minute or 90-minute play you are creating your own world, with your own characters, in your own style. Your writing is likely to be at its best and its most convincing.

2. There is the possibility that you will achieve something wonderful, and that your play will be read by a producer who likes it and has the opportunity to put it on. There is also the possibility that your play will be read and remembered later.

   It does happen. A completely unknown writer sent a 90-minute film script to BBC Pebble Mill. It was liked by a script editor who pushed it for production, but without success. Months later a production collapsed and there was a search for a replacement. The unknown writer – who had given up hope – received a phone called saying her play would start pre-production the following week, with Jane Lapotaire in the lead role.

3. There is a good chance that if your play shows genuine talent you will be considered as a writer for another slot. Most writers on soap operas and series dramas first attracted attention to their skills by submitting single plays.

Step by step for the new writer

- Unless you have a story that needs 90 minutes, write for a 60-minute slot. There are more of these available than 75- or 90-minute slots.

- On no account write for longer than 90 minutes.

- For the BBC and Channel 4 your idea needs to be big and bold and say something controversial, fascinating, or frightening, about contemporary life or society.

- ITV will be interested in family drama, or comedy drama, or social drama – but you need to bring to it a new slant, a new voice.

■ Do not write period drama, because it is very expensive and single plays almost always concern themselves with life today.

■ If you have specialist knowledge use it. Try to take us into a world that you know better than anyone else. If you have given birth to a baby and spent a year under the Pacific in a nuclear submarine you have at least two experiences that put you one up on the majority of TV dramatists.

■ Write for a reasonably small cast (i.e. don't demand hundreds of participating extras) and avoid elaborate and expensive set-ups (i.e. don't demand that filming takes place at a hot air balloon rally at the South Pole) because producers might be looking for a lower-cost drama (in BBC terms perhaps £700,000 an hour rather than £1,000,000) to compensate for the high budget 'events' to which they have previously committed themselves.

■ Write for film, with outside locations. Few if any single dramas are now shot in the studio.

■ Try to think of interesting but low-cost locations: fairgrounds give colour and visual interest, and fairgrounds are not too difficult for the production to find. Canal barges, the seaside, a hot air balloon rally that *isn't* at the South Pole – these are locations that get us out and about without costing the production a fortune. Try to think of locations that are cheap but different!

SERIALS

A serial tells an on-going story and has a set number of episodes. Often serials are in four parts, or six parts, but this is a matter of fashion and changes year by year. Serials include original dramas and adaptations of popular novels and classics.

There have traditionally been few opportunities here for the new writer. A drama department might make three or four serials a year, and will have a huge choice of materials and writers to select from. If it is rare for television to commission a new writer for a one-off play, it is almost unheard of to commission four or six hours of drama from somebody with no track record. BBC One has said that it is looking for 'signature writers' which is another way of saying big names.

But television is constantly changing, and if you have a strong idea for a serial – say a thriller, or comedy drama in four or six episodes – then you should go for it. Channel 4 and BBC Two are always asking for ideas for late-night, low-cost drama, and BBC One says it is interested in original drama ideas for 'post-peak' (around 10pm) slots that 'can be realised at a much lower cost through innovation and/or experiment'. What they mean by innovation and experiment is unclear, unless they are suggesting the use of puppets, but there must be opportunities here for the new writer.

Step by step for the new writer

- Write an opening episode and a synopsis of the other episodes. Each synopsis should be at the most two pages long (reasonably spaced out and easy to read). Don't break your synopses down into scenes but tell the broad sweep of the story, showing that each episode has an exciting opening, strong development, and a cliff-hanger climax.

- Your best chance is to write for a low-budget slot (for the production team this means around £450,000 for a 50-minute episode). Both Channel 4 and BBC Two would be very, very happy if a strong well-scripted story was offered that they could make for £350,000 an episode. BBC Two has said that it has late-night opportunities for those who embrace 'new technology and/or ways of working' which is yet another way of saying low cost. From a writer's point of view: make it a small cast with no car chases and few locations.

■ As with the one-off single drama, give us something fresh and original. Script editors yearn for something vivid and exciting, that hasn't been done before.

Adaptations

Whether it be classic period adaptations like *Bleak House* or *Sense and Sensibility*, or a modern novel like *The History Man*, the television company embarking on a multi-million pound project is going to look for a writer of experience to adapt the original material. This is the most difficult market to get into.

Like most writers, though, you probably have a favourite book (let us call it *Pigs Might Fly*) which you believe would make a terrific television serial. It is just possible that you could offer your adaptation at exactly the right time to a producer who (a) is also passionately fond of *Pigs Might Fly*, (b) thinks you have done a terrific adaptation and (c) has the muscle to get both the book and you accepted by the network scheduler.

In the case of classic novels, you should write a synopsis of the dramatic ground you would cover in each episode, and then write the first episode as an example of your work.

With modern novels, it is a more interesting situation. The work is in copyright, and the television rights could easily have been sold elsewhere. You might spend weeks toiling on an adaptation only to find that another writer is doing the same – but under commission for a television company that has taken out an option on the book.

If you believe your skills lie in the field of adaptation, do not be put off trying, but check the following before you start.

- Has the novel been done on television before, and if so how long ago was it? Generally speaking television does not worry about things previously done in black and white.

- Are the television rights in the book available? The publisher will gave you the name of the writer's agent, who will have this information.

- If the rights are available, will the writer agree to you adapting their work? Many writers, sensibly, are careful about who they allow to adapt their novels.

- If the rights are available, and the writer has no objection to you as adaptor, all you have to do is find a television company interested in putting it on.

Can I acquire rights in a book myself?

Yes, of course – again if the writer is willing to give you an option. Independent producers often take out options on books and then try to sell the idea to a television company.

In the general run of things an option on a book is not expensive. You can secure an option for 12 months for a few hundred pounds. This gives you the exclusive right to make a television programme out of the book during the period of the option. As you would expect, to option a best seller or a book by a very successful author will be much more expensive.

Of course you might be lucky enough to buy the rights in a book just before it becomes an international best seller – and then have the satisfaction of having the BBC, ITV and Channel 4 desperate to get hold of it, and happy to commission you as the adaptor. Everybody can dream...

13

Programmes Looking for Writers

WHICH ARE THE BEST PROGRAMMES TO TRY?

The television slots that offer the most opportunity to new writers are:

- series dramas;

- short plays;

- children's drama;

- situation comedy.

(Soap operas are covered separately in the next chapter.)

SERIES DRAMAS

Series dramas generally run for an hour, and there are a lot of them on television. In a series we have an established situation and established central characters, but each week we have a new story that also brings in its own characters.

A series will sometimes have only six or seven episodes, but more often it will have a magnificent 13, and will run for a quarter of the year.

Programme schedulers love series dramas because they build up an audience week by week. New writers ought to love them because of the opportunity they present.

How to write for a series

In its first run a series might have been written by a picked team of three or four writers (usually including the series devisor), but when a further series is planned the script editors instantly start to look around for fresh blood. Thirteen scripts might not seem too difficult to find, but to get them 40 or 50 storylines might be considered, and many of those will be put through two or three drafts. Then, perhaps 15 scripts will be commissioned – and when the first five come in and are hopeless the editor will panic and commission a whole lot more.

This may seem profligate, as fees can be over £10,000 for a 60-minute slot and the first half payment (50% up front) will be paid whether the script is accepted or not. Consider, though, that each programme is going to cost up to a million pounds to make, and that the BBC or ITV scheduler will rely on it to deliver an audience of 7 to 10 million contented viewers who will not only enjoy this episode, but turn on again the following week.

With so much at stake it is well worth commissioning three or even four scripts in order to get one that is good.

A 13-part series might therefore provide gainful employment to more than 25 writers. And still, at the end of the day, weak scripts will be accepted and go into production with the producers and script editor blindly relying on production values, in other words excitement on screen and glitzy casting – 'if in doubt cast up' – to save the day.

The writer shortage

The shortage of good writers in this area is acute. Script editors are often in despair, wondering where to turn next. All too often the choice is between the script editor's chum who works in the fringe theatre and rather despises television, or the weary old hack who has been churning them out since Z *Cars* and the first series of *Howard's Way*. When a new writer with sparkle, imagination and technical skill comes along he is sobbed over, cosseted, commissioned for new episodes and taken out for extravagant lunches. This could be you.

Step by step for the new writer

Select the series you would most like to write for.

1. In doing this, consider both your tastes in drama and any specialist knowledge you might have. A series about barristers will look favourably on a promising new writer who has been a barrister or a legal secretary; a series set in the medical world will always be interested in a script from a midwife or doctor.

2. Ideally, make your approach when the series is being transmitted and is getting a good audience response. This is often the time a decision on a further series is made.

3. Look the programme up on the internet e.g. for *Robin Hood* look on the Tiger Aspect website, for *Being Human* look on the Touchpaper website to see if there is any helpful information regarding future commissions and the number of writers used. Otherwise phone the production company and ask if another series is going to be made. Find out whether they want letters/scripts by e-mail or through the post.

4. Attempt to speak directly to the script editor or producer, and ask if they are willing to read an example of your work.

5. If they say 'yes' send them a copy of an original play you have written.

6. If you cannot speak directly to them, find out their names so that you can write to them personally.

7. Send an example of your writing. Say you would like the opportunity to submit a storyline. Ask if there will be changes to the basic format in the new series, i.e. are major characters being written-out, is the location changing? Ask for a copy of any new format notes for writers.

You can try to get new format notes during your first phone call, but the production office is unlikely to send out details of format changes to somebody who has phoned out of the blue and has not written for television before.

If the script editor is looking for new writers, though, and likes the writing sample you have sent, then she will encourage you to submit a storyline and will give you the same format notes that are being sent to experienced writers.

Common queries

Does it matter what sort of writing sample I send?
Yes. If you are hoping to write for something like *Midsomer Murders* or *Larkrise to Candleford* it is not helpful to send a gritty play about urban deprivation in Brixton. The script editor is trying to judge whether your talents for characterization, dialogue and plotting would make you suitable for the series she is editing. Don't make life difficult for her.

Should I send an episode of the series I want to write for?
No. Editors are not impressed by pale imitations of what you are seeing on the screen, and you do not have the current information regarding format. Editors want an example of what you, the writer, do best on your own initiative: your own characters, dialogue and style.

Should I send in lots of ideas for the series to show my ability and interest?
Again you do not have the relevant format information, and editors are not really interested in storyline ideas until they know you have the ability to write. That said, if you put forward a first-class storyline, well structured and succinctly told, so gripping that the editor can't put it down – then you are likely to get an interested response.

How do I write a storyline?
You have to put forward, in a clear, easy to understand manner, the story you are proposing. You have to make it exciting to the reader. You have to show that your drama opens in an interesting way, sustains itself, and has a good ending. It does not matter if your storyline is one page or six pages long, if what you write does the job. But the following guidelines might be useful to the beginner.

- Give an interesting summary of your story or stories: 'Wealthy Sir Solomon Featherstone leaves £50,000 in his will so that his friends can enjoy the party of a lifetime. And so they do – until a group of shaken guests swear they saw Sir Solomon himself dancing at the disco. Det Insp Friday disinters the coffin – and uncovers more than he expects'.

- For a 50-minute series episode an editor will normally expect a three- or four-page storyline. (Between 500 and 1,200 words.)

■ If you are writing for ITV the editor will look for strong endings to part one and part two – preferably edge-of-seat endings that keep viewers interested, and stop them from slipping away to other channels during the adverts.

■ If the storyline has two or three strands – perhaps a main story, a secondary story and a comic sub-story – the editor will look to see how skilfully stories develop and intertwine, and how you propose to contrast quiet moments in one story with action in another (see Chapter 4).

■ Take care not to get bogged down in detail – 'He says to her, then she goes out and he turns to somebody else and says...' – but stick to the main story developments. You are writing a synopsis, not a blow-by-blow account.

SHORT PLAYS OR 'SHORTS'

Short plays – either 30-minute slots or the 10-minute slots pioneered by Anglia's *First Take* and *10x10* by BBC Bristol are usually aimed at encouraging new directors rather than new writers. It is the would-be director, often from film school, who approaches the television company with a show-reel of their work and a script. But where do the directors get their scripts from? They have little money to buy scripts, and no access to professional writers. If you have an idea for a film it is worth ringing film schools to see if there are talented unknown directors desperately seeking talented unknown writers. Check with the Film Council, which sponsors 'shorts' as part of its brief to 'develop and nurture emerging film making talent' and which operates not only in London but in Scotland, Wales, Northern Ireland, and the English regions (see Chapter 18). Check online for universities that run post-graduate courses in film directing and film making (often the same as those that run courses in scriptwriting, see Chapter 18). It is also worth ringing regional arts associations who bring together local writers and directors and occasionally help with co-funding. Watch Internet sites like the BBC's Writersroom (*www.bbc.co.uk/writersroom*) and Channel 4 Ideas Factory (*www.channel4.com/ideasfactory*) for news of competitions or planned series.

Step by step for the new writer

■ Watch any series of short dramas being broadcast and if you are confident that you could write for the slot (take into account the type of stories told, the number of characters, the mix of studio/video) note the name of the producer or script editor.

■ Phone and ask if another series is planned. Ask if you can submit a script. Ask if the programme works in conjunction with any particular film schools or arts funding bodies.

■ If you are directed to the BBC's Writersroom, send your script in with a covering letter stating the strand for which it is intended, and giving the name of the producer or script editor who you want to read it.

■ Monitor Internet sites (like the Film Council regional and national sites, and writers' sites like Screenwriter Store, see Chapter 18) that are likely to provide information about low-budget drama strands and/or competitions.

■ Approach film schools and/or local arts associations to let them know that you are interested in writing a script for a new director.

■ If you are in Scotland, Northern Ireland, or Wales, look at low-cost drama specific to where you live – like *Tartan Shorts* in Scotland.

■ If the television production offices are non-committal, and the film schools not wildly enthusiastic, write a script anyway. This is only a ten-minute or 30-minute drama and you can afford to make the effort.

■ Remember that 'shorts' are low budget – this means perhaps £15,000 to £50,000 – so the fewer actors you use the better. Also remember that 'shorts' are primarily aimed at developing director skills. Your story must have the potential to be visually interesting.

■ Send your script to arts associations that encourage local writers, to film schools, to Channel 4's Independent Film and Video Department, and to the BBC's Writersroom. The BBC warns writers not to send uncommissioned and unrequested scripts to individual producers and programme production offices (saying that they always end up in the Writersroom anyway) but times change, and it does no harm to try your luck if you know a producer or script editor by name.

CHILDREN'S DRAMA

The requirement for children's drama is exactly the same as for any other kind of drama, be it one-off plays (of which very few are made) or series and serials (of which there are a lot). The BBC produces the most children's programming through CBeebies aimed at 4–6 year olds, and CBBC focusing on 6–12 year olds. ITV has cut back drastically on its children's TV output, possibly because producers of sugary sweets are no longer allowed to advertise heavily within children's TV commercial breaks. Children's drama is almost always low budget (though *The Roman Mysteries* cost over £1m an hour to make) so historical dramas are more difficult to sell than contemporary themes. Classical adaptations often have period settings, but in this area experienced writers are always used. Prominent drama slots on CBBC are generally 15-minute dramas in the early evening aimed at 6–8 year olds, and 30-minute dramas, either original (like the comedy series *Young Dracula*) or adaptations at around 5pm.

Children's programming guidelines

When writing for children certain guidelines have to be observed which essentially means being careful with the following.

1. Situations arising from adoption, desertion, cruelty in the home, which could threaten a child's emotional security.

2. Portrayal of injury or disablement, or embarrassing personal disabilities like stuttering.

3. The use of weapons or poisons to cause injury or death.

4. Joke stunts that could be copied with disastrous results: stretching wire across a path, for example, to dismount a cyclist.

5. Heroes and heroines who smoke and drink alcohol.

6. The infliction of pain or humiliation on others. Suffering of children or animals.

BBC script guidelines

The BBC's Children's Development Unit warns against having very large casts, too many sets, exotic foreign locations, and massive special effects (although they add that a certain amount of 'magic' is fine.) They get too many scripts and ideas relating to pop bands, computer games, 'green' issues and time-slip stories. They advise new writers to bear the following in mind.

- Series or serials normally run for six episodes. Write the first episode and provide synopses of the rest.

- Do not have long speeches. Keep dialogue short and crisp.

- Make sure there is plenty of action.

- Keep the plot going, with constant new developments.

- Write short scenes.

- Start with something exciting that will grab attention.

SITUATION COMEDIES

Everybody is looking for comedy scriptwriters. They are the best paid writers, they are the most in demand – and they suffer the most rejection. Every year the BBC, ITV and Channel 4 produce their crop of new situation comedies (often from new writers) and every year the critics and viewers are mercilessly dismissive. For every *The IT Crowd* there are a clutch of sitcoms that bite the dust, desperately unfunny, mourned only by the sad writer who worked so hard at the jokes and the poor actors who had to play them.

Does the script run for 30 minutes (the standard narrative comedy length)? Does the script tell a self-contained story that introduces the main characters and sets up the series premise? Is the script consistently funny? Is every character three-dimensional, with a defined personality and recognisable tone of voice?

BBC Comedy Department advice to new writers

It is because comedy is so difficult to judge that both the BBC and ITV are prepared to spend large sums of money making pilot programmes of sitcoms, and why there are now several comedy workshops where scripts – often by new writers – can be tried out on live audiences.

What programme makers say they want

■ Comedies that are 'intelligent, character-based, and up-market'.

■ Stories that are unpredictable with twists to keep an audience guessing.

■ Comedies which 'draw their strength from realistic and relevant situations and characters'. (BBC One)

■ Comedies that have a 'simple and funny high-concept premise which immediately suggests comic possibilities'. (BBC Comedy Script Unit)

■ Comedies that will attract a younger audience and appeal to younger women. (BBC Two)

In all cases, these ideas must have the potential to generate and support future storylines.

What programme makers say they don't want

■ Familiar themes: flat-sharing, the chap who's won the pools, mothers-in-law situation, grandads who come to stay and won't go home.

- Contrived situations and elaborate contrivances to keep the characters together.

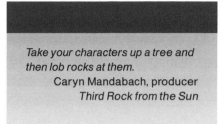

Take your characters up a tree and then lob rocks at them.
Caryn Mandabach, producer
Third Rock from the Sun

- 'Down-market, class-ridden comedies'. (ITV)

- Comedies that rely on 'strings of gags and funny lines'. (BBC) In other words the old time, third-rate ITV sitcom with artificial situations and farcical stories.

- Comedies that need expensive filming. Almost all situation comedy is studio-based, sometimes with a small amount of OB.

Step by step for the new writer

1. Use the internet to find out about situation comedy competitions and current script development plans. The BBC site is *www.bbc.co.uk/newtalent/* and there is useful information on *www.bbc.co.uk/writersroom*. Look also at the BBC's Get Writing site (*www.bbc.co.uk/dna/getwriting*) and at Channel 4 Ideas Factory (*www.channel4.comideasfactory*).

2. Write a brief outline of your idea, its premise, and your main characters. First try to sum up the idea in around 25 words (e.g. a sleepy, old-fashioned rural community suddenly finds its new vicar is a bubbly, enthusiastic, female who is determined to make things happen!). Your entire proposal should not be more than two pages long (well presented without too much dense writing) because the script reader will have already assessed several other proposals before reaching yours, and she will need all the mental assistance you can give her.

3. Write the first three half-hour episodes. Try to decide, as objectively as you can, which is the best (the best opening, the fastest, funniest story, and the really cracking ending). This is the script that you must send in. If it turns out to be the second or third script, ask yourself if it can possibly work as script one. If it can't, send it in with a brief outline of the series opening.

4. Send your script and outline to independent production companies as well as to the BBC. If an independent likes your idea they can offer it to the BBC, ITV, Channel 4, and Channel 5.

5. Send your script to independent producers who are making comedies that are currently being shown. They will be actively looking for new projects to replace programmes that are reaching the end of their life. (Situation comedies like *Fawlty Towers*, *Black Books*, and *The Office* burn brightly, but often only run for two or three short series).

6. If your script is rejected by the BBC don't let independent production companies know. 'My script has been turned down by the BBC but I thought you might still like to see it' might be honest, but it will not help you.

7. The BBC comedy unit likes scripts to be bound with a metal paper binder in the top left hand corner (which is how finished scripts are bound), and pleads for a self-addressed stamped envelope to be included.

8. See Chapter 19 for addresses of programme makers.

9. Send your script and outline to at least two independent companies at the same time. If you go round the independents one by one you could be a hundred and receive your telegram

from the Queen before you get the final rejection letter. If one company takes you up, you can tell the others that your work is no longer available.

10. Don't give up on a script too soon. Comedy is so individual that your work could be rejected by half a dozen producers – and then be taken up with enthusiasm by the next. At the same time, if several producers give a very clear and consistent reason for rejection ('Dear Sitcom Writer, you may not have noticed but there has already been a comedy series about a jolly lady vicar in a rural community...') then they are probably telling you something that you ought to know.

14

Soap Operas

A LARGE AND GROWING MARKET

Many new writers get their first chance in television by writing for soap operas. Many stay in the world of 'soaps' and become seriously well-off, particularly those writing for the major serials – *Coronation Street*, *EastEnders*, and *Emmerdale*. Soap operas do not always succeed – *Families* and *Eldorado* were costly mistakes, ITV's relaunched *Crossroads* failed, as did the more critically approved *Night and Day*, but *Hollyoaks* has established itself, as has the BBC's *Doctors* with its slightly different format. ITV is once again actively seeking a new daytime soap. If you live in Scotland there's *River City*, and if you are both Welsh and a Welsh language speaker there's *Pobol y Cwm*.

Some soap operas bring in extra money from overseas sales. *Jupiter Moon* can be seen on cable and satellite in the USA, and the Scottish Television soap *Take the High Road* was, for some reason, so popular in Sri Lanka that at one time it filled the Saturday evening prime-time slot.

Soap operas represent a huge market. Even the established soaps are using more writers, as they expand to make more programmes. At any given moment half-a-dozen script editors will be actively on the look-out for new writing talent.

Pot-bellied, whisky-pickled union shop convenor BILL
HODDER is all set for tomorrow's freebie visit to a
Bayonne engineering works.

In the meantime he and wife LIZ have been promised a
wedding-anniversary outing by son CLIVE.

CLIVE, though, has forgotten his filial duties and
fixed a date with SANDRA BREWSTER.

JOHN SCHOFIELD, project engineer at Alfred Holt, is
worried by a sudden, mystifying cut in development
funds.

GILLIAN BREWSTER, 13, is within an ace of getting
her own pony.

SANDRA BREWSTER is having a terrible time. Last week
she was told she wasn't good enough for the
shorthand/typing job her father FRANK got for her.

At the end of the last episode her father found out.

We last saw her sitting, anguished, on her bed,
while FRANK stormed up the stairs....

Fig. 21. A serial drama script editor will write either a 'Story So Far' or an
episode synopsis to accompany each script.

```
1. INT. HALLWAY. BREWSTERS. DAY  (From Episode 11)

Opening theme music as we see FRANK turn at the bottom of
the stairs and start to climb them, a grim, set look on his
face.

                    FRANK
               Sandra! Sandra!


2. INT. SANDRA'S BEDROOM.  DAY (From Episode 11)

17 year-old SANDRA sits hunched up on her bed. Hearing her
father's voice she looks in distress towards the door.
She's for it now!

CUT TO:


               OPENING TITLES


3. SANDRA'S BEDROOM. DAY

FADE IN on FRANK pacing up and down, exercising his powers
of mental creativity. SANDRA still sits hunched up on the
bed, but is now snivelling over a shorthand pad.

                    FRANK
               And in conclusion I would like to express
               my gratitude for the esteemed honour---

                    SANDRA
               We haven't done esteemed!

                    FRANK
               The esteemed honour of the valued custom
               you have so kindly given to us---

                    SANDRA
               I've never had esteemed said to me in me
               life---

                    FRANK
               So kindly given to us and I confirm
               delivery of same by the fourteenth ult.
```

Fig. 22. A writer picks up the story from a previous episode – in this case
there is a reprise of the final scene of the previous programme.

To write for a soap opera you need to:

■ take a lively interest in the domestic drama of everyday life;

■ respect popular drama and regard it as worthwhile and important;

■ have the ability to work with other writers, and to help formulate stories in storyline meetings;

■ be able to write imaginative, lively scripts within the restrictions of length, sets, locations and cast that are imposed;

■ thoroughly understand the nature of long-running serial drama: the 'soap formula'.

THE SOAP FORMULA

I remember, in those early days, likening the Crossroads *cast to birds in a nest, with their beaks wide open, yelling for 'More plot, more dialogue, more problems, more solutions...'*

Reg Watson, producer of *Crossroads* and *Neighbours*

Soap operas use up a ferocious amount of dramatic material. There are always at least three running stories that are not interconnected, and once those stories are exhausted new ones involving different characters must take their place.

The vital part of the formula is that we must be able to go, effortlessly, into the homes of our characters for an inexhaustible supply of domestic dramas.

There might be a big story of love and passion at Domicile A, a running tale of ambition and money at Domicile B and a running comedy theme at Domicile C. It is important that these dramas need only relate to each other (be it in the pub, shop, factory) when we want them to.

The simpler the structure and more ordinary the location the better. The identity of a soap opera is created by its characterization, plotting and view of life, not by any originality or novelty in format.

SOAP OPERA STORIES

Soap operas are popular dramas, aimed at every age and class. They have inherited the mantle of the minstrel and the teller of folk tales, the mantle worn by Trollope and Dickens and a host of less talented but equally prolific writers. At their worst (and there is a lot of their worst) they are bland and repetitious; at their best they are as good as any drama on television.

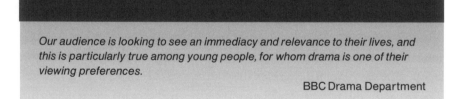

Our audience is looking to see an immediacy and relevance to their lives, and this is particularly true among young people, for whom drama is one of their viewing preferences.

BBC Drama Department

Opinion polls have told us what viewers look for.

- Different generations of people – babies and teenagers, adults and senior citizens.

- Love affairs, engagements, marriages, divorces, and all the complications resulting from male-female relationships.

- Young people and young people's problems – teenage 'going off the rails', school activities.

- Young couples living together. Homebuilding, pregnancy, unemployment.

- Humour.

- Community gossip, scandal, intrigue and curiosity.

- Larger-than-life characters – rogues, tarts, stirrers, snobs, gossips... people who ordinary folk can identify with.

SCRIPTS AND WRITERS

If you have 12 writers on your team, then at any given moment at least two of them will be on the way out. A writer might be going abroad for a few months, or want to take time off to write a novel, or might simply want to get off the soap opera treadmill. Then again the writer might not know he is on the way out, that sadly his time will be up just as soon as the script editor can find a replacement.

Many writers are kept on the team long after the producer, editor and cast have been sent screaming mad by boring, empty dialogue, pathetic characterization, repetitive and unimaginative scenes. They are kept on – often to their own surprise – because at the end of the day they can be relied on to deliver a script that:

- is the right length with a commercial break reasonably near the middle;

- has the right number of characters;

- uses the right sets with the right amount of OB;

■ covers the stories that the storyline says it should cover;

■ does not steal stories the storyline has allocated to the next writer.

The script editor opens the tired writer's script with a sinking heart, knowing she is going to have to stay up half the night trying to inject a modicum of sparkle and believability into the dialogue – but also knowing that on a primitive, basic level the script will work. It won't have to be binned. It will be pretty awful, but the cast will act their little socks off and it will get by.

And in the meantime, the search for a replacement writer will continue.

Step by step for the new writer

The first thing you must do is to choose your soap opera.

1. Identify the soap opera that you, as a viewer, most enjoy watching.

Among the urban TV soaps *Coronation Street* and *EastEnders* are identical in structure (working-class homes focusing on a pub; one in its time had a factory making jeans and the other a street market selling them), but vastly different in style. *Coronation Street* draws strength from Northern values and Northern humour, and often gives us a laugh. *EastEnders* reflects, indeed, sometimes seems to prey on, a glum world where life is gritty and grim. *Emmerdale* has its own characteristics, and they are far from being the characteristics of *Hollyoaks*. There was once a writer who, using two names, was on the team of both *Coronation Street* and *Crossroads*, but generally speaking writers are faithful to one programme because their view of life and writing style suits only one programme.

2.   Identify the programme you are best qualified to write for.

It might seem that if you grew up on a farm in Yorkshire, trained as a vet, regard all southerners as effete, and would rather go down a coal mine than watch dramas about lesbians, then you would find a warm welcome on *Emmerdale*. In fact, you would be better off – assuming you can write brilliant dialogue and have a good sense of humour – at *Coronation Street*.

3. Have a sample of work to show.

Evidence of your ability is vital. Editors want to see how you handle characters, plots and above all dialogue. In the first instance editors usually prefer to see a single play you have written and do not want to see your attempt at writing their soap opera.

Make sure your writing sample is something that will help the script editor to assess your suitability – in other words contemporary drama based on dialogue and character rather than action.

4.   Find out the name of the script editor, either by watching the credits or by phoning the production office.

5.   If you do phone the production office ask if the programme has its own system of assessing new writers – trial scripts, perhaps, or new writers' seminars.

6.   Send your sample script with a short covering letter.

If there is something in your background you think might be useful (you've been a social worker/vet; you're the Director of Programmes's mistress/boyfriend), say so. Otherwise the letter should be short and to the point, as in the example shown in Figure 23 on page 167.

7.   Make sure you know the programme thoroughly.

If the script editor likes your original script she will either write encouraging you to submit a trial sample script (unpaid!), or she will speak to you on the phone (curious to know more about you) or invite you in to talk.

If you are lucky she will just have had one writer bundled into a drying-out clinic, another run off to Latin America, and been forced by the producer to sack another. If you are unlucky the programme will have recently received three or four scripts from very promising new writers, and not be looking for more.

Either way, you have to be ready. You have to know about the programme – the characters, the locations, the stories in recent episodes. You must be able to say, instantly, what the current three running stories are. You must be able to say which characters you think are being written well for, and which are not. You must be able to project enthusiasm and have sensible, realistic ideas.

If you are encouraged to write a sample script, ask for a couple of back scripts, preferably by different writers, and any writers' guidance notes that exist.

8.   Do not copy the style of other writers.

Other writers' scripts, and episodes you have taped and studied, will give you a feel for the programme. But the script editor is not looking for a pale imitation of the past, she is looking for dialogue that is new and fresh; characters that ring true and honest, but are illuminated in a brighter, more vivid, more believable way; stories that are developed with verve and energy.

Ms Zia Wanascript
'Coronenders'
Friendly Television Company,
Moneygalore Road
London 1AA 6BQ

9 June 200X

Dear Zia Wanascript

I am interested in writing for Coronenders and enclose as an example of my work a 60-minute television play called 'Promise'.

I would be happy to write a sample script for Coronenders if you think this would be worthwhile.

If so, I would be grateful for any guidance notes for writers that you might have.

(or)

I understand that you occasionally hold seminars for new writers. I would be grateful for the chance to attend one of these.

I hope you enjoy reading 'Promise'.

Your sincerely

Julian Goodwriter

Fig. 23. How to write a covering letter for a sample script.

What next?

Assume your sample script was brilliant and you have been commissioned to write an episode. The script editor will not object to being sent flowers at this point. You will be asked to the studio, shown round the set, lunched in the canteen. You are a professional writer. Congratulations! You now have your first **scriptmeeting** to face.

How soap operas are written

Every soap opera varies slightly in its script production methods. Some programmes (like *EastEnders*) try to give scriptwriters an element of creative freedom, other soaps are very much a production line, with every scene, and the reaction of every character to every event, mapped out by storyliners. What follows is a typical fortnight on one of the more chaotic soaps.

Scriptmeeting

Up to a dozen writers meet for a day with the producer, two script editors and storyliners. They already have a long-term storyline. On this occasion they thrash out the stories for a fortnight of episodes. At this point the writers do not know which episode they will write or even if they will write at all. They are expected to contribute ideas for all the episodes. If they do not show keenness and enthusiasm, they might not be commissioned to write.

I like to write with the world shut out and completely naked. Who knows – some of the stuff I write might not be as good if I had kept my kit on.

Al Hunter Ashton,
EastEnders script writer

Scripts commissioned

The storyliners (who are almost always young, stressed-out, would-be writers themselves) work feverishly to prepare a storyline for each episode, showing commercial breaks and episode cliffhangers. Writers are phoned and offered an episode. They are told the schedule this time is very tight, and that they can only have four days to write their script.

Storyline approved

There is a delay while producers and executive producers read the storylines and demand changes. Writers are phoned and told that their storylines are going to be late, but will be faxed or e-mailed to them. They ask if they can have a later delivery time. They are told no they can't.

Episodes written

The storylines reach the writers. They start work. After several hours they are phoned again and told that their storyline has to be changed because of story objections from the channel head of drama. Writers again ask if they can have a later delivery date. Again they are told no they can't.

Scripts back

The scripts come in by e-mail, and are edited by the script editors. Rewrites might be demanded by phone and will need to be completed within a matter of hours. The scripts go to the producer, are edited onscreen, and go into production.

Six weeks or so later

The episodes are made, both in the studio and on location. On five-episodes-a-week soaps there is little or no rehearsal.

15

Other Markets for Scripts

Almost all television work for freelance writers is in drama and situation comedy, but a few opportunities exist in other areas.

CHILDREN'S PROGRAMMES

Children's drama has been covered in Chapter 13. Otherwise opportunities are few. The BBC uses some unpublished stories and says that ideas for children's programmes will be considered. Writers, it is said, should watch the department's output carefully to see the types of programmes being made.

For ITV watch the output carefully, note which regional company (or Independent) is putting Children's ITV on the network, and then approach the executive producer directly.

EDUCATION

The BBC transmits more than 2,000 hours of educational programming each year, an amount roughly matched by ITV and Channel 4. Many schools programmes are drama or dramatised documentary and ought, in theory, to provide excellent opportunities for new writers. The BBC says, however, that most of its schools programmes are written either by the producer or by a teacher/academic who has been approached by the production team.

Apart from schools broadcasting, BBC Education is looking for history programmes that encourage an active interest by viewers, for programmes that deal with citizenship and the community, and for programmes that deal with parenting. Costs must be similar to daytime prices (see below).

For ITV and Channel 4 note the television companies making the programme in which you are interested, and ring them directly (for contacts see Chapter 19).

SCIENCE PROGRAMMES

Most writers are expected to be involved with the actual production – which in practice means that writers are either BBC staff, or experts approached by either the production team or the independent production company that has been commissioned to make the programme. The BBC stresses, however, that consideration is given to scripts or ideas that are sent in. It is clearly an advantage to be an expert – if your idea is a programme showing the bizarre effects of quantum mechanics on daily life it is more likely to be taken seriously if you are a physicist rather than a stockbroker.

Treatments should be about two or three pages long, outlining the subject and making clear the way the writer would tackle the script.

HISTORY PROGRAMMES

The BBC and Channel 4 have discovered the appeal of history in recent years, and although most resources go into series like *Timeteam* and *Meet the Ancestors* there is a market for one-off features and part series, and these often include scripted sequences, even if it is only cavemen sitting round a fire going 'Ug'. If you have an idea for a history programme featuring dramatized sequences your best option is to approach an independent company that has a track record making historical documentaries. If they think the idea has appeal, they can put the proposal forward as a package.

LIGHT ENTERTAINMENT

Comedy sketch shows use a huge amount of material and there is a market for freelance sketches and one-liners. The BBC is at pains to say 'that there is no call for comic songs or verse'. Write directly to the producer of the show you are interested in, or to the head of light entertainment at ITV and Channel 4 and the BBC.

HUMAN INTEREST, CONSUMERS AND LEISURE

This is a vast and growing area of television. There are innumerable programmes about cookery and gardening, and specific interest programmes like *Sky at Night* and *Crimewatch UK*. Sadly there is virtually no work here for the freelance writer, but ideas and formats are always wanted. What next after the fashion for house-buying programmes pioneered by *Location, Location, Location* and *Property Ladder*? What next after the success of 'makeover' programmes pioneered by Trinny and Susannah? Many commissioning editors and daytime TV controllers would like to know the answer.

See which independent production companies are making the programmes you like, and approach them directly with your own idea.

DAYTIME TELEVISION

Daytime television is invariably low cost. In practice this means that the BBC expects to pay an independent company around £15,000 for a 30-minute programme. There is a market for documentary series (like *City Hospital*), panel games, quizzes, and interactive topical shows (i.e. chat shows). If you can come up with an idea for a 25–40 minute documentary type programme that only costs £4,000 then BBC Two would love to hear from you (programmes in this area normally utilize news or sports archive material). Again, your best bet is to make an approach through an independent.

SCOTTISH, WELSH, IRISH AND REGIONAL PROGRAMMING

Both the BBC and ITV in Scotland, Wales and Ulster devote resources to programmes that will not be shown throughout the United Kingdom and which reflect Scottish, Welsh and Irish interests. BBC Scotland, for example, is the BBC's most varied production centre outside London. Apart from making the Scottish soap *River City* it makes factual programmes like *End of Story* and *Writing Scotland* – both designed to encourage writing talent. BBC Wales not only produces the soap opera *Pobol y Cwm* but also drama-documentaries specifically for Wales.

Watch output, identify the slots devoted to regional programming, and if you have an idea approach the producer.

All the main ITV companies make programmes for their own regions. The BBC makes specific regional programmes from Birmingham, Newcastle, Manchester, Bristol and Plymouth.

Again, watch the regional slots (usually on BBC Two) and if you have an idea, write to the producer.

Telephone numbers for BBC and ITV production centres are included in Chapter 19.

We aim to add more peak time talent to our schedule. We should also be a launch pad for bright, new talent both on-screen and off – a place of enterprise and creativity.

Jane Lush, Head of BBC Daytime Commissioning

16

Common Queries

CHARACTER LISTS

Should I include a list of characters at the front of the script?

Yes, but keep it short, don't worry about minor characters and make your descriptions pithy and pertinent. 'Julian is late forties, a chartered accountant, married for around 20 years to Rose. The only apparent interest in their lives is who will reach the menopause first.' Do not write half a page of description on each character, and do not insist that they be tall or short or red-haired or bald, unless this characteristic is vital to the story.

SYNOPSES

Should I include a synopsis of the story?

A short indication of what the play is about – perhaps 50 or 100 words – can be useful in that it tells the script editor the sort of play she is about to read. 'A man claiming to be an MI6 agent breaks into a remote Welsh farmhouse. He tells the farmer and his family that he is pursuing a cell of cult fanatics intent on poisoning the water in a nearby reservoir. But why won't he say who he plans to meet at the farmhouse? And why does he force the family, at gunpoint, to hand over their mobile phones?'

This gives the editor a good idea of what is to come – a drama about a family torn out of normality into a nightmare situation. Even better, ITV's 2007 two-part thriller *Instinct* was summarised in production as 'a talented young detective's traumatic past returns to haunt him during the hunt for a serial killer stalking the Lancashire Pennines.' This is the kind of synopsis that will engage a script editor's interest. She will go on reading to see how well or badly you tackle the subject.

Do not write a three- or four-page synopsis. The script editor or professional reader might just as well read the play, and anyway the reader will be required to write a synopsis to prove that she has read the script carefully.

PROTECTING YOUR WRITTEN COPYRIGHT

Do I need to write 'copyright' and put a 'C' inside a circle?

It is curious but true that the very worst writers submitting the most unlikely scripts are those most anxious not to have their material stolen – and they very often put on their script a very firm copyright line. Very few professional writers or agents do this (your work is your copyright whether you draw little circles on it or not), although it is always a good idea to put the date on each draft you submit. If you want to protect your script further you can register it with the **Writers' Guild** providing you are a member (see page 217), or you can seal a copy in

> *Ideas don't interest us in themselves... Ultimately there is no point in stealing ideas, since ideas are never in short supply. What is rare is the writer who can take a good idea and execute it well.*
>
> BBC Writersroom

an envelope and send it to yourself by registered mail, and then keep the package unopened. There are also enterprising internet sites (e.g. *www.thescriptvault.com*) that will register and store your script electronically for you.

PROTECTING YOUR IDEAS

Will my ideas be stolen?

If they are going to be stolen, a copyright line will not help you. Many unsuccessful writers are convinced that their ideas have been stolen and used later, and it is easy to see how suspicions are aroused. A writer sends in an outline for a series of dramas set in a university, say, and it is rejected. Then, a year later, a university series pops up on the *same channel* that rejected his idea!

There have always been university/student ideas floating around, just as there have always been outlines for series set in airports, hospitals, city parks, animal sanctuaries, riding stables, factories.... There have recently been two rival proposals for series set on trains.

It must have happened that a writer's work has been stolen but it is a very unlikely occurrence. Nobody is going to plagiarise an actual script – they have no need to. If your script is good they will buy it anyway, and besides you would be very likely to find out and complain. Again if your idea for a series is *very specific* nobody is going to be foolish enough to try to pass it off as their own.

There is, however, a grey area when it comes to ideas. Say you have submitted an idea for a comedy series about two rival pleasure boat operators on the Thames. The idea is read and rejected. A year later the editor who rejected you is involved in another project, and suddenly has a flash of brilliance: 'We could have a chap who hires rowing boats, and somebody could try to move in on his patch...'

The editor has probably no idea where the thought came from. Even if she does remember your offering she will not regard the idea as exclusively yours. Intellectual copyright is a very difficult area of law, but basically you cannot copyright ideas (unless they are worked out in detail) and you cannot copyright titles.

SCRIPTING COMMERCIAL BREAKS

Are there rules about where to put the commercial break?

Weirdly, yes, there is a convention (which does work, artistically, most of the time) that the scene following a commercial break must be either (a) in a different location to the scene immediately before the commercial break, or (b) there must have been a time lapse of at least five minutes in your drama.

In other words you cannot do this:

DIANE: OK, right, so who is the little
tart?

MARTIN: This is not doing any good, this
is just upsetting you.

DIANE: Will you tell me who she is,
damn you!

MARTIN LOOKS UP, SUDDENLY DEFIANT.

MARTIN: OK, if you really want to know.

                    COMMERCIAL BREAK

SCENE FIVE. THE KITCHEN AS IN SCENE FOUR.

MARTIN: The woman I am leaving you
for is Lisa Strombali from the petfood factory.

DIANE: My best friend Lisa? You rat!

The scene before the commercial break is fine. After the break you
would need to assume a short time lapse and preferably take us to
a different location.

SCENE FIVE. EXT. PARK. DAY. DIANE IS LEANING OVER
THE FOOTBRIDGE. MARTIN IS WITH HER.

DIANE: I suppose you met her at the
petfood factory.

MARTIN: Yes.

And so on.

Must the commercial break be exactly halfway through the script?

It is more important that it should come at a natural, dramatically
effective point.

That said, a 30-minute slot on ITV is just over 24 minutes long, and
it is usual for the break to be somewhere in the middle four
minutes.

A one-hour serial or series slot is 52 minutes long, and generally has two commercial breaks. The first should be at least 15 minutes into the script, and the last not less than 15 minutes from the end.

When submitting to the BBC *take the breaks out*.

HOW TO TIME SCRIPTS

How do I time my script?

If you follow either of the script layouts suggested in Figures 1 and 2 on pages 107 and 108 your script will be running at around 45 seconds a page – depending, of course, on the pace and mood of the play and the amount of description you include.

If you read your script out aloud (preferably with another person, alternating lines), and also *read out loud the movements of the characters and action sequences*, you will get a rough timing. Nobody expects more of you at this stage.

SCRIPT LAYOUT

Why do television scripts only use the right-hand side of the page?

There are three versions of a television script.

1. The first is by the writer, and is written for the script editor and producer to read. There is no practical reason why this should only run down half the page – it is wasteful and leads to high postage costs. However, it is commonly done.

2. The second version is the rehearsal script, typed up by the production secretary after the first version has been edited, rewritten, changed for continuity, or cut for time. This version

traditionally runs down the right-hand side of the page so that:

3. The director's PA can add the camera directions to the production secretary's computer file without having to retype it. And in the studio or on location, the PA and floor managers can use the left-hand space to make continuity notes.

The examples in Figures 24, 25 and 26 on pages 182–184 are from a studio play, and show these three versions of the script.

What if my script is altered?

For a script editor to alter your script and rewrite bits presupposes that you are in the happy position of having sold it, that your script is in production and other creative influences are now at work.

Essentially, having accepted several thousand pounds for a script, it is no longer your property: at least not insofar as the rights you have sold are concerned. After all, if you buy a chair and take it home you can do what you like with it – chop a bit off one leg because of your uneven floor, or add a structural support – and you do not expect the carpenter to come and interfere and shout at you.

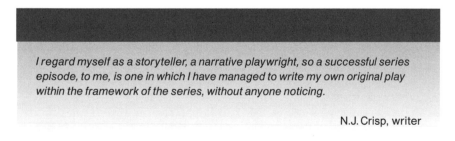

I regard myself as a storyteller, a narrative playwright, so a successful series episode, to me, is one in which I have managed to write my own original play within the framework of the series, without anyone noticing.

N.J. Crisp, writer

```
3. CAFE
DAISY brings ANNA a coffee and sits with her.

            DAISY
            Did you go to the meeting? Did he ask you out?

            ANNA
            Yes I went and no he didn't. I don't know why -
            I can't understand it. I wore my best suit, you
            know, the pretend Chanel one with the little
            gold chains.

            DAISY
            To a CND meeting?

            ANNA
            There's no reason not to look my best, Daisy,
            whatever the occasion. And my black patent
            heels, because Simon's so tall I thought he
            wouldn't feel threatened.

            DAISY

            No. Well what happened?

            ANNA
            What happened? They kept talking about the bomb
            and all that sort of thing, that's what
            happened.

            DAISY
            They would at a CND meeting. I don't think you
            take it seriously.

ANNA chokes on her coffee.

            ANNA
            Seriously - my God I'm dead serious! I joined
            didn't I? If Simon doesn't ask me out soon I
            don't know what else I can do-
```

Fig. 24. A page as originally written.

```
         SCENE 5    THE CAFE

----------------------------------------------------------------

                         DAISY
                         ANNA

              DAISY
              All I meant was he might notice you
              more if you could talk to him about
              his interests.

              ANNA
              I've joined CND.  I went on a march
              - in my red slingbacks with four
              inch heels all through London, past
              all the shops and I didn't go in,
              not even down Sloane Street.   I can
              talk about his interests. I don't
              suppose he's going to want me to
              know more about them than he does.

              DAISY
              No ---

              ANNA
              Men never do.  He gave me a lift
              home after the meeting.

              DAISY
              You see!  He must like you.

              ANNA
              He must, really, mustn't he.  Well,
              I did ask him if he would.  I left
              my car at home on purpose and said I
              had a tube phobia.


        - 13 -
```

Fig. 25. The rehearsal script.

```
"FLOGGING A DEAD PRINCE"              SCENE 6


                                      DAISY COMES OVER WITH HER PAD.

                                      DAISY
                                      One egg mayonnaise and salad, three
         See DAISY in +               coffees and a chocolate fudge cake.
         hold her away L to
         2S DAISY/GIORGIO
                                      GIORGIO
                                      We need more egg mayo, OK?


                                      DAISY GOES THROUGH TO THE KITCHEN.

52.   3                               GIORGIO
      CU GIORGIO                      I saw a traffic warden
                                      earlier.  I hope your cab's all
  53.  5                              right out there.  /
       CU A?B

                                      BRIAN
 54.  2                               She  won't bother my cab.  What were
      2S  GIORGIO/MARIA               we saying about Gustavus Adolphus.  /

      /5 repo KitchenL/
                                      MARIA
                                      (PATIENTLY)  Gustavus Adolphus, the
      Hold 2S with her                Swedish Meteor, took Pomerania in
      cross                           1630 only to face the obstacle of
                                      Brandenburg and Saxony.


                                      GIORGIO
      Hold her away R to              (WHISPERS) Stop encouraging him.
      BRIAN & ease in to CU
                                      BRIAN
                                      That's right.  Now then, a lot of
                                      people have got the wrong end of the
                                      stick about the 30 years war.


      /SHOT 55 ON 5 NEXT/             END OF SCENE
```

Fig. 26. The camera script.

In practice, having bought the script the television company can cut it, but cannot *add lines* without informing you, the writer. You cannot actually stop them adding lines – but if you disagree strongly, you can take your name off the play.

IMPORTANCE OF TITLES

How important are titles?

It is quite likely that the script editor will first open and start to read your script without even looking at the title. Many television plays – and in particular series – go through half a dozen titles (known as **working titles**) before the final name is agreed.

There is no doubt that a strong title is a good thing, and titles with sexual connotations and hints of intrigue always do well: *Desperate Housewives*, *Bad Girls*, *Footballers' Wives*, *Mistresses*, *The Year of the Sex Olympics*. Action titles are good: *Licking Hitler* and *Spend, Spend, Spend* and titles that conjure up memorable images like *The Saliva Milkshake* and *Deadhead*. There is a theory in America that any title with a number in it cannot fail: *The Third Man*, *The Fourth Protocol* – and indeed it is said that films are now being made with titles like *Godmother 6* without there having been any Godmothers one to five.

ARE AGENTS NECESSARY?

Do I need an agent?

A good agent is an enormous help. A good agent is known and respected by producers. When a script from such an agent arrives on a producer's desk it is taken seriously, read quickly, and the assumption right from the start is that it is good. Many programmes (like *The Bill*) say they will not look at a script at all unless it comes through an agent.

It is unlikely, as a new writer, that an agent can get you a higher fee than you could get for yourself. But an agent will make sure your residual rights and repeat fees are as they ought to be, particularly when dealing with independent production companies.

The problem is: how do you get a good agent to take you on? Good agents are careful to guard their reputation. They will not send a script to a producer unless they have confidence in it. They will not take on a writer unless they are confident in his ability. Persuading a decent agent to read your script and take you up is probably as difficult as getting a television company to buy your script in the first place.

If you approach a top television agent you are likely to be told that she already has more writers than she can handle, and is not looking for new clients at the moment. Occasionally this might be true. But at the end of the day all agents are interested in new, exciting writers – it is the 12.5% of your talent that keeps them fat and prosperous and if you have genuine ability an agent will eventually take you up and devote much time and effort to helping you.

It is best to approach an agent once you have either:

- won a playwriting competition, particularly one for television, or a London pub theatre writing competition; or

- had at least one play – either for television or radio – accepted.

A list of agents dealing in TV scripts is on page 233.

HOW MUCH YOU WILL BE PAID

How much will I be paid?

Writing for television is generally considered lucrative – but some slots pay a lot more than others, often because they attract automatic repeat fees. A good agent will fight to get you as much as possible, but most series and serials pay set rates, particularly for new writers. If you don't have an agent you can check on current agreements with the Writers' Guild or – a wise move – you can join the Society of Authors and they will check through your contract for you free of charge (see Chapter 18, page 216).

Some examples of television drama fees are as follows.

- A new writer will get around £12,000 for a 90-minute original television play. This might sound a lot, but is actually not much for many weeks – if not months, or years – of work. If the programmes is reshown or 'bought out' the writer will get a further payment – often 100%.

- On the other hand, an established writer will be paid up to £6,000 for an episode of a 30-minute soap opera like *Hollyoaks* that has been largely storylined by others, and that will take less than a week to write.

- A 45-minute script in a BBC series like *Robin Hood* will pay an experienced writer around £15,000 (plus fees for other rights).

- An ITV series like *Heartbeat* or BBC series like *Holby City* will earn more than £10,000 for a new writer, and around £13,000 for an established writer.

- *The Bill* pays a new writer around £12,000 and an experienced writer over £17,000 – and there can be further fees from foreign sales.

- An episode of *EastEnders* will earn around £8,500 including the omnibus fee.

- Writers become 'established' after writing four or five scripts. A good agent will make sure it happens sooner rather than later.

- BBC and ITV rates of payment are now very similar (ITV used to pay much more).

- Channel 5 pays less.

- Independent production companies have been notorious for asking writers to work on ideas, storylines, and scripts, without payment. Producers that belong to the Independent Producers' Association, PACT, will pay writers to develop a storyline (between 5% and 10% of an eventual script fee) or a treatment (between 15% and 25% of an eventual script fee). In practice, though, a new writer will still be expected to do a great deal of work without payment in order to show that they can deliver what they promise.

- The rate for children's drama or educational drama series and serials (both areas where the new writer might find an opening) is around £90 a minute, though in practice much higher rates can be paid on prestige projects. Religious drama, if there were ever to be any, would be paid at the same rate.

- When you are invited to attend the read-through of your script and attend rehearsals, you will be paid around £85 a day, and the BBC and ITV faithfully promise to pay this within 30 days of attendance.

- The most lucrative work is on serials or series where one writer writes all the episodes. A three-part original serial, with each episode running for 90 minutes, will earn the writer around £75,000 – and the possibility of at least as much again from overseas sales and repeats.

- An established writer on a soap opera like *Coronation Street* who also has income from previous programmes (residuals) might easily earn in excess of £150,000 a year.

- If you are a poet, however, and one of your published poems is read on television, you will be paid around £30 per half minute, and might well starve to death.

17

TV Talk: Common Words and Expressions Used in Scripts and in the Television Industry

Action props   Props used by actors in the course of a scene – swords if there is a sword fight, pen and paper if the scene calls for them to be used. The food consumed on set is an action prop.

Ambient noise   Background noise like traffic or air-conditioning. Often referred to as 'atmos'.

Backing   In the studio a piece of scenery put behind a door so that we do not see the studio when characters go in and out. Windows on sets similarly have backing scenery.

BCU   Big close up. The camera shows only part of the face or object.

Bible   When a drama series is given the go-ahead the first thing to be commissioned from the creator is the Bible. This is a full format with story idea, setting, locations, notes on style, character notes and usually the initial storylines.

Binned

A script is 'binned' if it is not acceptable and cannot be re-written. The writer will already have been paid 50% of the fee, but will not be entitled to the 'second half fee' if the script is not accepted. In practice writers are often paid the full amount in order to shut them up.

Boom

The microphone is held over the actors' heads on a boom or poked towards them behind the furniture. If you see actors on location, strolling over the hills with not a boom in sight, it means that either the sound operator is disguised as a sheep or the actors are using radio microphones.

Camera script

A studio script with the camera moves and technical directions on it. (See Figure 26, page 184.)

Captions

Opening captions show the title of the play or series, the individual episode title if there is one, the creator, the leading actors and usually the writer.

Ciné-vérite

Fly-on-the-wall documentary style, often involving a hand-held camera, giving a feeling of realism.

Credits

The names of actors, production staff and crew, and usually the producer and director. It used to be the case that the director always had the final credit, on a caption all to himself, but television is increasingly a producers' medium, and producers (or executive producers) are commonly taking the last place. To achieve this without aggravation directors are now sometimes credited among the opening captions. They like this because it is what happens on feature films.

CU

Close up. The face of a character or object fills the screen.

Cut away

If you want to leave a scene or set for a moment, to indicate a time lapse perhaps, or remind us of things happening else-where, or to give pace to a scene, the quick shot of something else is called a cut away. For instance, a tense scene of a couple waiting for a blackmailer to turn up might be interspaced with cut aways to show the blackmailer in his car driving towards the house, parking, coming up to the door. Or a scene showing a character dashing to save a victim might include quick cut aways of the victim bound and gagged and suffering terrible things.

Day for night

Filming on location at night is extremely expensive. Every shot has to be separately lit, which involves unbelievable numbers of electricians, exorbitant hire charges on lighting equipment, and massive overtime payments to the crew (this last item is changing as independent companies negotiate more effectively than the old ITV companies).

A traditional way to include night scenes on a low budget is to shoot during the day but with special filters on the camera. This day for night trick results in sequences that look murky and have strange colour tones. However skilled the cameraman, the sky is usually much too bright. Directors and producers dislike having to shoot day for night.

DBS

Direct satellite broadcasting.

Digibeta

Broadcast quality digital videotape, a format commonly used for shooting drama.

Digital editing

It used to be that when you copied tape it lost quality – 'went down a generation' – but digital technology means that edits can be dissolved and then reformed as new. Practically all editing – sound and picture – is now done digitally. Editors can do marvellous things, but cynics note that editing tape now takes ten times as long and costs ten times as much as it did in the old days when you had a piece of film and a razor blade.

Dress   A set is dressed when it has all its bits and pieces in place – cushions, tablecloth, ornaments, the movable items that have been stored away to stop them being stolen or damaged while the set was not being used.

Dry   An actor dries when he totally forgets his lines.

Dubbing mixer   Or sound supervisor. The person who mixes and adjusts sound effects, dialogue and music once the programme is filmed or recorded.

Ext or Int   Exterior or interior.
                           Although still very commonly used, Int and Ext survive from the days when Int meant anything done in the studio, and Ext was the bit of exterior shooting to show characters out and about in the world.

                           Nowadays most dramas are shot entirely on location, either on film or video, and directions as to Int or Ext are often superfluous. The direction INT. JULIA'S BATHROOM is pointless, unless there is a possibility that Julia's bathroom might be open to the skies, or somebody might be clinging to the outside wall peering in. The description EXT. EXMOOR is equally redundant, as INT. EXMOOR would be a nonsense. Int and Ext are still used, however.

Extras

Actors who do not have lines and are not individually and specifically directed to carry out particular actions. People sitting drinking and chatting in the background of the Rover's Return are extras. Generally speaking, writers need not worry about extras – the production will hire as many or few as it can afford. It is not a good idea, however, to write a play that positively must have a battalion of the Grenadier Guards milling around – you are likely to end up with four or five extras desperately trying to look like a battalion by moving about a lot.

Extras who are required to speak or to actually do something are called **walk ons**. A walk on can have ten words or so and can be directed. Thus if the barmaid in the Rover's Return says 'Now then Charlie, what was it a pint of mild?' and an extra nods and says, 'That's right' the extra will be classified as a walk on and be paid a few pounds more. Similarly if you want us to come across your hero entwined in the arms of a beautiful girl who is kissing him passionately and murmuring 'Cuddlebundle', the actress will be a walk on providing she does not say 'cuddlebundle' more than ten times and providing it is agreed that 'cuddlebundle' is one word and not two. The eleventh 'cuddlebundle' will officially, though not in practice, qualify her as a speaking character and put up her fee from around £100 to around £400. In practice actors are grateful for every word given because it increases their exposure on television.

Lines for a walk on should not be written in the script as dialogue but given to the actor on the day. You should thus write:

9. INT. DISCO. NIGHT

WE DISCOVER RORY IN CLOSE EMBRACE WITH YET ANOTHER BLONDE. SHE IS MURMURING WORDS OF ENDEARMENT AS MARIAN APPROACHES AND STARES AT THEM WITH A GRIM EXPRESSION.

Fade to black   When you want the screen to go to black, often used between scenes as a time passage. This device used to be popular, then was regarded as terribly clumsy, and now is regarded by some as quite artistic.

American dramas tend to fade to black every few minutes, but this is because the advertising breaks have been taken out.

Film editor

The film editor or VT (videotape) editor assembles the programme from the material shot, usually under the instruction of the director. In film the first assembly or **rough cut** will be viewed by the producer and script editor, who make their comments. A writer should endeavour to be present at this stage, although there may be resistance.

Fluff

When an actor muddles up a line or says the wrong word. An actor who does this will often do it again and again, at exactly the same place. Sometimes this is because of stress and tension – studio time costs hundreds of pounds every minute – and sometimes because the line or word is genuinely difficult to say. 'Probably' is often a word to cause fluffs, and actors will always thank you for writing 'I expect I'll potter to Pettifers' rather than 'I'll probably potter to Pettifers'.

Footprint

Satellites have different 'footprints' – their programmer can only be seen on television sets within their area of broadcasting as they travel round the Earth.

Format   A document explaining an idea for a series
                      or soap opera. A format is usually about
                      ten pages long. A shorter document of
                      two or three pages might be called an
                      outline. Nobody knows which term is
                      correct and nobody really cares. (See also
                      Bible.)

Genre   A type of programme. Soap opera is a
                      genre. So is science fiction. Critics, script
                      editors, directors and producers are all
                      fond of the word.

Gun mike   A microphone that operates in a very
                      narrow band, but over a long distance. It
                      can be used to pick up the speech of an
                      individual in a crowd.

High angle shot/ The camera looking down or looking
low angle shot   up.

Indie   Independent production companies are
                      known as Indies. Twenty-five per cent of
                      television production is supposed to be
                      made by Indies. Some of them are very big
                      like Tiger Aspect and Touchpaper, but
                      others are very small – often just one or
                      two hopeful people working from home
                      with a phone, fax, and headed notepaper
                      saying Megaworld Productions UK Ltd.

In frame   A person or object is in the camera's view.

In the can

A scene that is 'in the can' has been successfully (technically, if not artistically) recorded or filmed.

Libel

When your script is commissioned you will sign a contract stating that you will use your best endeavours to ensure that no defamatory matter is included in your work. The most obvious danger of libel comes from the choice of a character's name, or the name of a place. On page 22 there is an outline for a play about a man called Slime who starves to death the residents of the Hardtimes Residential Home for the Elderly. If this play were transmitted and it transpired that there really was a Mr Slime in charge of a Hardtimes Residential Home for the Elderly then he would be likely to claim damages for defamation of character.

The trouble with a real television play is that you cannot fall back on patently invented names like Slime.

So what can you do to protect yourself?

Basically, you should be certain that you have *not* libelled somebody you know. If there is an accountant called Fidgetwig living next to you, do not write a play about a crooked wife-beating animal-loathing accountant called Fodgetwog, because your neighbour will successfully sue you and the television company for a large amount of money.

In practice the script editor will carry out what is called a **neg check**. Thus if you have a crooked security organization in your play a check will be made (there are specialist firms who do this) on company registers to make sure that no security organization with the name you have chosen actually exists.

Using a very common name is not necessarily a protection. It is true that if you call a sex maniac teacher Smith, you will not be liable for prosecution by the thousands of teachers called Smith in Britain. But if your play is about a sex maniac teacher Smith who has four daughters, a water spaniel and a Volvo and lives in Chipping Dodsbury, and after transmission you get a call from a Mr Smith of Chipping Dodsbury who has four daughters, a King Charles Spaniel and a Saab – then you are in big trouble.

Again, though, the television company will in practice have done a neg check on teachers in the Chipping Dodsbury locality.

Library film   Film or videotape material not shot specifically for your play. If you have a scene with a teacher explaining the life cycle of the kangaroo, you might ask to see library film of kangaroos on a video screen behind the teacher's head. Use of library film is costed at so much per second, and the price depends on whether the production needs UK rights or world rights. Don't write it in without consulting the script editor.

LS
Long shot – figures in the distance, obviously not possible in a studio production.

Mix
Cross fade as it is known in radio, or **dissolve** on film, is when one scene merges gently into the next rather than a straight **cut**.

MLS
Medium long shot – generally a group of figures.

MS
Mid shot – this would show figures from about the waist up.

Narrative
The narrative is the story told through the plot. It is what happens scene by scene, and when script editors says a script has a strong narrative they mean that on the superficial storytelling level it holds their attention and develops well.

A script can have a strong narrative and still be empty of new ideas or originality.

OB

Filmed, or recorded on video, away from the studio.

Off the page

Good dialogue is said to come 'off the page' if it has energy and life and is believable. It is very bad news when a script editor says: 'This dialogue just doesn't come off the page'.

Option

If a television company or independent production company wants to adapt a novel they first take out an option with the copyright owner, usually the writer. Even small independent production companies take out options, as this then gives them a 'property' that nobody else can touch during the period of the option. (See page 142.)

Offline edit

Working on videotape rather than film, the director uses a small offline edit suite to produce the equivalent of a film rough cut or first assembly. This saves time when the director moves into the vastly more expensive **online edit suite** where the final editing actually takes place.

OOV

Out of vision. Sometimes called **OS** (**off screen**). We are listening to a character who is in the scene but is not visible. (But see VO below.)

Pan	The camera remains in a static position but the lens moves along a row of people, round a room, or across a landscape. The camera does not change its focus.
POV	The camera shows us something from a particular character's point of view.
Producer's run	When studio plays (nowadays mainly soap operas) have been rehearsed and actors are 'off the book' (know their lines) the play is run through without costumes or cameras for the producer and script editor to watch. At this point the producer can cut things and change interpretations she does not like, and the script editor can insist that the actors go back to the lines that were written for them, rather than the ones they've made up in rehearsal.
Production values	Are what everybody wants. If a show has good production values it means that visually the budget is being well spent, that the show looks lavish and interesting without costing an arm and a leg.
Pull back	The camera pulls back from a close up or medium shot to show more of the scene.
Reader	Most ITV companies and large independent production companies employ readers to assess unsolicited scripts. These readers are often would-be script

editors, usually female, often not long out of university. They are paid anything between £20 and £75 to read your script. They then have to summarise the story (to prove they have read it through) and give their opinion in around 100 words. Readers are sometimes more skilled and perceptive than you might expect.

Read through

On the first day of production the cast, technical staff, production staff and the writer come together for the first time, to read through the play. Whilst some actors are happy to give a performance, others read through the lines in a dull monotone. This is not because they dislike the play, but because they dislike interpreting the lines before rehearsal.

Residuals

The extra money you get when your play is repeated in the UK or sold elsewhere in the world. (See **How much will I be paid?**, page 186.)

Script unit

The BBC has a script unit that processes 10,000 unsolicited scripts a year and the bigger ITV companies and Indies have heads of drama development (often young graduates from Oxford who want to work in television). Readers are employed to process unsolicited material (see Chapter 19). Often they will give useful advice if they think you show ability. Unlike script editors assigned to particular programmes who are paid to find an exact number of scripts to fill an exact number of slots and do not have time or inclination to run a free advice service, script editors working with script units have a duty to encourage and help promising talent.

The drawback is that however much a script unit editor likes your work she is never in a position actually to *buy it*. At the end of the day it is a producer or editor working on a series that you have to please.

SFX

Sound effects. Denotes a particular sound effect that you want over a shot – if somebody is lying in bed dreaming about the sea and you want the sound of seagulls it would be an SFX. Rather old-fashioned radio phrase – it is as easy to write 'we hear the sound of seagulls and crashing waves'.

Slow zoom

The camera moves slowly in.

Stock shot

A shot that can be used over and over again. Often a three- or four-second shot of the exterior of a house in a series or serial drama.

Storyline

In series drama, a storyline is what the writer submits. It gives the basic story and shows the development of the plot stage by stage. In soap operas the storyline is drawn up by the script editors and details the stories that will be covered by individual writers. (See page 120.)

Talking heads

A play in which people talk to each other all the time, in boring locations, without any action. 'Talking heads' is generally regarded as a pejorative expression. 'It's nothing but talking heads' a director will moan.

Tighten

A zoom in, but gently and not as dramatic or as much.

Tracking shot

The camera moves with the characters – perhaps two people walking towards us, and the camera moving away at the same speed. The camera itself can also track in on a group. This is different from the **zoom** in that the camera itself moves, so that the angle on the subjects changes. We might, for example, start on the backs of the two characters as they sit on a sofa, and then track round with the camera until we see their faces.

Treatment

Development of an idea, showing how it will break down scene by scene, and often including examples of dialogue.

Two hander	A scene with only two characters.
Two shot (2S)	Two people on the screen.
VO	Voice over. A narrator voicing over a scene in a sound studio, or dialogue from scene A that is put over scene B for artistic effect.
Whip pan	A pan at speed – again not used in studio and only when being artistic on film.
Working title	If a writer cannot think up a good title for a play or series he gives it a working title just to be going on with. On the first page this will be indicated by:

BOOT MAN
(Working Title)
by Veronica Jane Rumble

Wrap	The time recording or filming ends. A location will wrap at a certain time. 'It's a wrap' means that shooting has finished for the day. 'We wrapped at one minute to six,' says the production manager to the associate producer, who is worried about overtime.
Zoom	The camera focus moves in or out on a person or object.

18

Organizations That Will Help You

- Writing courses.

- Residential courses, day seminars, and workshops.

- Grants and development funds.

- Internet help sites for new writers.

- Writers' organizations.

- University courses.

WRITING COURSES

Your aim, at all times, should be to *make contact with a professional, working, script editor*. Sending a script cold through the post might be your only option if you live in the Orkneys (where script editors rarely stray in a professional capacity) but for those able to do so, attending scriptwriting courses can prove fruitful. Some examples are given below.

- A biochemist with no contacts in the television world attended a weekend writing seminar in the Cotswolds (advertised in *The Guardian*) and her script was assessed by a professional working script editor. She went on to write for *EastEnders*.

■ Three young graduates on a scriptwriting course at the Northern Media School, Sheffield, were among students who had their work assessed by an assistant producer from Channel 5. They were all offered contracts on *Family Affairs*.

■ A young playwright attended a TV-writing course organized at the Liverpool Playhouse. His script was read by a senior script editor from Thames TV. He went on to write for *The Bill*.

When you consider a scriptwriting course of any kind you should always look carefully at the quality of advice you will be getting.

■ **Do** go for scriptwriting courses where your work will be looked at by professionals currently working in the industry. Always, if you can, opt for a course where you meet your tutor.

■ **Be wary of** courses where the tutors are media-course academics who have never actually worked in television – or are said to have had a distinguished career in as script consultants on TV drama in the Seventies.

■ **Be very wary of** correspondence courses. Quality of advice can be very uneven. You might be given an able tutor who has recently worked in television, but you might equally get somebody who has never worked in the business at all. Always ask to be told your tutor's credits. Avoid courses which ask you to do 'exercises' or to keep revising a piece of work. Some of the correspondence writing schools that advertise 'your money back if you have not sold a script by the end of the course' are reputable and give sound advice – but, clearly, there are not many people who ever finish their courses. You are better off improving your skills by writing new 10-minute dramas that have a chance of being bought and made into programmes.

■ Quality advice is not always cheap. A professional script editor or producer working on a major top-twenty series is not going to assess scripts by unknown authors for £5 an hour. Consultancies can charge up to £100 for a script analysis. Some residential weekends cost over £400. On the other hand, professional working script editors sometimes attend seminars and short courses run by arts associations, universities, and organisations like the Screenwriters' Workshop (see below). These might be heavily subsidised or even free to local aspiring writers.

■ Check with your local arts association on forthcoming script-writing courses (often run by university departments of continuing education) and writers' organisations in your area.

■ Look out for scriptwriting courses advertised on internet sites like Script Factory (*www.Scriptfactory.co.uk*) or in *Scriptwriter* magazine (*www.twelvepoint.com*). Avoid courses aimed primarily at feature film screenwriters, unless you enjoy delving into the theory of script structure and want to know how to write film treatments and make a 'pitch'.

RESIDENTIAL COURSES, DAY SEMINARS, AND WORKSHOPS

Residential writing courses, seminars, and workshops are usually run by enthusiasts and can be excellent – but they often survive for only a few years and then, sadly, fade away. As with everything else, check on the internet to see what is on offer. If you have had a radio play accepted, or a play performed by a professional theatre, apply to the BBC Drama Production Writers' Academy which will 'give you the specific skills required to write for some of the BBC's most popular format series such as *Doctors, EastEnders, Holby City* and *Casualty'*. This course pays you £400 a week during training and is advertised online at both the BBC Writersroom and at *broadcastfreelancer.com*

Two organizations that are well established and have a high reputation are Euroscript and The Arvon Foundation.

Euroscript

Formerly the London Screenwriters' Workshop, Euroscript helps new writers with seminars, workshop events, and tuition. The largest organization of its kind in Europe, the workshop was founded in 1983 by a group of film and television writers as a forum for contact, discussion, and practical criticism. Courses cover every aspect of script writing, from how to write a treatment to how to do a re-write. Some courses last for several weeks, other subjects are covered in afternoon or evening workshops. There is also a script-reading service that offers a professional assessment of your script with suggestions on storylines, character, plot, and dialogue.

Euroscript,
64 Hemingford Road,
London N1 1DB.
Tel: 07958 244 656
E-mail: *ask@euroscript.co.uk*
Website: *www.euroscript.co.uk*

The Arvon Foundation

High quality guest tutors run five-day residential courses at Hebden Bridge in Yorkshire, Totleigh Barton in Devon, Craven Arms in Shropshire, and Beauly in Inverness-shire. The foundation runs courses in many forms of creative writing, including film scriptwriting, television comedy and television drama. Courses are informal and friendly – students and tutors make their own breakfasts and lunches and share the cooking of the evening meal – and are open to anybody over the age of 16. The foundation is supported by the English and Scottish Arts Councils. Fees are low – around £450 including accommodation and food – and there are various bursaries available.

The Arvon Foundation,
Totleigh Barton,
Sheepwash,
Devon EX21 5NS.
Tel: 01409 231338
E-mail: *t-barton@arvonfoundation.org*
Website: *www.arvonfoundation.org*

GRANTS AND DEVELOPMENT FUNDS

Arts Council

The Arts Council works through Arts Wales (*www.artswales.org.uk*) Scottish Arts (*www.scottisharts.org.uk*), and regional offices covering the East of England, the East Midlands, London, the North East, North West, South East, South West, West Midlands, and Yorkshire. Information is now very much internet-based. Look at the main website and you will be directed to the different regional sites where you can find contact numbers to get information about pending writers' festivals, scriptwriting workshops, or drama events.

Tel: 0845 300 6200
Website: *www.artscouncil.org.uk*

Euroscript

A curious but admirable EU scheme to promote European scriptwriting. It provides funding to develop several screenplays a year, runs a film story competition (deadlines are 30 April and 31 October each year) and supports international workshops. In the UK it has absorbed the Screenwriters' Workshop – which actually created Euroscript in 1995.

Address as for Euroscript (see above).
Tel: 07958 244 656
E-mail: *ask@euroscript.co.uk*
Website: *www.euroscript.co.uk*

UK Film Council

The UK Film Council is primarily concerned with funding aspiring film-makers – but this can often involve funding scripts, particularly for short films. Check its website for details of current script funding in the different regions – North East, North West, Yorkshire and the Humber, East of England, East Midlands, West Midlands, the South East, and the South West.

The Film Council,
10 Little Portland Street,
London W1W 7JG.
Tel: 020 7861 7861
Website: (*www.ukfilmcouncil.org.uk/regions*)

Film London

Part of the Film Council, it gives grants to writers, producers, and directors in the capital. Send a sae for details or look at the website.

Film London,
20 Euston Centre,
London NW1 3JH.
Tel: 020 7387 8787
Website: *www.filmlondon.org.uk*

PAWS Drama Fund

PAWS (Public Awareness of Science) drama fund gives grants to writers (currently £2,000) who come up with good ideas for science-based television drama, and also organizes informal discussion evenings where scientists outline areas of their work they believe have dramatic potential, and television drama producers add their comments. There is generally an opportunity for writers to talk informally to both the scientists and the television people (it's the television people you want to meet!). PAWS is supported by companies like Zeneca, BP, and Unilever. For details write to:

PAWS,
1st Floor,
155 Regent's Park Road,
London NW1 8BB.
Tel: 020 7483 4545
E-mail: *pawsomni@globalnet.co.uk*

INTERNET HELP SITES FOR NEW WRITERS

Internet sites for television scriptwriters are in a state of constant flux. Many sites have fallen by the wayside. Channel 4 now provides little or no help and the excellent Writernet closed in 2009. There is a core of sites, however, that is immensely useful. The three top sites are:

BBC Writersroom (*www.bbc.co.uk/writersroom*) has onward-going details of BBC drama requirements, competitions, internet-based scriptwriting help, and script assessment.

Twelvepoint.com has evolved from *Scriptwriter* magazine, and is a place where you exchange experiences with other writers, can find information about writing seminars and competitions, and follow links to many other useful websites. It works closely with The Film Council and the Writers' Guild.

Writing for Performance (*www.writing.org.uk*) gives excellent free advice and valuable links to other sites. It is particularly strong on situation comedy.

Other sites worth looking at are:

BBC Get Writing (*www.bbc.co.uk/dna/getwriting*) encourages new writers to talk to each other and publish their own work on the internet.

BBC Talent (*www.bbc.co.uk/talent*) is another BBC initiative to discover and promote new writers and performers. Look at this site for details of competitions and regional events.

Farnham Films (*www.farnfilm.com*) is one of the most useful sites on the net. It provide a list of TV drama commissioning editors – invaluable as the list is regularly updated – and has plenty of advice for new writers.

Ideas4writers (*www.ideas4writers.co.uk*) is not specifically aimed at script writers, but provides useful links to other sites.

Screenwriters' Store (*www.screenwriterstore.co.uk*) sells software and training material, and provides news about courses and workshops for new writers.

Scriptfactory (*www.scriptfactory.co.uk*) provides training and development for scriptwriters, and is sponsored by organisations that include the UK film Council, and BBC Films.

Scriptunities (*www.xerif.com*) lists all UK and European script competitions, and links to scriptwriting workshops at Birkbeck College, University of London.

The Script Vault (*www.thescriptvault.com*) will archive your script electronically (thus helping to protect your copyright), and offers a script assessment service.

ORGANIZATIONS FOR WRITERS

The Society of Authors has an active broadcasting section with more than 800 members. There are occasional talks given by people working in the television industry – often producers and editors. The society has a permanent staff, including a solicitor who will vet contracts for you (useful if you do not have an agent). The society will take legal action on your behalf if the issue is considered of general concern to the profession. The society's magazine *The Author* comes out four times a year and has a broadcasting section which sometimes gives information about scripts in demand. The society also publishes free guides on such subjects as television agreements, copyright, libel, and authors' agents. If you do not qualify for membership of the society (you need to have had work accepted for publication or broadcast) you can buy *The Author* on subscription. There is also a category of associate membership for those who have not yet had a full-length work broadcast but have either received a major contract or have had occasional items broadcast. More information can be obtained from:

The Society of Authors,
84 Drayton Gardens,
London SW10 9SB.
Tel: 020 7373 6642
Website: *www.societyofauthors.net*

The Writers' Guild of Great Britain negotiates television fees (and radio fees jointly with the *Society of Authors*) and gives help and advice on everything from contracts and agents to fees. The Guild holds frequent meetings for members, and publishes a very useful range of booklets. If you are not a professional writer, the Guild has a category of membership specifically for those 'who are taking their first steps in writing but who have not as yet received a contract'. For information on membership, contact:

The Writers' Guild,
15 Britannia Street,
London WC1X 9JN.
Tel: 020 7833 0777
Website: *www.writersguild.org.uk*

University courses

Astonishingly, more than fifty universities or colleges in the United Kingdom currently offer MA courses in creative writing or scriptwriting. Before embarking on what might seem an arduous, and expensive, way to learn the writer's craft, ask if the course will include lectures, seminars, and (most particularly) script assessment by producers or script editors currently working in the industry. If there is no contact with the actual world of televison drama, the course is unlikely to help you to become a professional scriptwriter.

Universities offering courses that focus on film and television scriptwriting include:

Liverpool John Moores University,
St James Road,
Liverpool LI 7BR.
Tel: 0151 231 5052

University of Salford,
Adelphi, Peru Street,
Salford M3 6EQ.
Tel: 0161 295 6027

University of Sheffield,
388 Glossop Road,
Sheffield S10 2JA.
Tel: 0114 222 8177

Leicester De Montfort University,
The Gateway,
Leicester LE1 9BH.
Tel: 0116 255 1551

University of Glamorgan,
Treforest,
Pontypridd,
CF37 1DL.
Tel: 01443 482570

King's College,
University of London,
Strand,
London WC2R 2LS.
Tel: 020 7848 2184

University of York,
Heslington,
York YO10 5DD.
Tel: 01904 433369

National Film and Television School,
Station Road,
Beaconsfield,
Bucks HP9 1LG.
Tel: 01494 671234

Of the above Leicester De Montfort University is said to have a very good course, very much focused on the practical side of writing. It has produced a number of promising writers. Salford is also said to be good.

19

Where to Send Your Script

APPROACHING A SCRIPT EDITOR

■ You now have to get a producer or script editor to read your calling card script.

■ Send a copy of your script to the BBC Writersroom. If you want to write for a particular programme (e.g *EastEnders*) say so. If your script shows promise it will be forwarded to the producer or script editor concerned. Alternatively you might be invited to meet a BBC script editor, or to take part in a workshop.

■ As well as sending your script to the Writersroom, it does no harm to send a script directly to an editor or producer if you believe it will appeal to them. (The BBC discourages this approach and the producer concerned will probably pass it unread to the Writersroom, but you never know...)

■ With ITV and the Independents, try to find out the name of the script editor or script executive – either from the on-screen credits, by a telephone call to the programme company switchboard, or by looking at the company's website.

■ If you are a bold person, phone them and in a confident voice ask to speak to the script editor by name. Nine times out of ten you will not be put through, but you might be lucky. If you are, tell them you know they've got plenty of writers, but you would be grateful for any advice – do they perhaps have a writers' pack that they could send you? Try to engage their sympathy without irritating them. Ask if they will look at a script as an example of your work.

■ Whether you have made contact or not, send your script directly to the person you want to read it. If you've spoken to them on the phone, make your letter personal ('Thank you for your advice. As discussed on the phone, here's my script *Happy Days*. It was good of you to offer to read it.') Keep your letter short but friendly.

■ A good excuse for a phone call is to check on any special seasons for new writing talent, or to ask if the company produces a writers' pack for a particular programme.

■ Send a copy of your script to the BBC Writersroom and to at least one other possible buyer.

Things you should **not** do:

■ **Don't** send a tatty manuscript decorated with coffee ring stains.

■ **Don't** tell the script reader things about yourself that are not relevant, eg: the funny incident at Ibiza that first made you become interested in writing; the friends who said 'You've got a real gift for words'.

■ **Don't** mention that your script has been turned down by others, eg: 'Morag Veryweary at ITV Yorkshire read *Happy Days* with interest but unfortunately was not producing plays of this type at the moment and regretfully had to return it to me. Nat Goaway at Granada also liked it very much but felt he had to return it as he would not have a slot until Autumn 2049...'

Main drama department addresses are listed below, as are the names of some drama department contacts. People move about rapidly in the television world, possibly to avoid writers catching up with them. Before sending in your script, look online or telephone to make sure that the office holders have not changed (a good website for this is *farnfilm.com*).

BBC CONTACT ADDRESSES

BBC Writersroom

First Floor, Grafton House, 371–389 Euston Road, London NW1 3AU.
Website: *www.bbc.co.uk/writersroom*

This is your most important port of call. This is where you are wanted. The BBC says: 'BBC writersroom is always on the lookout for fresh, new, talented writers for a changing Britain. When we find them, we do everything we can to get their voice heard.' The BBC promises that all scripts sent in (some 10,000 a year) will be read, and the writers considered for 'highly targeted writing schemes and workshops'.

- Don't send scripts via e-mail.

- Don't send ideas or treatments, or novels/short stories you might like to adapt.

■ Don't send scripts for existing programmes (like *EastEnders*).

■ Chase up your script if you have not had an acknowlegement in one month and a response in three months.

BBC Drama

BBC Television Centre, Wood Lane, London W12 7SB.
Tel: 020 8743 8000

Behind the Writersroom are the controllers, commissioners, and producers of the BBC's output, now organised within a division titled BBC Vision. If you are able to wriggle round the Writersroom and make personal contact do so. Here are some of the key people in Vision and Vision Productions:

Head of Drama Commissioning: Ben Stephenson
Controller, In-house Drama Production: John Yorke
Director, Drama Production: Nick Brown
Head of Drama Series and Serials: Kate Harwood
Head of Drama, Manchester: Phil Collinson
Head of Drama Series, Birmingham: Richard Langridge

Children's Drama (CBBC)
CBBC used to look at unsolicited scripts, but now wants new writers to make an approach via the Writersroom. If you feel like chancing your luck, you could pretend to be an established writer and make an approach directly via Anne Gilchrist or Jon East (address as for drama, above).

Comedy
Controller of Comedy Commissioning: Lucy Lumsden

Multiplatform

This is an area of expansion, a growing market for new writers at home with the style and language of the internet. It is best to be young. If you are asked about yourself, and are 60, knock off the 0.

Drama Commissioning Executive: Rosie Allimonos
Children's Drama Multiplatform Executive: Rebecca Shallcross

Learning and Interactive

BBC White City, 201 Wood Lane, London W12 7TS.
Tel: 020 8752 5252

This unit commissions online and interactive factual programmes rather than drama – but it is looking for new writers.

Controller: Liz Cleaver

Northern Ireland

Broadcasting House, Belfast BT2 8HQ.
Tel: 028 9033 8000
Website: *www.bbc.co.uk/ni*

Produces a wide range of drama programmes including serials and single dramas. Will look at unsolicited scripts.

Development: Susan Carson
Head of Drama: Patrick Spence

Scotland

Broadcasting House, Queen Margaret Drive, Glasgow G12 8DG.
Tel: 0141 338 2000
Website: *www.bbc.co.uk/scotland*

The most varied production centre outside London. Watch its

website for opportunities for new Scottish writers.

Head of Drama: Anne Mensah
Commisioning Editor, Television: Ewan Angus

Wales

Broadcasting House, Llandaff, Cardiff CF5 2YQ.
Tel: 029 2032 2864
Website: *www.bbc.co.uk/wales*
E-mail: *writerswales@bbc.co.uk*

Broadcasts the Welsh soap opera *Pobol y Cwm* and produces popular drama, documentaries, and education programmes for network transmission including *Dr Who* and *Torchwood*. The writers' unit reads scripts written in both English and Welsh.

Head of Drama: Julie Gardner

INDEPENDENT TELEVISION

Channel 4 Television

124 Horseferry Road, London SW1P 2TX.
Tel: 020 7396 4444
Website: *channel4.com*

Channel 4 commissions programmes from independent companies and buys in ready-made programmes, but does not make programmes itself. Channel 4's remit is to provide programmes of interest to minority audiences and to be distinct and different from other channels. It aims at the 16 to 34 age group. Channel 4 says is it developing long-running series alongside big event dramas. 'Any series should be based around a bold, provocative idea.'

Head of Drama: Liza Marshall
Commissioning Editor: Camilla Campbell
Editor, Events: Ben Stoll
Controller, Film and Drama: Francis Hopkinson

Channel 5

22 Long Acre, London WC2E 9LY.
Tel: 020 7550 5555
Website: *www.five.co.uk*

Is committed to spend the money saved from its dead soap *Family Affairs* on popular drama. Watch the website and send in ideas and scripts (always low budget).

Drama Editor: Abigail Webber

ITV Network Ltd

200 Gray's Inn Road, London WC1X 8HF.
Tel: 020 7843 8158
Website: *www.itv.co.uk*

Broadcasts on ITV1 and ITV2. Check the website to see the drama series and serials coming up, and which production companies are making them. The ITV companies that make up the network do not encourage unsolicited scripts, but the big companies (now pretty well amalgamated within Granada) do make a lot of drama.

Controller, Drama: Sally Haynes
Commissioning Editor, Continuing Series: Steve Frost
Network Centre, Director of Drama: Laura Mackie
Head of Factual Drama: Jeff Pope

ITV Granada/ITV Productions

Granada Television Centre, Quay Street, Manchester M60 9EA.
Tel: 0161 832 7211
Website: *www.granadatv.co.uk*

Head of Drama: Hugh Warren
Head of Drama, Manchester: Kieran Roberts
Controller of Drama: Kate Bartlett
Director of Children's Drama: John Whiston

ITV Wales

ITV Wales, The Television Centre, Culverhouse Cross,
Cardiff CF5 6XJ.
Tel: 029 2059 0590
Website: *www.itvwales.com*

Head of Drama (ITV Wales): Peter Edwards
Head of Development, Indie Productions: Sue Shephard

Scottish Television (STV)

Pacific Quay, Glasgow G51 1PQ.
Tel: 0141 300 3000
Website: *stv.tv*

Makes drama and children's programmes for the ITV network, including *Taggart* and *McCallum*. Ideas for long-running series and serials are said to be welcome (with or without a Scottish flavour).

Controller of Drama: Eric Coulter

ITV Yorkshire

The Television Centre, Leeds LS3 1JS.
Tel: 0113 243 8283
Website: *www.itv.com*

If you are interested in writing for *Emmerdale* note down the name of the current producer or story editor from the screen and send your calling card script (not your attempt at an *Emmerdale* script) to them directly.

Group Controller of Drama: Keith Richardson
Controller, Drama Features and Comedy: David Reynolds

BSkyB

Grant Way, Isleworth, Middlesex TW7 5QD.
Tel: 020 7705 3030
Website: *www.sky.com*

Now making a profit, there are hopes that BskyB will plough money back into drama commissioned from independents.

Drama Commissioning Sky 1: Elaine Pyke
Head of Film: William Turner

INDEPENDENT PRODUCTION COMPANIES

Some independents are bigger and more important than many of the smaller ITV companies. Other independents are one-person affairs that occupy West End offices when they're in production, and shrink back into the spare bedroom in Hendon when they're back 'in development'. Big or small, however, there is little enthusiasm for reading unsolicited scripts and offering constructive advice to new writers.

WARNING

Beware of independent production companies that want you to develop your work without a fee. A company might well say: 'Get this script right and we'll bust a gut trying to get it on...'. Busting a gut in this context means that you spend weeks revising your script and the independent producer takes a Channel 4 commissioning editor to lunch and rapidly pitches a dozen different projects – including yours – in the hope that one will go forward into development. Too many writers are hacking away for nothing, paid only with words of encouragement and visions of hope. A company that really believes in your script will put money on the table, even if it is only a storyline or treatment fee.

Most independent production companies live in a state of flux. They come and go, amalgamate, change their names, change their address; and their willingness to read scripts changes just as abruptly, depending on their need for new ideas and their current staff levels. An Indie can have a Head of Script Development one week and just a part-time cleaning lady the next. Few, at any time, will admit that they welcome unsolicited scripts – but at the end of the day, of course, they can't do without new writers, scripts, storylines, and ideas. It's best to check the website for contact details then e-mail or phone to find out what (if anything) they are looking for. Below are some of the bigger Indies that make television drama and comedy.

The Comedy Unit

6th Floor, 53 Bothwell Street, Glasgow G2 6TS.

Tel: 0141 220 6400

Website: *www.comedyunit.co.uk*

E-mail: *info@comedyunit.co.uk*

New comedy writing encouraged. New writers encouraged. Asks for material to be submitted by post or by e-mail.

Script Editor: Niall Clark

Ecosse Films

Brigade House, 8 Parson's Green, London W4 4EU.

Tel: 020 7371 0290

Website: *www.ecossefilms.com*

Prefers scripts through agents, but worth checking the website to see what they are planning to make.

Hat Trick Productions

10 Livonia Street, London W1F 8AF.

Tel: 020 7434 2451

Website: *www.hattrick.com*

Specialises in situation comedy and drama comedy.

Contact: Jimmy Mulville

Hartswood Films Ltd

Twickenham Studios, St Margarets, London TW1 2AW.

Tel: 020 8607 8736

Website: *www.hartswoodfilms.co.uk*

Drama and comedy.

Contact: Elaine Cameron

Kudos

12–14 Amwell Street, London EC1R 1UQ.

Tel: 020 7812 3270

Website: *www.kudosproductions.co.uk*

Makes a lot of drama serials from *Spooks* to *Hustle* to *Moving Wallpaper* and consequently uses a lot of writers. Watch the website.

Shed Productions

2 Holford Yard, London WC1X 9HD.

Tel: 0207 239 1010

Website: *www.shedproduction.com*

'We know drama,' says Shed Productions, makers of *Waterloo Road*, *Rock Rivals*, *Bad Girls* and *Footballers' Wives*.

Talkback Thames Productions

20–21 Newman Street, London WIT 1PG.

Tel: 020 7861 8000

Website: *www.talkbackthames.tv*

E-mail: *reception@talkbackthames.tv*

Specialises, very successfully, in situation comedy and popular drama including *The Green Room* and *The Bill.*

Send your script to PA to the Managing Director.

Tiger Aspect Productions

5 Soho Square, London WIV 5DE.

Tel: 020 7434 6700

Website: *www.tigeraspect.co.uk*

Makes a huge amount of drama and comedy, from *Secret Diary of a Call Girl* to *Murphy's Law* to *Robin Hood* and the comedy drama *Benidorm.*

Head of Drama: Greg Brenman
Head of Comedy: Sophie Carke-Jervoise

Wall to Wall Television

8–9 Spring Place, London NW5 3ER.

Tel: 020 7267 5292
Website: *www.walltowall.co.uk*

Wall to Wall has been voted as the most respected independent production company, praised for the fact it is 'always creative and producing something edgy' and 'produces consistently high concept, classy, commercial ideas'. Drama includes *New Tricks*.

Working Title
76 Oxford Street, London W1D IBS.
Tel: 020 7307 3000 (films)

77 Shaftesbury Avenue, London W1V 8HQ.
Tel: 020 7494 4001 (television)
Website: *www.workingtitlefilms.com*

Scripts for drama, comedy, and low budget films.

Head of Development, Films: Debra Hayward
Head of Television: Simon Wright

World Productions
12–14 St Christopher's Place, London W1U 1NH.
Tel: 020 3179 1800
Website: *www.world-production.com*

Since it began in 1990, World Productions has produced over 250 hours of network drama, supplying one-hour series, mini-series and single films. It prides itself on being a company of producers. Each one makes their own relationships with writers and directors. Programmes include *Goldplated*, *Lilies*, *Hancock and Joan*, and comedy series *Never Better*.

TELEVISION AGENTS

As with independent production companies, agents are private businesses that cannot afford to spend time reading and commenting on scripts that they do not believe – if only from a cursory look at the subject matter and first page of dialogue – are going to make it. At the same time, of course, agents need new writers. You are always, therefore, in with a chance.

■ Look in *The Writer's Handbook* or the *Writers' and Artists' Year Book* for agents willing to look at scripts or outlines by new writers.

■ Give a succinct account of yourself, your ambitions and your circumstances. The agent will want to be assured that you have the determination, as well as talent, to be a full-time professional writer if the opportunity arises.

■ Indicate the type of programmes you believe you could write for.

■ Make sure your script is laid out in a clear and professional manner.

■ **Always** enclose a stamped, addressed envelope.

Below are some agents who specialise in television work, are interested in new writers, and in some cases are willing to look at unsolicited scripts.

The Agency (London) Ltd
24 Pottery Lane, London W11 4LZ.
Tel: 020 7727 9037
E-mail: *info@theagency.co.uk*

Founded in 1995, The Agency brings together a number of London's most distinguished television agents. You will need to have won a scriptwriting award or competition, or had a script on radio or the stage, to be considered. Send a preliminary letter describing yourself and outlining your script.

Blake Friedmann Ltd

122 Arlington Road, London NW1 7HP.
Tel: 020 7284 0408.

Send letter with a synopsis and sample pages.

Contact for scripts: Julian Friedman

Casarotto Ramsay and Associates Ltd

Waverley House, 7–12 Noel Street, London W1F 8GQ.
Tel: 020 7287 4450
E-mail: *agents@casarotto.uk.com*

Send a preliminary letter describing yourself and outlining your script.

Curtis Brown Ltd

Haymarket House, 28–29 Haymarket, London SW1Y 4SP.
Tel: 020 7396 4400
E-mail: *cb@curtisbrown.co.uk*

One of the biggest and most respected agencies, handling television scripts of all kinds. Send a preliminary letter describing yourself and outlining your script.

Contact: Nick Marston

Jill Foster Ltd (JFL)

9 Barb Mews, Brook Green, London W6 7PA.
Tel: 020 7602 1263

Particularly interested in TV comedy and drama. Send a preliminary letter describing yourself and outlining your script.

David Higham Associates

5–8 Lower John Street, London W1R 4HA.
Tel: 020 7434 5900
E-mail: *dha@davidhigham.co.uk*

Send preliminary letter with synopsis in first instance.

Valerie Hoskins Associates

20 Charlotte Street, London W1T 2NA.
Tel: 020 7637 4490
E-mail: *vha@vhassociates.co.uk*

Specialises in film, television and radio. Send a preliminary letter describing yourself and outlining your script.

Contacts: Valerie Hoskins or Rebecca Watson.

Andrew Mann Ltd

1 Old Compton Street, London W1D 5JA.
Tel: 020 7734 4751
E-mail: *info@andrewmann.co.uk*

Send a preliminary letter, synopsis, and sample pages of script. E-mail your letter and synopsis if you wish, but attachments will not be opened.

Contacts: Anne Dewe, Tina Betts, Sacha Elliot

PDF

Drury House, 34–43 Russell Street, London WC2B 5HA.

Tel: 020 7344 1000

Website: *www.pdf.co.uk*

E-mail: *postmaster@pfd.co.uk*

Peter Fraser and Dunlop, as it used to be known, is one of the most respected and successful agencies in the world – and what is more, it will look at scripts by unknown writers (perhaps this is why it has become so successful). Look at the website for script submission guidelines, or send your script to the 'Film and Script Dept' making sure you enclose return postage.

Sheil Land Associates

52 Doughty Street, London WC1N 2LS.

Tel: 020 7405 9351

E-mail: *info@sheilland.co.uk*

This agency 'welcomes approaches from new clients either to start or to develop their careers'. Send a preliminary letter first, describing yourself and outlining your script.

Further Reading

TV PLAYS

Some are paperbacks currently in print, others can be ordered through libraries.

Plays that might be said to have influenced contemporary television drama are marked:*.

Soldier, Soldier, John Arden (Methuen, 1967). *Soldier, Soldier* was broadcast in 1960; one of the first great television plays by one of Britain's most important playwrights.

*Talking Heads**, Alan Bennett (BBC Books, 1988); The *Writer in Disguise* (Faber and Faber, 1985).

*The Boys from the Blackstuff**, Alan Bleasdale (Granada, 1983); *The Monocled Mutineer**, (Hutchinson, 1986).

*The After Dinner Game**, Malcolm Bradbury (with Christopher Bigsby) (Arrow Books, 1989). Four plays for television.

*Deadhead**, Howard Brenton (Methuen, 1987).

The Last of the Summer Wine, Roy Clarke (BBC Publications 1976).

Churchill and the Generals, Ian Curteis (BBC Publications, 1980); *The Falklands Play**, (Hutchinson, 1987).

Z Cars, Keith Dewhurst (Longman, 1968). Classic scripts, but note that today series drama is shot on location rather than in the studio.

The Long March, *A Woman Calling*, Ann Devlin (in Ourselves Alone,

Faber and Faber, 1988).

Hancock's Half Hour, Galton and Simpson (Woburn Press, 1974).

After Pilkington*, Simon Gray (Methuen, 1987).

All Good Men, Trevor Griffiths (Faber and Faber, 1977).

Abel's Will, Christopher Hampton (Faber and Faber, 1979).

Licking Hitler, David Hare (Faber and Faber, 1978); *Dreams of Leaving**, (Faber and Faber, 1980).

Still Waters, Julia Jones (Longman, 1978).

Episodes from 'The Liver Birds', Carla Lane (in *Situation Comedy*, Studio, 1980).

Solid Geometry, Ian McEwan (in *The Imitation Game: Three Plays for Television*, Cape, 1981).

Collected Television Plays, David Mercer (2 vols, John Calder, 1981).

Juliet Bravo, Paula Milne (Longman, 1983). Compare the scene structure and ratio of studio/OB between a *Juliet Bravo* script and a *Z Cars* by Keith Dewhurst or Alan Plater.

Annie Kenny, Alan Plater (in Act Three, Hutchinson, 1979); *Z Cars*, (Longman, 1968).

Pennies From Heaven, Dennis Potter (Quartet Books, 1981). *Waiting for the Boat*, (Faber and Faber, 1984). *The Singing Detective**, (Faber and Faber, 1986).

Bar Mitzvah Boy, The Evacuees, Spend, Spend, Spend, Jack Rosenthal (in Three Award Winning TV Plays, Penguin, 1978); *Three Plays*, (Penguin, 1986).

Penda's Fen, David Rudkin (Davis-Poynter, 1975).

Our Day Out, Willy Russell (in *Act One*, Hutchinson, 1979).

Soldiers Talking, Cleanly, Mike Stott (Eyre Methuen, 1978).

The Ballard of Ben Bagot, Peter Terson (in *Scene Scripts Two*, Longman, 1978).

BOOKS ON WRITING TV DRAMA

Hazel: the Making of a TV Series, Manuel Alvaredo and Edward

Buscombe (BFI/Latimer, 1978).

The TV/Film Script, Rodney Bennett (Harrap, London, 1976). A director's viewpoint.

British Television Drama, George W. Brandt (editor) (Cambridge University Press, 1981).

Writing Comedy for Television, Brian Cooke (Methuen, 1983).

Debut on Two, Phillippa Giles and Vicky Licorish (editors) (BBC Books, 1990). Writers' viewpoints, including Jeanette Winterson on adaptations and Paul Jackson on comedy, plus a script editor's advice from Roger Gregory, a former senior script editor at BBC Pebble Mill, and eight 15-minute plays that featured in the BBC Two *Debut* series. The editors say: '*Debut on Two* – both the book and the series – aims to inspire new writing for television.' Valuable reading for new writers.

How Plays are Made, Stuart Griffiths (Heinemann Educational, 1982).

Writing for Television and Radio, Robert Hilliard (Focal Press, 1976).

Writing for Television, Malcom Hulke (A & C Black, 1980). Includes television techniques, plotting, dialogue, with excellent examples. (The example of *Three Into One Won't Go* as a characterization on page 85 comes from this book.)

Writing for Television, Gerald Kelsey (A & C Black, 1990). Covers plots, formats, story construction, dialogue and characterization, and includes very useful script excerpts from *Howard's Way*, *Brookside* and the film drama *Sun Child* by Angela Huth.

Writing for the BBC, Norman Longmate (BBC Books, 1989). Tells you all about the BBC script unit, which no longer exists, and lists the many programme slots that do not require scripts from outside sources. More a round-up of the BBC's overall output than a useful guide for the new writer. Devotes more space to radio, and in particular local radio, than to television. Of little use until a revised edition appears.

Screenwriting for Narrative Film and Television, William Miller

(Columbus Books, London, 1988). Excellent in-depth study of techniques by American film maker and professor.

The Boys from the Blackstuff – the Making of TV Drama, Bob Millington and Rob Nelson (Comedia/Routledge, 1986).

The Way to Write for Television, Eric Paice (Elm Tree Books, 1981). Very good introduction for new writers.

Ah, Mischief: the Writer and Television, Frank Pike (editor) (Faber, 1982). A number of television dramatists including David Edgar put forward their views on the problems of working in television drama.

Television Drama: an Introduction, David Self (Macmillan, 1984).

Play for Today: The Evolution of Television Drama, Irene Shubik (Davis Poynter, 1975).

The Largest Theatre in the World, Shaun Sutton (BBC Publications, 1982). Shaun Sutton, highly respected former head of BBC Television Drama Group, gives a history of British television drama.

Film Scriptwriting: a Practical Manual, Dwight Swain (Focal Press, 1982).

Writing for Television Today, Arthur Swinson (A & C Black, 1965). Gives an account of television drama in its early days, and studies outstanding television plays like *Soldier, Soldier* by John Arden and *June Evening* by Bill Naughton.

Writing Scripts for Television, Radio and Film, Edgar Willis (Holt, Rinehart and Winston, 1981).

REFERENCE BOOKS

Writers' and Artists' Yearbook (A & C Black) contains general information and lists agents and publishers. It has a section on broadcasting.

The Writers' Handbook edited by Barry Turner (The Macmillan Press), covers markets for radio, film and television scripts.

Index

ROYAL BOROUGH OF GREENWICH

Follow us on twitter  @greenwichlibs

Please return by the last ~~date~~ shown

11/16	28 JAN 20__ / 10 AUG 2019	10 APR 20__
16 FEB 2017		01 MAY 2022
23 APR 2017	28 SEP 2022	
21 APR 2018		
20 OCT 2018		

Thank you! To renew, please contact any
Royal Greenwich library or renew online or by phone
www.better.org.uk/greenwichlibraries
24hr renewal line 01527 852384

PRAISE FOR *HALF A CREATURE FROM THE SEA*

"If anything will encourage teenagers to start
writing, it is this superb masterclass in how setting,
dialogue and character can convey powerful
emotions in a few words."
Daily Mail

"Almond cements his prolific, beloved place among
writers of magic realism for today's young readers."
Booklist

"The sights, sounds, smells, and emotions evoked in
these stories will long resonate with readers."
Publishers Weekly (starred review)

"This is powerful, top-notch storytelling
from Almond, who, as ever, fluidly blends past
and future, the living and the dead, the
ordinary and the transcendent."
Kirkus (starred review)

"The work of a writer of great power, and
a living insight for teenage readers into
the power of imagination."
The School Librarian

"He writes sparingly and beautifully ...
fiction to treasure."
Books for Keeps

ALSO BY DAVID ALMOND

A Song for Ella Grey

The Boy Who Climbed Into the Moon

The Boy Who Swam with Piranhas

Clay

Counting Stars

The Fire-Eaters

Heaven Eyes

Kit's Wilderness

Mouse Bird Snake Wolf

My Dad's a Birdman

My Name Is Mina

The Savage

Secret Heart

Skellig

Slog's Dad

The Tightrope Walkers

The True Tale of the Monster Billy Dean

half a creature from the sea

A Life in Stories

DAVID ALMOND

illustrated by Eleanor Taylor

WALKER
BOOKS

This is a work of fiction. Names, characters, places and incidents
are either the product of the author's imagination or, if real, are used fictitiously.

First published 2014 by Walker Books Ltd
87 Vauxhall Walk, London SE11 5HJ

This edition published 2016

2 4 6 8 10 9 7 5 3 1

Introduction and story introductions © 2014 David Almond

"Slog's Dad" © 2006 David Almond (First published in *So, What Kept You?*)

"May Malone" © 2008 David Almond (First published in *The Children's Hours*)

"When God Came to Cathleen's Garden" © 2009, 2010 David Almond
(First published in *Sideshow: Ten Original Tales of Freaks,
Illusionists and Other Matters Odd and Magical*)

"The Missing Link" © 2008, 2014 David Almond (First published in *The Times*)

"Harry Miller's Run" © 2008 David Almond
(First published in conjunction with Great North Run Culture)

The right of Dav... ...author... and
illustrator respec... ...ely of this work has be... ...nce
with ...the C... ...Designs a... ...Act 1988

This bo...

Printed a... ...in Great Britain by... ...Co Ltd, ...

All rights reserved. No part of this book may be reproduced, transmitted or
stored in an information retrieval system in any form or by any means, graphic,
electronic or mechanical, including photocopying, taping and recording,
without prior written permission from the publisher.

British Library Cataloguing in Publication Data:
a catalogue record for this book is available from the British Library

ISBN 978-1-4063-6559-7

www.walker.co.uk

For Tim and Rachel

CONTENTS

"I'll

start

with

things I can hardly

remember,

things I've

been told about,

things that are like

fragments of a dream.

I grew up in a town called Felling-on-Tyne. My first home was an upstairs flat in White's Buildings, a cluster of houses at the edge of the town's main square. It had high white walls and wide dark doors, and a tiny kitchen where the sink perched on a timber frame. The tin bath hung on the kitchen wall. Steep, crumbling steps led to a small back yard and the outside toilet. My mother used to say that before she opened the door to any room, she'd tap on it to make sure the mice scattered to their holes in the skirting boards and floors. There were hundreds of them, she told me. Thousands! I remember the smell of damp, of the outside loo. Dust cascaded through the shafts of light that poured through the narrow kitchen windows. Dead flies clustered on dangling fly papers. Sirens blared from the factories by the river, foghorns hooted from the distant sea. There were four of us then: Mam, Dad, my brother Colin, and me.

Mam said that I was just a few months old when she first took me to visit my Uncle Amos. She'd wheel me in my pushchair through the square, past the Jubilee pub, Dragone's coffee house, Myers' pork shop. Down onto the steep, curving High Street, lined with a butcher's, grocer's, tailor's, pubs. A pink pig's head would be grinning out from Myers' window. There'd be boxes of bright fruit stacked outside Bamling's. A great cod fish, bigger than a boy, would lie on the marble slab outside the fishmonger's. You could smell the fish and chips from Fosters', the beer from the open windows of the Half Way House, oil and rust from Howie's cluttered junkyard behind its swinging stable door. We'd pass by the cracked pale faces and legs of the mannequins of Shepherd's department store. All the way, Mam'd be calling out greetings to family and neighbours. They'd be leaning down to grin and coo at me, maybe to slip a coin into my little hand. Always, above the rooftops, the thin steeple of our church, St Patrick's, pointed to the blue.

Halfway down the street, my mother would turn into a narrow alleyway and carry me into Amos's printing shop. There'd been a few generations of printers in our family, and Amos was the latest. He printed the local newspaper in that dark small place, on a pair of ancient printing machines. Do

I remember it? I like to think I do, but I guess I only really remember my mother's words. She told a tale that one day when she was in there, with me lying in her arms, Amos pulled a lever, and the printing machines began to clatter and turn, and the pages of the newspaper began to stream out from them, and I started to wriggle and jump in her arms, and to point and giggle at the pages. Just as a baby's eyes are caught by flashing lights or flying birds, my eyes were caught by print – and I'd be in love with it for evermore. Maybe I began to be a writer that day in that little printing shop, a time I can't remember, when I was a few months old.

Amos was a writer as well as a printer. He wrote poems, stories, novels, plays. At family parties, after a couple of drinks, he'd take a piece of paper from his pocket and read a poem to us. Some would roll their eyes and giggle, but I loved him for it. I had an uncle who was a writer; I could be the same. None of his work was ever published or performed, but it didn't matter to him. He kept on writing for the love of it, and for his family and friends. I was just a boy when I told him shyly of my own ambitions. "Yes," he said, "do that!" He also told me, "Don't let your writing separate you from the people and places that you love."

White's Buildings was eventually classified as a slum and was demolished. We moved to a brand-new council estate, The Grange, beside the brand-new bypass on the eastern edge of town. I went to St John's Catholic primary school, a sombre stone-built establishment next to the river. Amos closed the printing shop and moved away, but the sign above the alleyway remained for years:

ALMOND PRINTER

I passed beneath it a thousand times as I continued to grow.

I played with my friends on the fields above the town. I roamed further, to the hills beyond the fields, where there were abandoned coal mines and spoil heaps, tussocky paddocks with ponies in them, newt ponds, ruined stables. From up there, you could see the whole town sloping away: the streets leading to the square, the factories below that, the river lined with shipyards, the city of

Newcastle with its bridges and towers and steeples. To the north, the distant bulges of the Cheviots in a haze. To the west, the hills of County Durham, the pitheads and winding gear of the coal mines. To the south, more fields, lanes, hawthorn hedges, then Sunderland, then the towns of Teesside on the far horizon. To the east, the dark North Sea. It seemed that much of the world, in all its variety, was visible from this little place.

I started to scribble stories of my own. I read books from the local library. I dreamed of coming back to this library one day in the future, to find books with my own name on them standing on the shelves. Once or twice I dared to admit to others that I wanted to be a writer. I remember one day getting the response, 'But you're just an ordinary kid. And you come from ordinary little Felling. What on earth will you write about?'

As time has gone on, I've found myself writing more and more about that little place. Many of my stories spring from it. They use its landscape, its language, its people, and turn it into fiction – half imaginary, half real. The stories in this book are

all in some way connected to that 'ordinary' place.
I try to do what many writers have done before me:
show that ordinary places can be extraordinary. **"**

"The story of 'Slog's Dad' takes place right in the heart of the town, in Felling Square. This was a small, low-walled area with an ancient fountain and water trough at the centre. There were benches where folk sat to while away the day, to take a rest after walking up the steep High Street or to sit and wait for the Black Bull or the Jubilee to open. On one side of the square was Ray Lough's barber's, with its plate-glass window, its short line of chairs. Ray would have no truck with modern styles. Boys might go in asking for a James Dean or a Beatles cut but they'd all get the same: short back and sides finished with lotion slapped on; the kind that set hard as soon as it hit the open air. Just next door was my grandfather's betting shop. The name in the window – John Foster Barber – caused some men to walk in for a haircut, but instead they'd find my grandfather puffing on his pipe behind the counter, men standing around earnestly reading *Sporting Life*, and crackly radio reports of horse race results coming from speakers on the walls. The square, and the High Street, and many of the shops and pubs, still exist. Not Lough's, and not the betting shop. My Uncle Maurice took it over when my grandfather retired, but then Ladbrokes opened in the square and Maurice moved the shop to Hebburn, a few miles away, to catch the custom of shipyard workers. But shipbuilding declined then quickly crashed, and the betting shop was one of the many businesses that went down with it.

Myers' pork shop sold the best pork pies, the best pork sandwiches, and the best saveloy dips in the area. Saveloys are a kind of sausage. They seemed to my friends and me to be the height of deliciousness, especially inside a soft bread roll with stuffing, onions and mustard and dipped into a shallow tray of Myers' special gravy. A saveloy dip with everything: a taste of Heaven!

I was a Catholic, like many of my friends. We were taught to believe that when good people died, they went to be with God. (The bad, of course, went to

Hell to burn for all eternity.) Sometimes, when the sun shone down and the sky was blue and the river glittered far below, the larks singing over the high fields, Heaven didn't seem too far away. We were constantly reminded of its inhabitants, too. There were statues of Jesus and his mother, and of saints and angels in St Patrick's. We all had prayer books and rosary beads and little statues and pictures in our homes.

Cheery priests were familiar figures in the streets – off to visit the sick, to comfort the bereaved or to have a glass of whisky with a parishioner. Tramps were often seen too. There was one in particular who lived, it was said, somewhere in the hills above town. No one knew his name, or where he'd come from. He was a silent, swiftly walking man with flaxen hair. He seemed at ease, untroubled by the world, and he was a romantic figure to boys like me. To live a life of freedom in the open air! Who wouldn't desire such a life? Sometimes I'd see him sitting alone on a bench in the square, just as Slog's dad does in the story. I longed to try to talk to him, but I never did.

This story came from a fragment from the

notebook of the great short-story writer Raymond Carver, which I used as an inspiration for a tale of my own. One line jumped out at me: 'I've got how much longer?' As soon as I wrote it down in my own notebook, 'Slog's Dad' sprang to life. I switched on the computer, began to write. There was a boy called Davie, walking across the square with his friend Slog. There was a bloke on the bench. There was Myers' pork shop with its delicious saveloys... "

Slog's dad

Spring had come. I'd been running around all day
with Slog and we were starving. We were crossing the
square to Myers' pork shop. Slog stopped dead in his
tracks.

"What's up?" I said.

He nodded across the square.

"Look," he said.

"Look at what?"

"It's me dad," he whispered.

"Your dad?"

"Aye."

I just looked at him.

"That bloke there," he said.

"What bloke where?"

"Him on the bench. Him with the cap on. Him with the stick."

I shielded my eyes from the sun with my hand and tried to see. The bloke had his hands resting on the top of the stick. He had his chin resting on his hands. His hair was long and tangled and his clothes were tattered and worn, like he was poor or like he'd been on a long journey. His face was in the shadow of the brim of his cap, but you could see that he was smiling.

"Slogger, man," I said. "Your dad's dead."

"I know that, Davie. But it's him. He's come back again, like he said he would. In the spring."

He raised his arm and waved.

"Dad!" he shouted. "Dad!"

The bloke waved back.

"See?" said Slog. "Howay."

He tugged my arm.

"No," I whispered. "No!"

And I yanked myself free and I went into Myers', and Slog ran across the square to his dad.

★   ★   ★

Slog's dad had been a binman, a skinny bloke with a creased face and a greasy flat cap. He was always puffing on a Woodbine. He hung on to the back of the bin wagon as it lurched through the estate, jumped off and on, slung the bins over his shoulder, tipped the muck into the back. He was forever singing hymns – "Faith of Our Fathers", "Hail Glorious Saint Patrick", stuff like that.

"Here he comes again," my mam would say as he bashed the bins and belted out "O Sacred Heart" at eight o'clock on a Thursday morning.

But she'd be smiling, because everybody liked Slog's dad, Joe Mickley, a daft and canny soul.

First sign of his illness was just a bit of a limp: then Slog came to school one day and said, "Me dad's got a black spot on his big toenail."

"Just like *Treasure Island*, eh?" I said.

"What's it mean?" he said.

I was going to say death and doom, but I said, "He could try asking the doctor."

"He has asked the doctor."

Slog looked down. I could smell his dad on him, the scent of rotten rubbish that was always on him. They lived just down the street from us, and the whole house had that smell in it, no matter how much Mrs Mickley washed and scrubbed. Slog's dad knew it. He said it was the smell of the earth. He said there'd be nowt like it in Heaven.

"The doctor said it's nowt," Slog said. "But he's staying in bed today, and he's going to hospital tomorrow. What's it mean, Davie?"

"How should I know?" I said.

I shrugged.

"It's just a spot, man, Slog!" I said.

Everything happened fast after that. They took the big toe off, then the foot, then the leg to halfway up the thigh. Slog said his mother reckoned his dad had caught some germs from the bins. My mother said it was all the Woodbines he puffed. Whatever it was, it seemed they stopped it. They fitted a tin leg on him and sent him home. It was the end of the bins, of course.

He took to sitting on the little garden wall outside the house. Mrs Mickley often sat with him and they'd be smelling their roses and nattering and smiling and swigging tea and puffing Woodbines. He used to show off his new leg to passers-by.

"I'll get the old one back when I'm in Heaven," he said.

If anybody asked was he looking for work, he'd laugh.

"Work? I can hardly bliddy walk."

And he'd start in on "Faith of Our Fathers" and everybody'd smile.

Then he got a black spot on his other big toenail, and they took him away again, and they started chopping at his other leg, and Slog said it was like living in a horror picture.

When Slog's dad came home next, he spent his days parked in a wheelchair in his garden. He didn't bother with tin legs: just pyjama bottoms folded over his stumps. He was quieter. He sat day after day in the summer sun among his roses, staring out at the pebbledashed walls and the red roofs and the empty sky. The Woodbines dangled in his fingers, "O Sacred Heart" drifted gently from his lips. Mrs Mickley brought him cups of tea, glasses of beer, Woodbines. Once I stood with Mam at the window and watched Mrs Mickley stroke her husband's head and gently kiss his cheek.

"She's telling him he's going to get better," said Mam.

We saw the smile growing on Joe Mickley's face.

"That's love," said Mam. "True love."

Slog's dad still joked and called out to anybody passing by.

"Walk?" he'd say. "Man, I cannot even bliddy hop."

"They can hack your body to a hundred bits," he'd say. "But they cannot hack your soul."

We saw him shrinking. Slog told me he'd heard his mother whispering about his dad's fingers coming off. He told me about Mrs Mickley lifting his dad from the chair each night, laying him down, whispering her goodnights, like he was a little bairn. Slog said that some nights when he was really scared, he got into bed beside them.

"But it just makes it worse," he said. He cried. "I'm bigger than me dad, Davie. I'm bigger than me bliddy dad!"

And he put his arms around me and put his head on my shoulder and cried.

"Slog, man," I said as I tugged away. "Howay, Slogger, man!"

One day late in August, Slog's dad caught me looking. He waved me to him. I went to him slowly. He winked.

"It's alreet," he whispered. "I know you divent want to come too close."

He looked down to where his legs should be.

"They tell us if I get to Heaven I'll get them back again," he said. "What d'you think of that, Davie?"

I shrugged.

"Dunno, Mr Mickley," I said.

"Do you reckon I'll be able to walk back here if I do get them back again?"

"Dunno, Mr Mickley."

I started to back away.

"I'll walk straight out them pearly gates," he said. He laughed. "I'll follow the smells. There's no smells in Heaven. I'll follow the bliddy smells right back here to the lovely earth."

He looked at me.

"What d'you think of that?" he said.

Just a week later, the garden was empty. We saw Doctor Molly going in, then Father O'Mahoney, and just as dusk was coming on, Mr Blenkinsop, the undertaker.

The week after the funeral, I was heading out of the estate for school with Slog, and he told me, "Dad said he's coming back."

"Slogger, man," I said.

"His last words to me. 'Watch for me in the spring,' he said."

"Slogger, man. It's just cos he was…"

"What?"

I gritted my teeth.

"Dying, man!"

I didn't mean to yell at him, but the traffic was thundering past us on the bypass. I got hold of his arm and we stopped.

"Bliddy dying," I said more softly.

"Me mam says that and all," said Slog. "She says we'll have to wait. But I cannot wait till I'm in Heaven, Davie. I want to see him here one more time."

Then he stared up at the sky.

"Dad," he whispered. "Dad!"

I got into Myers' pork shop, and sausages and bacon and black pudding and joints and pies sat in neat piles in the window. A pink pig's head with its hair scorched off and a grin on its face gazed out at the square. There was a bucket of bones for dogs and a bucket of blood on the floor. The marble counters and Billy Myers' face were gleaming.

"Aye-aye, Davie," he said.

"Aye," I muttered.

"Saveloy, I suppose? With everything?"

"Aye. Aye."

I looked out over the pig's head. Slog was with the bloke, looking down at him, talking to him. I saw him lean down to touch the bloke.

"And a dip?" said Billy.

"Aye," I said.

He plunged the sandwich into a trough of gravy.

"Bliddy lovely," he said. "Though I say it myself. A shilling to you, sir."

I paid him but I couldn't go out through the door. The sandwich was hot. The gravy was dripping to my feet.

Billy laughed.

"Penny for them," he said.

I watched Slog get onto the bench beside the bloke.

"Do you believe there's life after death?" I said.

Billy laughed.

"Now there's a question for a butcher!" he said.

A skinny old woman came in past me.

"What can I do you for, pet?" said Billy. "See you, Davie."

He laughed.

"Kids!" he said.

Slog looked that happy as I walked towards them. He was leaning on the bloke and the bloke was leaning back on the bench, grinning at the sky. Slog made a fist and a face of joy when he saw me.

"It's Dad, Davie!" he said. "See? I told you."

I stood in front of them.

"You remember Davie, Dad," said Slog.

The bloke looked at me. He looked nothing like the Joe Mickley I used to know. His face was filthy but it was smooth and his eyes were shining bright.

"Course I do," he said. "Nice to see you, son."

Slog laughed.

"Davie's a bit scared," he said.

"No wonder," said the bloke. "That looks very tasty."

I held the sandwich out to him.

He took it, opened it and smelt it, looked at the meat and pease pudding and stuffing and mustard and gravy. He closed his eyes and smiled, then lifted it to his mouth.

"Saveloy with everything," he said. He licked the gravy from his lips, wiped his chin with his hand.

"Bliddy lovely. You got owt to drink?"

"No," I said.

"Ha. He has got a tongue!"

"He looks a bit different," said Slog. "But that's just cos he's been…"

"Transfigured," said the bloke.

"Aye," said Slog. "Transfigured. Can I show him your legs, Dad?"

The bloke laughed gently. He bit his saveloy sandwich. His eyes glittered as he watched me.

"Aye," he said. "Gan on. Show him me legs, son."

And Slog knelt at his feet and rolled the bloke's tattered trouser bottoms up and showed the bloke's dirty socks and dirty shins.

"See?" he whispered.

He touched the bloke's legs with his fingers.

"Aren't they lovely?" he said. "Touch them, Davie."

I didn't move.

"Gan on," said the bloke. "Touch them, Davie."

His voice got colder.

"Do it for Slogger, Davie," he said.

I crouched, I touched, I felt the hair and the skin and the bones and muscles underneath. I recoiled; I stood up again.

35

"It's true, see?" said Slog. "He got them back in Heaven."

"What d'you think of that, then, Davie?" said the bloke.

Slog smiled.

"He thinks they're bliddy lovely, Dad."

Slog stroked the bloke's legs one more time then rolled the trousers down again.

"What's Heaven like, Dad?" said Slog.

"Hard to describe, son."

"Please, Dad."

"It's like bright and peaceful, and there's God and the angels and all that..." The bloke looked at his sandwich. "It's like having all the saveloy dips you ever want. With everything, every time."

"It must be great."

"Oh, aye, son. It's dead canny."

"Are you coming to see Mam, Dad?" he said.

The bloke pursed his lips and sucked in air and gazed into the sky.

"Dunno. Dunno if I've got the time, son."

Slog's face fell.

The bloke reached out and stroked Slog's cheek.

"This is very special," he said. "Very rare. They let it happen cos you're a very rare and special lad."

He looked into the sky and talked into the sky.

"How much longer have I got?" he said, then he nodded. "Aye. OK. OK."

He shrugged and looked back at Slog.

"No," he said. "Time's pressing. I cannot do it, son."

There were tears in Slog's eyes.

"She misses you that much, Dad," he said.

"Aye. I know." The bloke looked into the sky again. "How much longer?" he said.

He took Slog in his arms.

"Come here," he whispered.

I watched them hold each other tight.

"You can tell her about me," said the bloke. "You can tell her I love her and miss her and all." He looked at me over Slog's shoulder. "And so can Davie, your best mate. Can't you, Davie? Can't you?"

"Aye," I muttered.

Then the bloke stood up. Slog still clung to him.

"Can I come with you, Dad?" he said.

The bloke smiled.

"You know you can't, son."

"What did you do?" I said.

"Eh?" said the bloke.

"What job did you do?"

The bloke looked at me, dead cold.

"I was a binman, Davie," he said. "I used to stink but I didn't mind. And I followed the stink to get me here."

He cupped Slog's face in his hands.

"Isn't that right, son?"

"Aye," said Slog.

"So what's Slog's mother called?" I said.

"Eh?"

"Your wife. What's her name?"

The bloke looked at me. He looked at Slog. He pushed the last bit of sandwich into his mouth and chewed. A sparrow hopped close to our feet, trying to get at the crumbs. The bloke licked his lips, wiped his chin, stared into the sky.

"Please, Dad," whispered Slog.

The bloke shrugged. He gritted his teeth and sighed and looked at me so cold and at Slog so gentle.

"Slog's mother," he said. "My wife…" He shrugged again. "She's called Mary."

"Oh, Dad!" said Slog and his face was transfigured by joy. "Oh, Dad!"

The bloke laughed.

"Ha! Bliddy ha!"

He held Slog by the shoulders.

"Now, son," he said. "You got to stand here and watch me go and you mustn't follow."

"I won't, Dad," whispered Slog.

"And you must always remember me."

"I will, Dad."

"And me, you and your lovely mam'll be together again one day in Heaven."

"I know that, Dad. I love you, Dad."

"And I love you."

And the bloke kissed Slog, and twisted his face at me, then turned away. He started singing "Faith of Our Fathers". He walked across the square, past Myers' pork shop, and turned down onto the High Street. We ran after him then and we looked down the High Street past the people and the cars, but there was no sign of him, and there never would be again.

We stood there speechless. Billy Myers came to the doorway of the pork shop with a bucket of bones in his hand and watched us.

"That was me dad," said Slog.

"Aye?" said Billy.

"Aye. He come back, like he said he would, in the spring."

"That's good," said Billy. "Come and have a dip, son. With everything."

"We were kids. There were always tales of ghouls and ghosts and monsters going around. In my first school, St John's, a spooky stone place down by the Tyne, there were fiends waiting in the deep, dark cupboard just past the staffroom door. The ghosts of dead pit men and pit boys, killed in the Felling Pit disaster of 1812, could be seen during winter dusks in the school yard. A madman lived in that abandoned paint works by the river. Some folk had tails hidden beneath their clothes. Strange creatures were said to have been born in the Queen Elizabeth Hospital; creatures that could never be allowed out into the world – half human, half beast, born by weird couplings. When I camped with pals in their gardens – with Tex Flynn or Graham and Charlie Mein – we quaked as we whispered to each other about the witches and demons that waited in the darkness just beyond the thin canvas wall.

Our imaginings were intensified in church, especially during mission week. This happened every year or two, when teams of priests and fierce monks were sent to us. They roamed the streets and glared. They came to our homes to check up on our attendance at Communion or confession. They stood in the pulpit in a crowded St Patrick's and terrified us with detailed and gory descriptions of hellfire, burning flesh, demons, brimstone, red-hot pokers.

"Beware!" they snarled, gripping the pulpit edge and leaning towards us. "The creatures of Satan truly do walk among us. Perhaps they are with us now! Be alert! Keep away from them! Avoid all sin. Keep your mind on God!"

In this story, May Malone is lapsed – she used to be a Catholic, but she's lost the faith and has left the Church. Just like one of my friends did in real life, when we were eighteen, May stood up in church one day, yelled at the priest that he was a bliddy liar, and stormed out, never to return. To believers, May had put herself into a very perilous position. She was already headed for the fire. Not surprising, then, that there were rumours about her life, her child ... about her monster.

May lives in the dark terraced streets at the lower end of Felling, below the railway line. Norman lives in the new flats by Felling Square, Sir Godfrey Thomson Court, where my family lived for several years. I took Norman's surname, Trench (which I like a lot!) from Richard Trench, a nineteenth-century archbishop who wrote a strange and strangely wonderful book called *Notes on the Miracles of Our Lord*. Trench's book is one that I keep around me on the shelves in the shed where I write. Another book that's always near by is a collection of William Blake's poems. This story was written for a radio series called *Blake's Doors of Perception*. I was invited to take a line or two from Blake and use it as an inspiration, so I chose his poem "The Garden of Love", which contains these lines:

> *And Priests in black gowns were walking their*
> *   rounds,*
> *And binding with briars my joys and desires.*

There are more echoes of Blake in some of the
sentences. I like to think that, by the end, Norman's
own doors of perception have started to open. "

May Malone

The story was that May Malone had a monster in her house. She kept it in chains. If you went round to the back of the house and put your ear to the wall, you'd hear it groaning. You'd hear it howling at night if you listened hard. There were tales about May and a priest from Blyth. There was a baby, it was said, but the baby was horrible because it was born from such a sin. Even weirder tales were whispered. The Devil himself had come to May and it was the son of Satan living in her house. She'd been with horses, with dogs, with goats. Anyway, whatever it was you'd risk your body, your sanity and probably your soul if you got too close.

Norman Trench was ten or eleven at the time. He lived in the new flats in Felling Square. May's house was at the bottom end of Crimea Terrace, not far from the muddy green where the lads played football.

Norman's mam tightened her lips when he asked her about it.

"Them daft tales! Tek nae notice. What's done is done. Just keep away and leave her be."

To look at May you'd never think she had a monster. She was getting on, but she wore tight skirts, she dyed her hair, and she wore high heels that clicked and clacked on the pavements as she hurried along. She was lapsed. Everybody knew the tale of how she'd stood up in church in the middle of Mass and yelled that the priest was a lyin' bliddy bastard, then stormed down the aisle, spat at the altar, and never went again.

You could see people's faces closing down as she dashed through the streets. She hardly spoke to anybody and you could see that nobody wanted to speak to her. Except for some of the blokes, of course, the ones who sighed as she came near, and who couldn't help following with their eyes when she passed by.

Norman was a miserable kind of kid. Aye, he had

some reasons — the brother that'd died at three years old, a dad that'd gone wrong with the drink and ended up in the clink. But everybody's got something to put up with. Norman was just the kind that took it all too seriously.

People used to go, "Cheer up, man! It might never bliddy happen."

And sometimes he'd yell back, "It's happened albliddyready, right! So bugger off!"

Norman thought about illness and death and dying all the time. He thought about the Devil and Hell. And those nightmares! Boiling oil and scorching flames and red-hot pokers and devils' horns. He told the priest about it in confession and the priest sighed. Oh dear. Such fears and dreams were common enough among his flock. We all had such a cross to bear.

The priest leant closer to the grille, trying to get a proper look at Norman.

"Desolation of the heart," he said, "is often a sign of God's call. Do you ever feel you might have a vocation, my son?"

Norman's mam had been through everything that he had been through, of course, and far worse. The difference was, she had a cheerful heart.

"Let's have a smile," she used to say, and Norman would curl his lips up and try to please her, but it just made things worse.

"Oh, son," she'd say. "Don't grow up so sad. God is good, the world is beautiful and Heaven waits for us."

Made no difference. Norman believed in none of that. He was shutting down, getting ever more miserable. He couldn't stop himself, even when the lads started moaning.

"Why can't you just enjoy yourself, man? You're like a wet bliddy Monday morning."

No wonder they started to turn their backs on him, like he was May Malone, or running away from him and howling, like he was the monster.

It was October when Norman went to May's for the first time. The nights were turning cold and cutting in. He waited till dark, then down he went to the end of Crimea Terrace and into the back lane. He scrambled over the wall into May's back yard. He went to the house wall and pressed his ear to it. Nothing. Maybe a radio somewhere far away. The distant voices of the lads echoing on the green. He concentrated. All he heard was his heart, then the noises of monsters inside himself. He tiptoed to the kitchen window and cupped his hands, peered in and nearly yelled with bliddy fright. But it was just his own staring eyes that goggled back at him. Nothing else.

Next time he went, though, he was sure there was a bit of grunting, a bit of squeaking. May came into the kitchen and made a pot of tea and put some biscuits on a plate. She looked out. Norman pressed right against the back wall. Then she leant up and pulled the curtains shut. Norman climbed back over the wall and stood in the dark at the end of the terrace. He lit the cigarette he'd bought at Wiffen's shop that he'd said was for his mam. A river bell rang. A door clicked open and shut on Crimea Terrace and footsteps hurried up towards town. He drew deeply on the cigarette. He coughed. He stood looking down through the night towards the river. All this is pitching me closer to bliddy Hell, he thought.

"Where you been?" his mam said when he got back in.

"Football," he said. "With the lads."

"Good lad. That might cheer you up, eh? Or mebbe not."

He kept going back to May's. Maybe he had it in his head that he'd be able to go to the lads and say

"It's true. There is a monster. Come and see", and that that'd sort everything out. But there was nothing, and soon the lads were taking no notice of him at all. It was like they didn't even see him, like he wasn't there. Probably they'd even forgotten all about May's monster.

Then he steps out of Wiffen's one afternoon and there's May Malone right slap bang in front of him. She's wearing a green coat. Her eyes are green, her fingernails bright red.

"So," she says. "What have you got to say for yourself?"

Norman gulps.

"Come along," she says.

"Nothin', Miss Malone."

"Huh! Nothin'. So would you like to see my monster?"

Norman gulps again and blinks.

"Well?"

She doesn't smile. She isn't cross. Her voice is crisp and clear.

"Yes, please, Miss Malone," he says.

"You won't want to be seen walking with me.

Follow me down in five minutes or so. Come to the front door."

And away she clacks.

He smokes his fag as he walks down Crimea Terrace. He's trying to seem nonchalant.

The door's ajar.

"Don't just stand there," comes her voice from inside.

He sidles through and finds her waiting in a narrow corridor. She goggles, gasps and claps her hands across her mouth.

"Oh no!" she says. "You are in the house of May Malone! Lightning will strike at any moment!"

Then she laughs and tells him to stop his bliddy trembling and come properly in.

Everything is neat and clean, just as she is. Her green coat is hanging from a hook on the wall. There's a door open to a living room. He sees a couple of armchairs, a couple of ashtrays. There's a decanter with what looks like whisky in it, and two glasses. There's a painting of a Chinese lady on the hall wall. When May closes the front door, the hallway is deeply shadowed, and a red light shines down from upstairs.

She reaches out and takes his hand in hers. He

flinches and she holds his hand a little tighter.

"Don't worry," she softly says. "Come with me and see."

She leads him towards a dark door at the back of the house. She hesitates.

"You won't tell a soul, of course," she says. "Will you?"

She squeezes his hand.

"Will you?"

"No, Miss Malone."

"Good, for I am the one who decides who knows."

She turns the handle of the door.

"Now you may meet my boy. His name is Alexander."

It's a small room. Light falls from a skylight in the ceiling. There's a narrow bed against the wall. The boy is sitting on a small blue sofa. His head is slumped onto his shoulder.

May goes to him, kneels beside him, puts her arm around him.

"Alexander," she whispers. "Here is a new visitor for you."

She turns the boy's head to Norman.

He is very pale. One of his eyes is not there at all.

The other is very small, and it gleams, as if from a great distance. His mouth is red and crammed with uneven teeth. His legs and arms are shrunken, frail.

"The visitor's name," she whispers, "is…"

"Norman," says Norman.

"Norman. Come closer, Norman."

She looks at him.

"Surely you are not going to hesitate now, are you?"

Norman kneels beside them. May lifts one of Alexander's small hands and rests it against Norman's face. Alexander grunts. He squeaks.

"Yes," murmurs May Malone. "Yes, I know, my love."

She smiles.

"Alexander thinks you are very beautiful," she says.

Norman stares into the tiny distant eye. He searches for the boy's distant consciousness.

"And isn't he beautiful, too?" says May. "Isn't he?"

"Yes, Miss Malone," says Norman at last.

"Good. And Alexander says that you are like an angel. Now say hello. Go on. He can hear you, even though it might seem that he can't, just as he can see you."

"Hello," whispers Norman. "Hello, Alexander."

Alexander squeaks.

"See?" says May. "He answers you. He is a boy, just like you. Can you see that?"

"Yes."

"Good. Now sit beside him, Norman. Go on."

Norman does this. Alexander leans against him.

"And he is getting older, just like you," says May. "He needs a friend, just like you. And he needs to play."

She sits on the edge of the bed, facing the two boys. She smooths her skirt over her knees and smiles.

"You're lovely together," she says.

Alexander suddenly turns his face upwards. There is a pigeon there, looking down through the skylight. Alexander's mouth purses and he coos.

"Yes!" says May. "A bird! And look at the clouds, Alexander." He slowly, hesitantly, raises his hands and he opens them over his head. They flutter and tremble in the air.

"See?" says May Malone. "He knows that the world is beautiful, Norman."

Alexander trembles, and Norman can feel the excitement rushing through the boy as the bird flutters its wings above.

"Now," says May. "I would like you to take him out, Norman."

Norman catches his breath. He glances at the door and gets ready to run.

"Please do not leave us," says May Malone. "Not now."

She takes his hand again.

"Just take him out into the yard at first," she says. "What could be so difficult about that?"

"Who's his father?" Norman dares to say.

"You are a nosey bugger, aren't you?"

"Sorry, Miss Malone."

"Are you a churchgoer?"

"Yes."

"I thought so. Those black-gowned bloody priests. They blasted me. Don't let them blast you, Norman, with their *Thou shalt nots*." She touches her boy's head. "They said this angel is a devil. Never mind his father. Will you take him out?"

They help Alexander to rise from the sofa. May Malone opens the door. Norman holds Alexander's arm and guides him out into the place where he's only ever hidden in the dark. It is late afternoon. The sun is descending in the west. There are great streaks of red and gold across the sky. A storm of starlings sweeps over them from north to south. The city rumbles, the river bell rings, the lads' voices echo from the green. Norman imagines walking towards them with May Malone's monster at his side. He imagines the lads turning to him in amazement. He imagines May Malone watching them all from a bench near by. Alexander reaches upward, upward and he moans with joy. He leans against Norman and coos into his ear. May Malone watches from the doorway.

"See? It's easy enough, isn't it?" she says.

They soon go back inside. They take Alexander to his room and lay him down on the bed.

"He's tired out," said May. "But can you see how he is smiling, Norman?"

"Yes," says Norman, for he can. The distant gleam of Alexander's eye has grown brighter.

"He is as he is because he is as he is," says May. "No other reason. And he is quite as capable of joy as any of us. More so, in fact."

She leans towards Norman.

"You, for instance," she says, "must stop being so sad. You know that, don't you?"

"Yes, Miss Malone."

"Just open your eyes, Norman. The world is a strange and gorgeous and astonishing place."

She looks at her watch.

"Now," she says. "You will come back again, won't you?"

"Yes, Miss Malone."

"And you won't tell anybody, will you? Not until we're ready."

"No, Miss Malone."

"Good."

She kisses his cheek. He says goodbye to Alexander, and she leads him to the door.

"Goodnight," she says. "Until the next time. We will be waiting for you."

Norman walks up Crimea Terrace below the astonishing sky. He keeps touching his cheek where May Malone's lipstick is, where the memory of her lips is. He remembers the feeling of her red-fingernailed hand upon his. He keeps remembering Alexander's trembles of excitement.

A man is hurrying down the street, with the rim of his trilby tilted over his eyes.

"Hello," says Norman.

The man flinches, looks at the boy in astonishment,

then he gives a broad grin.

"Aye, aye, lad," he says, and he winks.

Norman keeps going. All the sadness is lifting away from him as he goes uphill, like he's opening up; like he's beginning to see this world for the first time.

"This story is filled with real people: my sisters Mary and Margaret; their friend Cathleen; Cathleen's mother; my mother; my mate Tex Flynn; the footballers Dave Hilley and Alan Suddick. And I suppose, as the narrator is called Davie, I'm in it too. Of course, as soon as you start to write about somebody, you start to fictionalize them. The person in real life isn't quite the same as the person in the tale. And the events in the tale, of course, never happened at all.

It's set on a small estate where we moved when I was eleven, by which time I'd passed my 11-plus and was at grammar school in Hebburn. Until then we'd lived on the council estate beside the new bypass, and then in a new council flat close to Felling Square. Now we were in the first and only house my parents ever bought. It was a short walk uphill from the square, in a ring of semi-detached houses formed by two streets, Coldwell Park Avenue and Coldwell Park Drive. The neighbourhood in the story isn't exactly like those streets. There was no gate in Cathleen's garden that led to the park and the playing fields, but there needed to be one for the story, so I put it there. That's a strange thing about writing stories – you put in something imaginary to make the whole thing seem more real.

I always loved football. For a time, I took a football everywhere I went. I dribbled it along the pavements, played keep-up in the back garden, kicked it about with my friends in the streets, on the patches of grass near our homes, in the fields around the town. Sometimes there'd just be a couple of us playing against a garage door, or a handful of us playing in somebody's little garden. Other times, teams of twenty or more would charge across the fields above the town. At the best of times we'd play all day, until we could no longer see the ball, then I'd walk home through the gathering dusk and sleep, and dream I was playing again.

I was crazy about Newcastle United. I roared them on at St James's Park. I collected photos, posters, programmes. I had a black-and-white scarf and a black-and-white hat. I used to go with my mates, Tex Flynn or Peter Varley, maybe, to watch the team training on Hunter's Moor at Spital Tongues. Sometimes we jogged alongside them in the streets around St James. I remember one day trotting past the shops in Fenham for a few hundred yards with Colin "Cannonball" Taylor, a stocky left winger with the hardest shot I'd ever seen. He teased me, letting me think I could keep pace with him, then laughed fondly and pelted away. I kept scrapbooks with signed photographs and match reports in them. It was such a thrill to stand beside the players, show them my books, watch them sign their names. I used to dream of playing with them: taking a pass from Dave Hilley on my thigh before lashing it into the net, sending an inch-perfect cross onto Alan Suddick's head.

I'd been brought up to believe that God was everywhere, and was always watching us. Maybe it's inevitable that I'd come to write a tale like this, one that turns my boyhood heroes into saints, and in which God seems to wander into an ordinary Felling garden.

The story has gone through a number of incarnations and has been rewritten several times. This latest version, set in a time of snow and ice, seems to work best of all. But maybe it'll seek another rewrite. Some stories seem never to be 'finished'; seem always to be on the point of change. **"**

When God came to Cathleen's garden

A Tuesday morning at the start of the Christmas holidays. Deep fresh snow lay on the ground and the sun was blazing down but I was pretty fed up. I'd packed a flask of tea and some sandwiches and crisps. I had my photograph albums and autograph albums and pens. I was supposed to be going to Newcastle with Tex Flynn. The plan was we'd watch the United players training and get some autographs. In those days you could wander about on the training ground with them. You could jog with them through the streets. They were brilliant and famous, they played in front of thirty thousand fans every week, but there they were right beside us. They played keep-up, head tennis, penalties, shots. They were always laughing and playing daft tricks on each other, but suddenly one of them would do something that seemed impossible. Sometimes they'd let us join in. They'd fall down when we dribbled past them, they'd dive the wrong way when we took penalties. They'd pretend to be amazed by our tricks, to be terrified by the power of our shots. They didn't keep the magic to themselves. One day Alan Suddick showed me how to swerve the ball with the outside of my foot. Dave Hilley told me it wasn't power that made a great shot, it was timing. He spent more than ten minutes with me, passing the ball to me, telling me to fire it back. "That's good, son," he said. "You'll get there. Practise, practise, practise, till you can do it without a thought." Lots of lads went, especially in the holidays. We all had autograph books and albums packed with photos we'd cut out of the papers. The players were great. They all signed our books. *Best wishes,* they wrote, or *Keep on kicking* or *Have a great life!*

But Tex had gone down with flu, which seemed pretty weird. He'd been fine on Monday afternoon.

"Are you sure?" I asked his mam when she answered the door with the news.

"Sure?" she said. "You want to go and see him and catch it yourself?"

I looked past her into the shadowy hall. I thought of his bedroom above. It was just like mine: black-and-white stripes everywhere, stacks of old football programmes, photographs of the heroes pinned to the walls. I thought of him lying there, sweating and shivering and taking Beecham's Powders and drinking orange juice and sniffing Vicks.

"But he was fine," I said.

"Aye, he was, Davie. Till he got to playing football in a blooming blizzard. Till he got back here in the pitch-black freezing cold, soaking wet and shuddering. A fine Christmas he's going to have, isn't he?"

"Yes, Mrs Flynn."

"Yes, Mrs Flynn! Huh! Anyway, they'll not be training today, not if they've got any sense."

And she said goodbye and shut the door.

I walked back home up Felling Bank. Not be training? Of course they would, just like me. I kicked a stone through the slush on the pavement. I dribbled it around the lamp posts and telegraph poles. I heard the crowd all around me, yelling me on. I heard them singing "The Blaydon Races". In my head I said, "He's beaten one man! He's beaten two! Can he do it?" I sidestepped a little dog that came out of nowhere. I dropped my shoulder, slid on a patch of ice, swerved one way then another and flicked the stone through an open gate. I slithered to a stop and punched the air. I raised my arms to the sky. "Yes! Yeeeees! What a goal!" And the dog danced and yapped around me.

Back at home, in the garden, I kicked the snow aside, sat on the back step and swigged some of the tea. I told my mam about Tex.

"That's the flu for you," she said. "One minute you're as right as rain, the next you're a shivering wreck."

"He was fine yesterday," I said.

"Yes, but I don't expect that playing football in a—"

"It was just a bit of snow!"

"And how would you like it, just before Christmas? The poor lad."

She folded her arms and looked down at me.

"Now I hope you're not going to be moping all day."

I tugged my black-and-white scarf around my neck. I pulled down my black-and-white hat. I got one of my albums out. I'd just stuck some new pictures in. There was a brilliant one from the *Pink*: Dave lashing in the winner against Swansea City under the headline **HILLEY SINKS THE SWANS.** There was an even better one of Alan. He was horizontal, four feet off the ground. His eyes were bright with concentration. The ball had just left his head and was on its way to the goal. His arms were spread wide, just like he was flying. Alan Suddick. Dave Hilley. They could do anything.

I played with my new biro and dreamt I was a famous player. I imagined kids lining up in front of me. I scribbled my name fast on scraps of paper.

"That's OK, son," I murmured. "It's a pleasure, lad."

I drank my tea, chewed my sandwiches, crunched the crisps. My breath drifted in the icy air. Maybe Tex was just putting it on, I thought. Maybe he was going off the team. Maybe he was going off me.

Lads' voices echoed across the roofs from the playing fields outside the estate.

"On me head! On me head!"

"Get stuck in!"

"Goal! Goal! Yeeeeees!"

I kept listening. Somebody was playing a trumpet somewhere. Somebody was banging a drum.

Mam came out again.

"You're wasting a beautiful winter's day," she said. "There's a million things you could do instead of sitting there and staring into space."

"A million?" I said.

"Yes."

"Like what?"

"You could go and play football with the lads. You could shovel some of that snow off the front path."

"That's two," I said.

"You watch your lip," she said. "One thing you could certainly do is stop staring at those daft pictures. There's nothing special about those fellers. They're people, just like you."

She went back in. What did she mean, just like me? She hadn't seen Dave Hilley dribble. She hadn't seen an Alan Suddick free kick. These "fellers" could work miracles! I closed my eyes. I tried to feel like Alan when he smashed the ball into the net. I tried to feel like Dave when he left a defender sprawling in the dirt. I practised Dave's signature until it was just like his. I wrote, *To Davie. Best wishes, Dave Hilley* on his picture.

"Thanks, Dave," I said.

I said, "You're welcome, son," in Dave's gentle Scottish accent.

I signed Alan's picture, *To Davie, a true fan. Yours in sport. Alan Suddick.*

I winked like Alan did.

"No bother, lad," I whispered.

I sat there, in the icy sunshine, in the dream.

Then there were footsteps and two of my sisters — Mary and Margaret — were there, wrapped up in their brown winter coats with wellies on their feet.

"What do you want?" I grunted.

Mary put her finger to her lips.

"Shh," she said.

Mam waved at them through the kitchen window. They waved back.

"It's a *secret*," Margaret whispered.

I sighed.

"What is?"

They turned so that Mam couldn't see their faces.

"God's come," said Mary.

"What?" I said.

"God's come. He's in Cathleen Kelly's garden," said Mary. "He was fast asleep and now he's woke up and he's sitting by the fish pond. Are you coming to see?

Cathleen said you should, but nobody else."

I rolled my eyes. What a pair.

"Please," said Margaret. "And hurry up, before he goes away."

I sighed again. Mam would have me shovelling that snow if I didn't do something soon. So I stood up. I still had my album and my biro in my hand. Mam waved as we left.

We headed down towards Cathleen's. I flung a couple of snowballs at some kids I knew across the street.

"How do you know it's God?" I said.

"Cathleen says it must be," said Mary. "She's been saying loads of prayers since Jasper died. She's been begging him to help her. And he's sitting just where Jasper's buried."

"And he looks *just* like his pictures," said Margaret.

"And he appeared like magic," said Mary. "Out of nothing."

"So it's true," said Margaret. "Isn't it?"

I flung some more snowballs. How did I know?

We went into Cathleen's front gate and down the side of her house and into the back garden. Cathleen was kneeling on a shopping bag in the snow beside the little fish pond with her hands joined. Mary and

Margaret pulled their coats over their knees, knelt down beside her and joined their hands too, as if they were in church. Mary looked at me like she thought I should kneel as well, but I didn't.

God was sitting on a folded blanket in the sunshine with his legs crossed. You could see how he'd shoved away the snow with his boots.

"This is Davie, Lord," said Cathleen.

God looked at me and smiled.

He had dark skin and dark eyes. He wore thick orange robes and brown leather boots. He had a black cap on but you could see he was bald. He had a pot belly and a big white beard.

He raised a hand in greeting. I nodded at him.

"Do your mam and dad know?" I asked Cathleen.

She shook her head.

"Dad's at work," she said. "Mam's doing some Christmas shopping."

"Does he talk?" I said.

"We don't know."

God smiled. He picked a stone up from the edge of the pond. He showed it in his hand, closed his hand then opened it again and the stone had gone. Then he took the same stone out of his left ear and put it back

71

by the pond again. Margaret clapped. God reached into the snow, found a stick, snapped it and put it back together again. He took another stick as long as his arm and opened his mouth and swallowed it and drew it out again.

He smiled and giggled, and the girls clapped.

I saw tears in Cathleen's eyes.

She clasped her hands tight and leant right towards God.

"Please, Lord," she said.

He turned his face towards her. She chewed her lips.

"I see your powers, Lord," she whispered. "Please, Lord, could you possibly bring Jasper back to us?"

God smiled. He reached up, plucked something from the empty air, then showed a handful of tiny silver coins to us. He dropped them into Margaret's hands.

"Please," Cathleen begged. "Please. I know you can."

He formed a little creature from a handful of snow, tossed it up into the air and off it flew, a silver bird. He smiled at Cathleen. He stretched and yawned. He rested his hands on his pot belly and turned his face towards the sun.

Everything was still. There were streaks of pink

in the blue sky. The air shimmered, the snow and ice glowed. I heard the trumpet again, high-pitched and far away. God heard it too. He tilted his head, listened and smiled. There was a gate at the back of Cathleen's garden that led to a park and then to the playing fields. Kids were yelling out there. There were mad cries from the lads as a goal was scored.

"Yes! It's in! Yeeeees!"

I looked at God and knew he wasn't God. His clothes were faded and patched. His boots were held together with string. His face was filthy. He looked like he'd walked miles. He was just some weird bloke that'd wandered in from the park for a nap in the shade.

I felt so stupid. I should have gone and played football. I should have gone to Newcastle on my own.

"We should tell somebody about him," I said.

"But who?" said Mary.

"Father O'Mahoney?" said Margaret. "Or the Pope, maybe?"

"*No!*" said Cathleen. "He came to *my* garden. He came just for us. Can you, Lord? Please, Lord. Please bring Jasper back."

I was stuck. I couldn't just clear off and leave them here with him.

"When's your mam coming back?" I said to Cathleen.

She just kept on staring at God.

God brushed the snow away from the ice at the edges of the pond. We saw goldfish shining in the depths. He broke the ice and dipped his hand in and let water trickle from his hand across his brow. Then he held his hand towards us. Cathleen reached out. She caught some drops and touched them to her own brow. God smiled at her. He opened his mouth, took three goldfish out of it, showed them to us and slid them gently down into the water, where they flickered and flashed.

"Will you sign my book?" I said.

God raised his eyebrows.

"They're all footballers in here," I said. "They play for Newcastle. But there's an empty page you could use."

I knelt down beside him. He smelt spicy and sweet, like the stuff Mam puts into the Christmas pudding.

I opened the book and God's eyes widened.

"They're footballers," I said.

God laughed softly and pointed to Alan.

"That's Alan Suddick, God," I said. "He's brilliant!

And so's Dave Hilley. Look, that's him scoring the winner against Swansea."

God ran his fingers over Alan's face, over Dave's face. He smiled, as if he knew them well.

I showed him where it said *To Davie. Best wishes, Dave Hilley.*

"That's how the footballers do it," I said. "Will you write that? And will you sign it from God."

I handed him the new biro. He smiled as he clicked the point in and out and in and out. He held it to his ear to listen to the clicks. He ran his fingers across the page in the book as if he loved the feel of it. He listened to the distant trumpet for a moment. Then he licked his lips and started to copy: *To Davie. Best wishes.* He concentrated hard, but he couldn't hold the pen properly, and his writing was all uneven and clumsy. He looked at what he'd written. It looked like:

7O DOVIC 13es4 NIL5He S

He shrugged, as if to say he was sorry but it was the best he could do.

"That's great, Lord," I said. "Thank you. Will you put your name now, please?"

He put the pen on the page again. I held his cold, smooth hand this time. I guided him as he wrote, *God.*

I read the words out loud. God giggled. I giggled with him.

"Now you're there in the book with Alan and Dave," I said.

Cathleen was furious. She glared at Mary and Margaret.

"I hope you two aren't going to ask for something now!" she whispered. "This is *my* garden!"

Mary and Margaret shook their heads.

"Good," said Cathleen. "Please, God. *Please!*"

I sighed. She might as well ask Alan or Dave to bring her dog back. I looked at a photo of Alan leaping over a clumsy defender. I looked at Dave balancing the ball on his knee. I closed my eyes and imagined kneeling before them on the training ground. *Please, Alan. Please, Dave. Please bring Jasper back again.*

I thought of Jasper. He was an ordinary little black-and-white dog. A jumpy, yappy, happy thing, part spaniel, part poodle, part something else. He'd come from a big litter from somewhere on Brettanby Road. He was just a few years old, but some disease got into him and there was no saving him. Mr Watkinson, the vet in Felling Square, had put him down. I'd seen Cathleen and her mam bringing him back in a brown shopping bag. Mary and Margaret had seen Cathleen's dad digging his grave. Sometimes at night I thought of him lying there, his little body turning, like all bodies, to dust, to earth.

God smiled at Cathleen. There was great kindness in his eyes. He stood up and rubbed his knees and his back as if they were aching. He picked up his blanket and put it over his shoulder. He stretched and yawned. He stroked his beard, like he was wondering about something, then put his hand deep into his robes and took out a little box. There was a picture of a beautiful faraway mountainous place on it. He opened it, and there were sweets inside. He held them out to us. They were delicious, soft and mysteriously sweet, and dusted with the finest sugar.

We licked our lips at their deliciousness.

"They're lovely, God!" said Mary.

He put the whole box into her hands. Then he raised his hand as if in farewell.

"But where are you going?" asked Cathleen.

"Aaaaah," said God.

It was the first thing we'd heard him say.

"And what about Jasper?" said Cathleen.

"Aaaaah," he said again, but much more sadly.

She jabbed her finger towards the earth.

"He's down there in the hard cold ground!" she said. "And I've been praying to you and praying to you and praying to you!"

God looked down at the earth beside the pond. He spread his hands and closed his eyes. He squeezed Cathleen gently on the shoulder, then he just turned and walked through the gate into the park.

He walked slowly and easily, rocking gently from side to side. He walked across the playing fields. Children ran to him across the ice and snow. He kept reaching into his robes, taking things out, giving them to the children.

Cathleen stamped her foot.

"See? Every single person gets something!" she said. "You get silver coins, you get sweets, you get his autograph, they get what he's giving them. And what do I get? Absolutely nothing!"

She yelled after God.

"What about Jasper? What about my *dog*?"

God didn't turn.

"You don't care!" she yelled. "I don't believe in you!"

He hesitated, but he didn't turn.

Cathleen stamped again then realized she was stamping right on top of Jasper. It just made her cry some more.

"Oh!" she yelled. "Why don't all you silly people just go home?"

But we didn't. We shared the sweets. I wished I had a picture of God to go with his autograph.

Someone thumped the far-off drum.

After a while I said, "It wasn't really God, you know."

Cathleen stamped her feet again. She raised her fists in the air.

"I know that!" she said. "Do you think I don't know that?"

I kept thinking I should go, but I didn't. I bet Tex has had a miraculous recovery, I thought. I bet he's out playing football right now.

"Was it not God, Mary?" whispered Margaret.

Mary shook her head.

"No. Of course not. Shh."

The sun fell lower and the sky above Felling began to glow red and gold.

Soon, Cathleen's mam came home, loaded down with shopping bags.

"Hello, everybody," she said. "And Davie as well! Hello, stranger."

She handed custard creams around and took a leaflet from her handbag.

"Town's full of funny folk giving these out," she said. "Look what's on its way."

A circus. There were pictures of a big top, a pony, a tiger, a girl swinging on a trapeze.

And on the back there it was, a picture of God in his orange robes and boots and with his great white beard.

★ THE MISTERIOUS SWAMI,
THE GREAT ORIENTAL MAGICIAN.
SEE SWAMI, AND YOU WILL BELEIVE IN MIRACLES!

Margaret gasped. Cathleen put her tongue out at me. She flicked some crumbs from her lips. I was already imagining the picture stuck in my book close to the pictures of Dave and Alan. Maybe I could find Swami again and get him to sign it with his real name.

"Is everything all right, love?" said Mrs Kelly to Cathleen.

"Yes!" snapped Cathleen.

Mrs Kelly smiled. She put her arm around Cathleen.

The trumpet and drum echoed through the late afternoon air.

"Oh, love," she said softly. "Jasper loved you very much, you know."

Mrs Kelly looked me in the eye and I knew she wanted us to leave.

"Come on," I said to my sisters, and we all got up.

We were heading down by the side of the house when the barking started.

"What's that?" said Mary.

"It's Jasper!" gasped Margaret.

"Don't be silly," I said.

But we all looked back. The barking came from the other side of the gate into the park. We could hear paws scratching and scratching there. We could hear the dog flinging itself against the gate. We stepped back into the garden.

"Somebody sounds very excited," said Mrs Kelly.

The dog barked and yapped and yelped.

"Go away!" she said, but it barked and barked.

"Do we dare to let it in?" she said.

Margaret clasped her hands together. She closed her eyes tight and tilted her face towards the sky.

"I'll go," said Cathleen at last. "I'm the one that's

good with dogs, aren't I?"

She wiped the tears from her eyes with her sleeve. She went to the gate. She stood on tiptoes and looked over it.

"Oh!" she cried.

She looked back at us with amazement in her eyes. Then turned to the dog again.

"Oh, welcome home!" she cried.

And she opened the gate and the little yappy black-and-white dog raced in.

"I didn't think this would turn out to be a ghost story. I knew it'd be a tale about an outsider, a boy separated from other kids by his appearance, by his background, by what others took to be his stupidity. I knew he'd be nicknamed 'The Missing Link' and he'd go through a lot of trouble. Once the story got going, it developed its own momentum and the ending seemed inevitable.

Back then, everyone took the 11-plus exam. If you passed, you went to grammar school. If you didn't, you were classed as a failure and you went to secondary modern. I had lots of friends and relatives who didn't pass – good, decent, bright boys and girls who at the age of eleven were already classed as failures, whose whole lives would be affected by this. And for some of them it was family circumstances, deprivation, poverty or illness that robbed them of this chance.

I passed and went to a Catholic grammar school in Hebburn, three miles downriver from Felling.

The boys in the story know they're supposed to feel clever, but they often don't. They try to adopt a pose of superiority, but it isn't tempered by compassion. Their toughness is a sham. As the narrator says, bullying was commonplace back then. Kids who were bullied were expected to toughen up, to laugh it off, or to just put up with it. The ones who showed signs of weakness were bullied even more.

There was always a tension between education and religion. The more you learned and the more you read and the more you matured, the more you started to question and to doubt. You began to doubt both the scary things (dominated by Satan, his devils and Hell) and the comforting things (dominated by Jesus, his angels and Heaven). This was scary indeed, because you were told that doubt was a dangerous thing. It might lead you from the one true path. It was scary even to *admit* to doubt. It was strange. We were learning about the universe, evolution, the human mind. How did such things tie in with what we were told in church or in our RE lessons? What did the Hail Mary mean to us, modern adolescents in a modern world?

But the faith still held us. We went to Mass and Communion and confession. We went along to services (like the novena services in the story) that promised to save our souls. Yes, we were tempted to say it was all a lot of nonsense, but we didn't dare. As the boys in the story know, and as the Hail Mary emphasizes, the hour of death is mightily important. *Holy Mary, Mother of God, pray for us sinners, now and at the hour of our death…* Will you be in a state of grace? Will you be prepared for Final Judgment? Will a priest be near by to hear your last confession? Our childhoods and adolescence were laced with such questions.

In that world, bullying and tormenting a boy like Christopher McNally was a far lesser sin than, say, missing Sunday Mass or taking God's name in vain. Our duties to retain the faith and to please and obey God were much more important than our duty to love and to care for our fellow creatures.

I wrote this story for an evening of ghost story readings at the Lit & Phil in Newcastle. (Its full name is the Literary and Philosophical Society

of Newcastle upon Tyne.) This is a wonderful
Georgian library near the middle of town, with high,
bright book-filled rooms on the ground floor and
appropriately spooky rooms below. It is democratic
and open to everyone, founded on the belief that
every single one of us is a worthwhile citizen, that
each of us can read, learn, flourish and play
an active part in our amazing world.
It's where I often go to write. It's
where I've just written this. 99

the missing link

It started when they came to town. There were just two of them, McNally and his mother. They seemed to come from nowhere, but it turned out they harked from West Ham, West Bromwich, somewhere like that. The story was, there'd been some trouble – nobody was sure what – and they were looking for a fresh start.

They came to Jonadab. It was a half-abandoned place down by the Tyne: all knocked-down streets and shuttered shops and boarded houses. It was the time of the slum clearances, families getting shifted from the old Victorian terraces and into the new pebbledashed estates further up the hill. Jonadab was almost gone. There were just a few families waiting to get re-housed. The McNallys would have to wait their turn. They'd be the last in line.

The mother was a little hunch-shouldered, weary-looking woman with the scar of some old wound on her face. She got work at Swan Hunter's shipyard: a cleaner, the lowest of the low, sweeping out the ships after the caulkers and welders and burners, mopping out the bogs.

There must've been a dad at one time, but there was no sign of him.

"He must have upped and offed," said my mate Nixon. "Or slit his wrists more likely. And who could bliddy blame him? A woman like that. A son like that. Bliddy Hell. Just imagine it."

We couldn't believe it when the lad arrived at school. The school was St Aidan's, a grammar school. We'd all passed the 11-plus. We were the bright ones, we were the chosen few. And now here came this ugly, stupid-looking thing. He was big and lumpy. Bulbous eyes. There was always dribble on his chin. He'd got a uniform from somewhere: crumpled trousers, worn-down shoes, a tight and tatty, worn-out blazer with the school badge peeling from the pocket. He stank, of course. And that voice! It was so weird and ugly he hardly dared to use it: stupid-sounding, thick and wet, half a grunt and half a whine, whistly and wobbly.

"Jesus bliddy Christ," said Nixon in disgust. "How the hell did a thing like that get let into a place like this?"

We'd started doing science, of course. We'd already found out about evolution. We loved the idea that we were all descended from apes, that everything had led to us, to clever *Homo sapiens*; that we were striding forward together into a bright new world. And now here was Christopher McNally. We took one look at him and pretty soon we were hooting and grunting. We were dangling our fists down to the ground and pretending to be throwbacks or thick.

I was the one who came up with his name. It was during English. We were writing about Shakespeare or somebody like that. I looked across and saw McNally dribbling, saw the way he clutched the pen with his clumsy fingers, the way his head rocked as he wrote. He was hardly human. I gagged, and nearly retched.

I nudged Nixon.

"It's him," I whispered.

"Who?" said McNally.

I stifled my sniggers. I nodded towards McNally.

"The Missing Link," I said. "We've found the Missing Link at last."

From then on, we were poking him with sticks, chucking bananas at him. The size of him, he could've taken any of us, but he never lifted a finger, and never said a word.

"It's like he thinks he deserves it," Nixon said.

"He does!" we said, and we mocked some more.

There was a little bit of pity from the girls. Some of them said we should be ashamed of ourselves. They even said it was us that was half evolved. But it didn't last long. It was hard for them to keep on feeling sorry for hunched shoulders and hairy moles and a grunty voice and smelly breath.

And the teachers? Well, they were different days. Bullying was everywhere. There was neither blood nor broken bones, so they managed to turn their eyes away, and to see next to nowt.

Soon after McNally arrives, we're in the school hall with the priest. You wouldn't believe it nowadays but back then it was all that ancient stuff about fighting temptation and avoiding sin, and about how God sees everything, even our most secret thoughts. It was all to make sure we kept our hands off the girls, of course. Not that it worked very well. Every year there were fifth-formers and sixth-formers slinking off with bairns in their bellies. Anyway, the lads are rolling their eyes like always, and the girls are blushing and sniggering and staring at their nails. Then we get the catechism for the millionth time: *Who made you?* Blah blah blah. Blah blah blah. *Why did God make you?* Blah blah blah. Then the dire warnings:

What if death came now, this very second?

Are you in a state of grace?

Are you prepared for Final Judgment?

The Final Judgment. My God, we still believed in that. Or even if we said we didn't, we were still half terrified of it.

"Hell lies in wait," they said. "How will you keep yourself away from it?"

Anyway, Link's at the back. We can hear his grunty breath, and it's like there's some weird snuffling beast among us.

Nixon pipes up.

"Have all creatures got souls, Father?"

"All creatures?" says the priest.

"Yes, Father. Even them from way, way back, like the apes and the half-human things we grew from and that?"

We all start nudging, giggling. We all start turning and looking at Link.

The priest sighs.

"An interesting question. But you are leaping into dark theological waters, my son. What is certain is that we have souls, and we must fortify them. Which leads me to my main topic – to introduce you to the First Friday Novena."

Novenas. We were always doing sodding novenas. Don't know what it was about the number nine, but we were always saying nine prayers for this and nine for that. We'd light nine candles in a row. We'd contemplate the nine orders of angels and the nine rivers of Hell. And this one?

"This novena," says the priest, "may be the most powerful of all. You must come to Mass and take Holy Communion on the first Friday of the month, for nine months in a row."

He pauses. We wait for whatever reward will be promised.

"Do this," he says, "and the hour of your death will not arrive without a priest being close at hand to administer the blessed sacrament."

We all listen. We know what that could mean. No matter what sins we have committed, a priest will be there to take our last confession, to give us his blessing. We will be kept out of the jaws of Hell.

"None of us is perfect," he whispers. "But do we not all dream of dying without a trace of sin on our souls? This novena helps that dream come true."

"Is it true?" asks someone.

"There is no infallible teaching. But the devout have always observed this novena, and many of our greatest saints. Isn't it better to be safe than sorry?" He peers at us. "Or perhaps you would prefer to take a risk. Perhaps you would prefer to toy with the fires of destruction."

Before he leaves, he says, "I see we have a new boy. What's your name, lad?"

Link grunts something. We all squeeze our eyes and hold our laughter in.

"He's the Missing Link," squeaks Nixon.

Our laughter bursts free.

The priest shakes his head.

"Take no notice, my son," he says. He pats Link

on the arm as he leaves. "You'll find they're not all badness. You'll surely find a pal among them."

He rolls his eyes.

"You lot! What are we going to do with you?" he says. "We begin this Friday. Don't forget."

We didn't forget. The church was full, and there we were, breakfasts in brown paper bags, stomachs groaning, souls yearning, tongues stuck out to welcome Christ's body and salvation into ourselves.

And there was Link, kneeling just along the altar rail from us.

"Who does he bliddy think he is?" muttered Nixon at my side. He groaned in disgust as the priest pressed the pure white host onto Link's horrible lumpy tongue.

"Novena?" he said. "I'll bliddy novena him."

After Mass, we waited in an alleyway between the church and the school. We dragged Link in and started on him.

That morning saw the first of the monthly beatings of the missing link between the age of stupid apes and the age of brainy men.

★   ★   ★

I don't know why he came to me. I was always there, those Friday mornings in the alleyway. I wasn't the worst of us, but I always did my bit. And I always urged the others on. I always laughed at Nixon – the way he slapped and poked and kicked and spat, leaving pain and fright but neither blood nor broken bones. I was always there hooting with laughter as Link scuttled off.

But it was me that Link came to, in the school yard, one bright and early morning. There was hardly anybody else around. I must've still been half asleep. I felt the touch on my shoulder. I turned round and Link was there, his wet eyes looking down at me, his tongue flapping in his horrible wet mouth.

I couldn't catch his words at first.

"Eh?" I said.

"It's an illness," he grunted.

I looked around, backed away.

"Eh?" I said.

"The thing that makes me h-horrible," he said. "Look at how me arms and legs is thickening and me chin's dropping."

He showed his thick, muscly, lumpy limbs, his grotesque chin, the hairs sprouting on his face.

"And me tongue," he said. "It's too big for me mouth. It's why I..."

"What're the doctors doing?" I said.

He took a big purple pill out. He shoved it in his mouth and swallowed it.

"The novena'll help and all," he said. "I'm praying for deliverance from it."

He swiped his sleeve across his mouth.

"D'you believe me?" he said.

"Dunno," I said.

Link moved closer. He reached out to me, held me by the collar, breathed on me with his rotten breath.

"Look through this," he said. "Look through all the ugliness."

I tried to pull away.

Beyond him, I saw Nixon swaggering through the school gates.

"Look right inside," said Link. "I'm just like you."

"Like what?" I said.

"Aye, like y-you."

Nixon quickened towards us. He started grinning.

"Hey, Nixon," I said. "I'm just having a nice chat with the Missing Link."

"Ah, isn't that nice," said Nixon.

"I know," I said. "And listen – Link says he's just like us."

"Is that right?" said Nixon.

"Aye," I said.

"Then Link," said Nixon, "is even stupider than we thought."

Link took his hand away from me. We laughed and watched him shuffle off.

We went round the back and lit a fag.

"What's he doing coming to you?" said Nixon.

"Mebbe he thinks I'll be his pal."

Nixon laughed.

"Funny, eh? You always look as sweet as pie. Mothers and old biddies and missing links think you're the bee's bliddy knees. They don't see to the inside. Not like I do."

I drew on the fag and showed my teeth.

"They don't," I said. "I'm a bliddy devil, eh?"

Even so, I think I did start to change that day. I thought about being dragged out of West Bromwich to a place like this; having no father, having a mother like that, having some horrible condition; being scared of what's happening to your own body; being all alone at school;

being scared of kids that should be your mates.

But what good's change if it's all inside yourself and nowt happens on the outside? What's the good of knowing that you shouldn't do something like beating up Link when you go on doing it? What's the use of it when your mate Nixon comes and tells you you're going to stop the Missing Link from finishing his novena, and you just answer, "Aye! That's a great idea! That'll be a real bliddy laugh!"

The trouble is, it's easy to go along with it all. And it's a laugh, especially when you get to plotting with your mates.

"Novena?" you say. "Ha! We'll bliddy novena him!"

Early morning, first Friday, ninth month. It was November, still dark, icy cold. We waited, half a dozen of us, in a deep doorway on the High Street. We smoked Woodbines and thought about salvation, and resisted the temptation to eat our breakfasts there and then. We felt good. We were going to escape the jaws of Hell today.

"Link alert!" whispered somebody at last, and there he was, lurching up from Jonadab beneath the streetlights.

We did it fast. He hardly struggled. We dragged him down the alleyway into a little abandoned printing shop. We tied him to a twisted doorframe and gagged him with his scarf. He kept his eyes on me but I did nothing while Nixon softly whispered, "Don't worry, Link. We'll soon be back to let you go."

We hurried churchward under heavy, sleety-looking clouds. Inside, we hung our heads and murmured the prayers. At the altar rail I cast my eyes over the ornate altar, the saints in their little niches, the crucifix, the monstrance. I felt no connection to any of it. I told myself I believed none of it. I stared through to the emptiness behind it all, then opened my mouth and stuck out my tongue when the priest came to me. I closed my eyes, felt the bread pressed onto my tongue then swallowed it down into the emptiness inside myself.

Afterwards, we clenched our fists in triumph at achieving our novenas.

"Hell is defeated!" said Nixon.

Then we went back to the alleyway to liberate the Missing Link.

He died in mid-December. We were hanging baubles on the classroom tree when the priest came in.

The boy had fallen into the river, he told us. He'd been washed up on a mud bank. He must have been out walking, maybe stumbled in the dark.

"You weren't there, Father?" I said.

"Me?"

"There was no priest there, Father?"

He spread his hands. How could there have been? But he saw the yearning in our eyes.

"Christopher was a good lad," he said. "He held to his faith. God will have recognized one of his own. Now let us pray for his soul."

I clenched my fists, and I begged God to hear us.

In the yard we leant together against a frosty wall. We smoked, and tried to imagine drowning all alone in the filthy Tyne, tried to imagine what waited afterwards.

"It's all ballocks," said Nixon at last.

"Eh?" we said.

"That novena stuff. It's just made up, man."

"Not just that," I said. "It's *all* made up. Every last little bit."

"Aye!" we said. "All of it. It's ballocks!"

We coughed and laughed and our breath swirled around us in the icy air. But we shuddered with the dread of what we might have done to Link, and to ourselves.

I've told nobody till now what happened next. I've tried forgetting it, I've tried not believing it, but there's been no escape.

Link came back, not long after that Christmas. I was in bed. I woke up in the middle of the night and there he was. He was standing over me, showing the massive distended bones and muscles of his arms, just like he had in the yard that day.

"It's stopped getting worse," he said. His voice was still all slobbery. "And there's no pain, and no fear."

I could smell the river on him.

"Did you jump?" I said.

He smiled.

"You could've saved me," he said. "You know that, don't you?"

"I?" I said.

"Aye. In the alleyway that day. You could've spoken up. But you didn't. You just looked away."

"Did you jump?" I said again.

He laughed and nodded.

"Yes. I did. I couldn't stand it any more so I jumped."

"Suicide," I whispered.

"Aye. Suicide."

Suicide. It was despair, a mortal sin. There could be no forgiveness. It meant eternal damnation.

I heard Hell's gates creaking open for both of us.

"So you're in Hell?" I whispered.

He smiled again.

"Because I jumped? No, that's all ballocks, just like First Fridays, novenas, all that stuff. All that matters is goodness, just simple goodness."

"And how d'you get that?"

He shrugged. He was so free, so easy, not like the Link I used to know.

"Dunno. But it seems I had it."

Then he shrugged again and he was gone.

He's kept on coming back, through all the years between. It's always the same: the smell of the river, the smile. He hasn't spoken again. Doesn't need to, I suppose. He said it all that very first time. He just stands there in the darkness, like he simply wants me to look upon him. And I do. Sometimes there's been years between his visits and I get to hope it's all over, but then he appears again, unexpected but expected, like last night. He disappeared as dawn came and then I started writing it all down at last.

It was long ago. Link's mum died soon after him.

We grammar school boys are all scattered. Some of us could well be dead. Most of us have forgotten Link, I'm sure. Nixon's ended up in California, surfing, playing golf and drinking. He sends me cards and says it's Paradise. Me, I've always talked of moving, but I keep on staying here. Funny, but the faith draws you back, even when you don't believe it. I've gone back to lighting candles, saying my prayers in nines. I try to keep in a state of grace. I'm even in the middle of a First Friday Novena. It's all because the end's not too far away, of course.

Mebbe after that I'll discover what simple goodness is.

I hope I don't.

"A story is a journey. Every word is a footstep. Every sentence, paragraph and page carries you a little further. You might know where it starts and where it's headed, but you can never be certain if you'll take the right turnings, or what you'll see and who you'll meet along the way. And, of course, a story is a life.

This story's inspired by the Great North Run, the half-marathon that takes place every year in the north-east of England. It starts in Newcastle, goes through Gateshead, Felling, Hebburn, Jarrow, and ends at South Shields, beside the North Sea. Famous athletes like Mo Farah and Paula Radcliffe take part. So do joggers and sports-club members, and people dressed as ducks and fairies. I went to the same school as Brendan Foster, the man who helped to set it all up. In Felling we lived next door to Brendan's coach, Stan Long, who started training runners when he was a welder in Gateshead. He was still Brendan's coach when he became an Olympic medallist and world record holder. The Great North Run started in 1981 and it grows bigger and more famous every year. Probably influenced by Brendan and Stan, I've run it three times myself.

To prepare to write this story I went to watch the run, of course. That morning I'd arranged to give a writing workshop in Low Newton women's prison in Durham, along with the writers Wendy Robertson and Avril Joy, who ran the educational programme there. When I arrived I was guided through a series of gates and doors by a uniformed prison officer. Each one was unlocked, opened, then shut and locked again. Keys jangled and steel clanged. I was taken to a library room with a few armchairs and tables in it. Then the women came in. They were shy at first, maybe suspicious, but they soon relaxed. I talked about my life and my writing. We did a couple of quick imagination exercises, made a few first scribbles. Some of the women began to tell me about their own lives and childhoods. They hinted at the difficulties, deprivations and abuses they'd endured. They talked about the constrictions of being in this place, about the fellowship they tried to develop with each other, and the inevitable frictions and fights. Many of them wanted to write about themselves, to somehow turn their lives into coherent stories. I said that fictionalizing a life can make it seem more real, and can make difficult personal experiences more bearable. We scribbled again, and began to shape the scribbles into narratives.

Before I left, one of the women suddenly said, "I'm like you, David. My childhood was like yours."

She laughed.

"And look where I've ended up!" she said.

I was led back through the clanging doors. At the exit Avril told me that there was much more the women could have said.

"They've had some awful journeys," she said.

I drove away from the prison towards Felling. I parked the car. There were crowds lining the bypass, closed to traffic on this special race day. I was early. I walked down into the pebbledashed estate where I'd spent my boyhood. I stood before the little house in which Mam, Dad, Colin, Catherine, Barbara and I had lived, and in which

Barbara had died. I watched the memories and imaginings rise for a few moments in my mind. Then I hurried back to the road.

Here came the runners, streaming past towards the sea, hundreds upon hundreds of them, sprinting, trotting, striding, dancing, exulting in their freedom, running for their lives.

Later, at home, I started to doodle a map of the route. I scribbled a few possibilities. Then the young narrator came into my mind, and he led me to Harry Miller, and both of them began to run, taking the story all the way to South Shields and back again. **,,**

harry miller's run

I don't want to go to Harry Miller's. It's Saturday morning. My entry for the Junior Great North Run's just come through the post. I'm already wearing the T-shirt. I'm already imagining belting round the quayside and over the bridges in two weeks' time. I'm imagining all the running kids, the cheering crowds. I'm dreaming of sprinting to the finish line. I phone Jacksie and we end up yelling and laughing at each other. His stuff's come as well. He's number 2594. I'm

2593. We can't believe it. But we say it's fate. We've been best mates for ever. We say we'll meet up straight away and get some training done in Jesmond Dene.

But soon as I put the phone down, Mam's at my shoulder.

"Don't go," she says.

"Eh?"

"Come with me to Harry's. It's his last day in the house. He'll need a friendly face around."

"But, Mam!"

"Come on, just an hour or two. Just for me."

"But I haven't got time, Mam."

She laughs.

"You're eleven years old. You've got all the time in the world."

So in the end I sigh, phone Jacksie again and put him off till the afternoon, and I slouch down the street with my mam.

Harry's ancient. We've known him for ever. He lives at the end of our street and he was fit as a lop till the heart attack got him. It looked like the end but he was soon fighting back. A few days in intensive care, a couple of weeks in Freeman Hospital, and before we knew it he was back home in Blenkinsop Street. He started tottering around his little front garden on his Zimmer frame, tottering past our window to the Elmfield Social Club. He stood gasping at street corners, grinning at the neighbours, waving at the kids. When he saw me out training, he'd yell, "Gan on, young'n! Keep them pins moving!" And I'd wave and laugh and put a sprint on. "That's reet, lad! Run! There's a wolf at your tail! Run for your life!"

Everybody knows Harry. Everybody loves him. The women in the street take him flasks of tea and sandwiches and plates of dinner. His mates from the club call in with bottles of beer to play cards and dominoes with him. The district nurse visits every day and she's always laughing when she comes out his front door. But one day she found him with a massive bruise on his head after he'd had a fall. One day he was out wandering the street in his stripy pyjamas. It couldn't go on. There was nobody at home to look after him. It was time for him to leave the house, get rid of tons of stuff and move into St Mary's, the new nursing home just off Baker's Lane.

Mam took it on herself to help him clear out. "Poor soul," she said. "How on earth'll he bear up?" But

Harry didn't seem to find it hard at all. Out went all his stuff, to charity shops and fetes and the town dump: pots and pans, dishes, tables and chairs, clothes, a radio, an ancient TV.

"What are they?" he said. "Nowt but things. Hoy them oot!"

He just laughed about it all.

"I'll not need much in the place where I'm gannin'. And for the place past that, I'll not need nowt at all."

We walk down the street to Harry's. Mam lets us in with a key. By now, just about everything's gone. The floors are bare. There're no curtains at the windows. He's sitting in the front room in a great big armchair with a box full of papers on his lap and the Zimmer frame standing in front of him. There's a little table with boxes of tablets on it. He looks all dreamy but he manages to grin.

"How do, petal," he says.

"How do, Harry."

Mam bends down and kisses him. She pushes some hair back from his brow. She says has he washed this morning, has he brushed his teeth, has he had breakfast, has he…

"Aye," he says. "Aye, hinny, aye."

He stares at me like he's staring from a million miles away.

"It's the little runner," he says at last.

"Aye, Mr Miller."

He reaches out and touches the T-shirt. His hand's all frail an' trembly.

"Great North Run?" he says.

"Aye, Mr Miller."

"I done that."

"Did you really, Harry?" says Mam. "And when was that?"

He reaches towards me again.

"How old are ye, son?"

"Eleven."

"That was when I done it. When I was eleven."

Mam smiles sadly at me.

"Must've been great," she says.

"It was bliddy marvellous, pet."

He closes his eyes. Mam lifts the box from his lap. It looks like he might be dropping off to sleep, but he jumps up to his feet and grabs the Zimmer frame. He leans forward like he's ready to run.

"It's the final sprint!" he says.

He giggles and drops back into the chair.

"Tek nae notice, son," he says. "I'm just a daft old maddled gadgie."

He looks at the box.

"Them'll need to be gone through," he says. "Ye'll help us, hinny?"

"Course I will," said Mam.

He sighs and grins, and stares past us like he can see right through the walls.

"I can see the sea, mates!" he says. "We're nearly there!"

And he falls asleep and starts to snore.

It smells of old bloke in here. Suppose it's bound to. Suppose he can't help it. Suppose I'll smell like old bloke myself one day. Pee and sweat and ancient clothes and dust. The sun shines through the window. Dust's glittering and dancing in the shafts of light. Outside there're the little trees in Harry's neat little garden, the rooftops of the street, Newcastle's towers and spires, then the big blue empty sky.

Mam lifts the papers out. She unfolds them from packets and envelopes while Harry snuffles and snores.

Here's his birth certificate.

Harold Matthew Miller
Born in 1927

Father:	*Harold, a turner*
Mother:	*Maisie, a housewife*
Address:	*17 Blenkinsop Street,*
	Newcastle-upon-Tyne

"Same address as now," I say.

"Aye. Lived here all his life. And look, this must be them."

It's a small faded black-and-white photograph. A young couple and a wrapped-up baby beaming through the years. Mam holds the photograph close to Harry's face. "Can you see them in him?" she says. And when we look at Harry and think of him with his wide and shining eyes, we have to say we can. The baby, the woman and the man are living on in the sleeping bloke.

More photographs: toddler Harry in a fat nappy with his dad in overalls on one side, Mam in a flowery frock on the other. Scruffy boys and girls on benches in an ancient schoolyard. A teacher at the centre with a big hooked nose and a fur wrap around her shoulders. Which one is he? We pick the same face, the grinning kid just behind the teacher's head, the one lifting his hand like he wants to wave at us from seventy years ago. A final school report from 1942.

Harry is a fine hard-working lad.
We wish him well in his chosen workplace.

There's his apprenticeship papers from the same year, when he started as an apprentice welder at Swan Hunter's shipyard. A photograph of him in a soldier's uniform. National service, says Mam. Harry with girls, one pretty girl then another, then another. They're on Tynemouth seafront, on Newcastle quayside market, sitting in a Ferris wheel at a fair. There's a folded piece of pink paper with a handwritten note:

Thank you, Harry. Such a lovely day.
Until next time.   Love, V

"V?" I say.

Mam shrugs.

"Who knows? I heard tell he'd been a ladies' man. Often chased but never caught."

She holds the photos to his face again.

"And there's still the handsome lad in him!" she says.

Then there he is in colour, in swimming trunks and with a sombrero on his head. He's linking arms with his mates on a beach in what Mam says must be Spain.

"That's Tommy Lind!" says Mam. "And Alex Marsh, God rest his soul."

There's more, and more. Photographs and documents, savings books, rent books, pension books. There's his dad's death certificate in 1954, then his mother's just a few months later, both of them with cancer, both of them too young. There're holiday bookings, airline tickets, outdated foreign money. Lists of medication, prescriptions, hospital appointment cards.

"A whole life in a box," says Mam as she lifts another envelope and opens it. "What's this?" she says to herself.

"It's what I telt ye," says Harry. He's wide awake. "It's the Great North bliddy Run."

There're four skinny kids on a beach, three lads and a lass. The sun's blazing down. The lads are wearing baggy shorts and boots, and they've got vests slung over their bare shoulders. The lass is in a white dress and she's wearing boots as well. They're all grinning and holding massive ice creams in their fists.

"Pick us out," says Harry.

We both point to the same lad.

"That's reet," he says. "And that one's Norman Wilkinson, and he was Stanley Swift." He pauses as he looks. He touches the girl's face and smiles. "She joined us at Felling. Veronica was her name."

He grins.

"It was took by Angelo Gabrieli, the ice-cream maker."

He keeps on grinning.

"It's South Shields," he says.

"South Shields?" says Mam.

"Look, there's the pier in the haze. There's Tynemouth Castle in the distance."

We peer closely.

"Oh, aye," we say.

"We run there from Newcastle," says Harry.

We just look at him.

"We were eleven years old," he says. "It was 1938. We were young and daft and fit as fleas."

He points to the envelope.

"Keep digging, hinny."

She takes out a sheet of paper. It crackles as she

unfolds it. It's faded at the edges. The writing's all discoloured. Mam reads it out.

THIS IS TO SERTIFY THAT

Harold Matthew Miller

RUN FROM NEWCASLE TO SOUTH SHIELDS ON

29 AUGUST 1938.

What a grate achevemente!
GOOD LAD! WEL DONE!

SINED

Angelo Gabrieli

MASTER ICE-CREAM MAKER OF SOUTH SHIELDS
29 AUGUST 1938

"He made one for all of us," says Harry. "And he sent the photographs to all of us."

We don't know what to say. He laughs at us.

"It's true," he says. "It was a lovely summer's day. Norman says, 'I'd love a swim.' So Stanley says, 'Let's go to Shields.'"

"But Harry…" says Mam.

He points to the envelope.

"And we got our swim," he says.

Another photograph. The same kids, in the sea this time, yelling with laughter as the breakers roll over them.

"Beautiful," he murmurs. "We were that hot and sweaty and fit to drop, and it was wet and icy and tingly and just that lovely. And Mr Gabrieli with the camera. Can see him still, standing in the sunlight laughing and urging us on. Dark hair and dark eyes and broad shoulders and dressed in white. A lovely man."

"But it's thirteen miles," says Mam.

He sighs, he leans back in his chair. "Giz a minute. Any chance of a cup of tea?" She makes it. It trembles as he lifts it to his lips. He drinks. He drinks again. "Lovely cup of tea," he says. "One of them tablets. Aye, the white ones, love." He takes the tablet, he drinks more tea. He blinks, takes a breath. "Thirteen miles. We weren't to know. Stanley said he went there with his Uncle Jackie on the train one day. Said it was just across the Tyne Bridge then through a place called Felling then turn left and a short bit more. Said it'd mebbe take an hour at most and we'd be back for tea." He giggles. "We didn't do geography at school, except to find out aboot Eskimos and pygmies and the River Nile."

"But what did you tell your mams?" says Mam.

"Nowt! Nowt at all." He looks at me. "We were

always shooting off to the town moor or Exhibition Park, or just pottering around the streets and lanes. They were used to us going out in the morning and not coming back till nearly dark. Don't believe it, de ye?"

"Dunno," I say.

"Different days, son. Mind you, by the time we got to Felling, we were starting to see what we'd took on."

He drinks some more tea.

"We started at ten o'clock. It was already hot. Stanley said, 'Just think of that icy watter on your skin, lads.' So we belted out of Blenkinsop Street and down to the bridge. What a clatter! All of us had studs in our boots that our dads'd hammered in te mek them last longer. We started off by racing each other, but after a while I said, 'Tek it easy, man, lads. No need for racing yet.'" He looked at me. "You'll understand that, eh? Save some breath for the final sprint?"

"Aye, Mr Miller," I say.

"Aye. Good lad." He looks at my T-shirt again. "It's not the full run ye'll be diying, is it?"

"No," I say. "Just the junior one. A couple of miles around the bridges and the quay. You've got to be seventeen to do the proper Great North Run."

"Seventeen. So we were even dafter than I thought.

Anyway, we trotted across the bridge and there were ships lined up along the river underneath, and seagulls screaming all around, and lots of folk walking on the bridge that we had to dodge past. We get to Gateshead and onto the High Street and we ask a fruiterer if we can have a drink of watter, please, cos we're running to South Shields today. 'To South bliddy Shields?' he says. 'You better have some apples an' all. Are ye sure?' he sez. 'Aye,' we say. 'It's just roond the corner, isn't it?' 'Depends what ye mean by roond the corner,' he says. We just laugh and take the apples and run on cos we're still full o' beans and it's great to be together on a summer's day. Then there's Sunderland Road that gets us to Felling, and it's a lang straight road and we've already been gannin' for nearly an hour. There's no sign of any sea, no end in sight. And we sit doon by Felling railway station and we look at each other and nobody says a word till Norman says at last, 'So where the hell's South Shields?' Stanley points along the road. 'That way, I think,' he says. 'I divent knaa exactly, but I'm certain we're gannin' the reet way.' Norman just looks at him. 'I'm getting knackered,' he says. 'Let's gan back.' And probly we would have. But then we seen her, across the street, lookin' doon at us."

"Who?" says Mam.

"Veronica."

He sips his tea again. He sighs and blows.

"You knaa," he says. "It comes to something when talking aboot runnin' gets as knackerin' as runnin' itself." He grins. "Divent get old, son. Promise us that. Stay eleven for ever."

"OK, Mr Miller," I say.

"Good lad. I bet you're fast, are ye?"

"Not that fast. I can keep going, though."

"Ye'd have been good that day, then. And ye'll be all set when you're seventeen."

"Aye. I think I will."

"Just wait till ye see that sea, shining before ye after all them miles."

"Veronica, Harry," says Mam.

"Eh?" says Harry.

"Veronica. Who was she?"

"Veronica? She was something else."

He turns his face to the ceiling. He closes his eyes like he's imagining it all again, then he opens them again and there's such a smile on his face.

"She was on the green at the end of a row of terraced houses," he says. "She was hanging washing oot. She stopped what she was diyin' and she had one hand up across her eyes to shade them from the sun. 'Gan and ask her for some watter,' sez Norman. 'Gan yourself,' sez Stanley. 'I'll gan,' sez I. And off I go. I can see her now, standing in her white cotton dress with the basket of washing under her arm and the way she watches us as I get closer. 'What do you want?' she sez when I get closer. 'Is there any chance of a cup of watter?' I say. 'We've been runnin' from Newcastle and we're parched.' 'From Newcastle?' she sez. 'Aye,' I say. 'From Blenkinsop Street. We were ganna run te South Shields but I think we're turning back.' 'Why's that?' she sez. 'Cos we're knackered,' I say. 'And South Shields is a lang way. And to be honest we divent really knaa where it is.' She puts the washing doon. 'Turning back?' she sez. 'And you don't even know where it is? What kind of attitude is that?' 'I divent knaa,' I say. 'But if you'll be kind enough to give us some watter we'll be on our way.' And she sez, 'Wait there,' and she turns round and walks away."

He says nothing for a while. It looks like he's going all dreamy again, like he might doze off again.

"Did she bring some water?" says Mam.

"Eh? Aye, she did. A big bottle of it. And she's got

jam sandwiches an' all, and she's got big boots on and she sez, 'There's no need to turn back. I know where South Shields is. I've left a note for my mother. I'll take you there.' And she puts a sandwich in me hand, and walks down to where the other two is. She tells them an' all while they're eating the sandwiches and swigging the watter. 'But we're half knackered already,' sez Stanley. 'By the time we run aal the way back again we'll be bliddy deed.' 'There's no need to run back again,' she sez. 'We can take the train. You'll be back for tea.' And when we start to laugh she goes into the pocket in her dress and takes some money out. 'I'll pay,' she sez. 'My Uncle Donald sends it to me. He lives in America. He says he works in Hollywood. I think he's fibbing but that doesn't matter.' Me and the lads look at each other. A train steams through the station. I look at her, I think of the train, I taste the lovely bread and jam, and I swig the lovely watter. 'I'm Veronica,' says Veronica. 'What're your names?' So we tell her, and so she says, 'What we waiting for?' She smiles her smile at me. Me and the lads look at each other. 'Nowt,' I say. 'Nowt,' say the other two. 'This way, then,' she sez, and we set off running again."

"Quite a girl," says Mam.

"Aye," says Harry.

He goes silent again. Mam says does he want more tea. He says yes. She goes to make it. I look at my watch, I think about Jacksie, I think about running through Jesmond Dene.

"Things to do?" says Harry.

"Aye."

He nods. "I'll not be lang. I cannot be. Or like Stanley said, by the time I finish I'll be bliddy dead. More tea. Good lass! Ha, and a slice of jam and bread and all!"

Mam smiles with him.

"Eat it up," she says. "It'll give you strength."

And he eats, and wipes his lips with his shaky hand, and after a moment he starts again.

"So we run out of Felling and down through Pelaw and Bill Quay and into Hebburn, and it's getting hot as Hell and staying bright as Heaven. And Veronica runs smooth and free beside us. And our feet clatter and beat on the tracks and pavements, and sometimes we walk and rest and gather our breath and run again. And sometimes we shout out to folks we pass that we're running to South Shields and we've run from Blenkinsop Street in Newcastle and from Felling station and they say they don't believe it. They say it's such a bliddy wonder! 'Good lads!' they say. 'Good lass! Run! Run! There's a wolf at your tail! Run for your lives!' And people give us watter, and a baker in Hebburn gives us cakes. And we run and run and run and run. And we get to Jarrow and we rest in the shade under the trees in St John's churchyard, and we watch a coffin bein' carried from a hearse through a group of mourners and put into the ground, and out of the blue Veronica stretches her arms out wide and says, 'They said I might not live at all. And just look what I can do!'"

"How do you mean?" says Mam.

"That's what I sez – 'How d'you mean?' Veronica shrugs. 'I was a weakly child,' she says. 'I was back and forward to the doors of death.' Me and the lads is hushed. They were different days back then. There were many little'ns took too soon. Stanley hisself had a sister gone before he was born. 'Are you all right now?' he whispers to Veronica. And she laughs, the way she did. 'Now how could I run to South Shields if I wasn't, Stanley?' And up she jumps with her big heart and her big soul and her strong legs and her big boots and we're off again, and as we leave Jarrow behind we start telling each other we can smell the sea. Which was more a matter of hope than truth. Nae sign of any sea. Nae sign of any South Shields. We've soon been gone more than two hours. It's afternoon. It's blazin' hot. We're absolutely knacked. We're slowin' doon. Nobody says it but we're all thinking of giving up. Even Veronica starts puffin' and pantin' and gaspin' for air, and Stanley's watching her with great concern. And then we hear it, the clip-clop-clip of Gabrieli's pony and the toot of Gabrieli's horn." He laughs at the memory. "It come upon us like a miracle."

"The ice-cream maker?" says Mam.

"Aye. Mr Angelo Gabrieli, master ice-cream maker of South Shields. He's on an ice-cream cart that's painted all white and red and gold. The pony's shining black. Mr Gabrieli's sitting there in his white shirt and his white trousers and his white cap with **GABRIELI'S** printed on it and there's a great big tub of ice cream at his side. He toots his horn again. He laughs. 'Buy a Gabrieli!' he calls. 'Best ice cream this side of Heaven!' And he tugs the pony to a halt at our side. We halt as well. We puff and pant. We drool. We watch the shining tub. I think of Veronica's cash. Never mind the train, I think. Buy some ice creams now! 'Good afternoon, my fine children!' says Mr Gabrieli. 'And where might you be going on this perfect day?' 'South

Shields,' I tell him. He grins in satisfaction. 'The perfect destination! Your names, my friends?' We tell him our names. I tell him we've run all the way from Newcastle and Felling. 'Indeed?' he says. 'I thought you looked a little hot. Perhaps a little ice cream would be rather helpful.' We daren't speak. We look at Veronica. Our eyes and hearts are yearning. 'Perhaps a little one now,' says Mr Gabrieli, 'and the biggest one you've ever seen when at last you reach the beach!' And he opens the tub and digs into it, and gives us each an ice cream for free. Ha! And nothing I've tasted in the seventy years since has tasted anything like that glorious gift. Mr Gabrieli smiles as he watches us. He ponders. 'I could offer you a lift,' he says and Norman's mouth is opening wide with joy. But Veronica's shaking her head and telling him no. 'Yes, you are right, Veronica,' says Mr Gabrieli. 'This is an achievement you will remember all your lives. Do not worry, boys. It is not far now. Along here then right and onto lovely Ocean Road, and then at the end of that – the shining sea itself! I will meet you there!' He snaps the reins. 'Onward, Francisco! Until we meet again, my friends!' And off he trots."

Harry rests. He gazes out at the trees and the sky. Mam brings more tea.

"You've not told anybody about this till now?" she says.

"I've told bits of it, pet, just like bits of crack and reminiscing at the club. But I've never telt it all with all the detail in. And even now, there'll be bits of it I must leave out."

"It was such an amazing thing, Harry," Mam says. "Like Mr Gabrieli said, such a great achievement."

"Aye, that's true. And it was a day of daftness and joy, and if we'd never started and we'd never kept on going, just think of what we'd've missed." He smiles, like he's slipping into a dream. "So we kept on going and we kept on going. We followed Gabrieli's cart until it went right out of sight, and we kept on going with the lovely thought of massive ice creams still to come. And then we're on Ocean Road, and there's seagulls in the air and a breeze on our faces, and this time we can truly smell the sea, and then, 'Oh, I can see it, mates! I can really see the sea!'"

And Harry's eyes are wide, like he can see the sea again.

"And he's there, like he said he would be. Mr Gabrieli. He's sitting up on his cart and he smiles to welcome us and holds his arms out wide. 'Now,' he says. 'Which should come first? The ice cream or the sea?' And we divent hesitate. We're straight onto the beach and plunging into the watter. And when we look back, there's Mr Gabrieli laughing at us as we jump and dive and tumble through the waves. Then we stand together and he photographs us, and we come out and he leads us to the cart and he gives us the biggest ice creams we've ever seen, then he photographs us again. And he has our certificates ready and we sit in the sand and read them to each other. And then Mr Gabrieli asks us if we know that we are wonderful, and he sings to us – something I never heard before and have never heard since, except in dreams, something Italian and strange and very beautiful."

He points to the envelope.

"Should be something else in there," he says. "He got some passer-by to take it."

Mam slips her fingers inside and takes it out, another photograph. Everybody's in it, standing smiling before the ice-cream cart and Francisco the shining pony. Harry, Veronica, Stanley and Norman with their certificates, and lovely Mr Gabrieli himself, all in white with **GABRIELI'S** printed on his cap, and past them is the beach and then the sea. And me and Mam don't say anything, though we can see that Harry and Veronica are standing right together, holding hands.

"And then," says Harry, "we give our addresses to Mr Gabrieli and we say goodbye. And back we go up Ocean Road and to the railway station. And then we get the train, and off it puffs, through Jarrow and Hebburn and Pelaw and Heworth, doing in minutes what took us so long. And then along the track to Felling."

"And Veronica?" says Mam.

"She got off there. And we went on. And we were home in time for tea."

"You know what I mean. Did you see her again?"

"Most nights, in me dreams."

"No more than that?"

He shakes his head, closes his eyes, then points into the box.

"That brown packet there," he says.

She lifts it out.

"Gan on," he says.

She opens it, and there they are, Harry and Veronica. They're on the Tyne Bridge, maybe eighteen years old. The breeze is in their hair and there're seagulls in the air behind them, and they're laughing out loud and holding hands again.

"Aye," he says. He takes the photograph and holds it. "We made sure we found each other again. And we were together for a time. And she really was something else. But then…"

His voice falters. He shakes his head.

"Not now, love. I'm knacked. The lad's got running to do, I've got a home to go to, and you've got some helping out to do."

"OK then, Harry," says Mam.

She kisses him. She tells him to close his eyes, to have a rest.

"Aye, I will," he says. He licks his lips and stares into the photograph.

"Do you think…?" he says to Mam.

"Think what, Harry?"

"Do you think there's a Heaven, like they used to say there was? A Heaven where we meet again?"

"I don't know, Harry."

"Me neither. And mebbe it doesn't matter. Mebbe this is Heaven. Mebbe you enter Heaven on the best of days, like the day we got to Shields, like other days."

"Days with her? With Veronica?"

"Aye. Days with Veronica."

His eyes flutter. He looks at me.

133

"You're a good lad. Get started, keep on going. You'll have a lovely life."

He closes his eyes.

"You know what?" he murmurs before he sleeps. "Me great achievement is that I've been happy, that I've never been nowt but happy."

"Go on, son," says Mam. "Go and see Jacksie. Get your training in."

Harry never got to St Mary's Nursing Home. He died that afternoon while I was running with Jacksie through Jesmond Dene. Mam said he just slipped away like he was going into a deeper sleep. She arranged the funeral. People came to our house afterwards. We played a CD of Italian songs. There was beer and a big tub of ice cream, and there was crying, and lots and lots of laughter. I ran again that afternoon with Jacksie, and I heard Harry deep inside me: "That's reet, lad! Run! There's a wolf at your tail! Run for your lovely life!"

A week later we ran the Junior Great North Run. We belted round the quayside and across the bridges, hundreds of us running through the sunlight by the glittering river and through the cheering crowds. We raced each other to the finish line, me an' my best mate Jacksie, numbers 2593 and 2594, and Jacksie just got there in front of me. It didn't matter. We stood arm in arm with our medals and certificates. We laughed into Mam's camera. We were young and daft. We'd run the run, and we felt so free and light I really thought we might have run into a bit of Heaven.

Next day she drove us all to Felling. We stood on the bypass and here they came, the thin, fast lines of professionals and champions and record-holders and harriers; then the others – hundreds after hundreds after hundreds of them – puffing and panting, grinning and gasping. Here came the young and the old, the determined and the barmy. They waved and grimaced and sighed and giggled. They squirted water over their heads and over us. There were gorillas and ducks and Supermans and bishops and Frankensteins and Draculas and nurses. And the watchers laughed and yelled.

"You're doing great!" yelled Mam. "Good lad! Good lass! Gan on! Well done!"

And then I saw them. They were kids, too little and young for this run. Three skinny lads in vests and boots that thudded on the road, a dark-haired lass in boots as well and wearing a white dress. They twisted and dodged and threaded their way through the crowd. And I looked at Mam a moment, and her eyes were wide with astonishment and wonder as well. As the four of them passed by, one of the lads lifted his hand high and waved at us and laughed, and then was off again. And they'd gone, lost again in the crowd, a crowd that kept on running past and running past, a crowd we couldn't wait to join, a crowd that seemed like the whole of Tyneside, the whole of the world, all running through the blazing sunlight to the sea.

"Sometimes, usually in winter, I get to wondering, why on earth do I live in the north? It gets so cold! It seems so far away from everywhere! Then I go to the coast, and I start to understand again. As a kid I used to stand at the top of the town and look down to the river, snaking its way past shipyards, warehouses, great cranes, the cluttered riverbanks of Hebburn, Jarrow, Tyne Dock, then flowing between the twin piers at Tynemouth and South Shields to merge with the North Sea. Sometimes the sea shone brilliant blue and sometimes it was almost black. When the wind was right, you could smell it. Seagulls squawked above our streets. When there was fog, the river bells rang, and distant foghorns droned. The lights of ships shone at night like stars. The sea was always with us, part of what we were, and it seemed we always wanted to be near to it.

On bright Sundays our family went on car trips to South Shields. There's a photograph of us all – we've put up a windbreak and spread our blankets on the sand, and the beach all around is packed with folk. Granddad's there, a huge, round, silent man, in his blue serge three-piece suit, his cloth cap, his big black boots, sitting with his legs straight out, puffing on his pipe as always. Grandma, almost as big as he is, in her floral frock, pours tea from a thermos. Dad's still got his glasses on, wearing his green trunks, hands on hips, poised for action. Three kids: Colin, Catherine, me, all in swimming gear. Mam's wrapped up in a cardigan and scarf because of her arthritis. I can hear her words.

"Go on. Run and play. Those that can run should run, those that can play should play."

Soon we'll wade into the water, dive and swim furiously out against the waves. Yes, it'll be bitterly cold, but so what? You quickly get used to it. And yes, we'll shudder and our knees will knock when we run back out again, but Dad'll wrap towels around us and rub us hard to get us warm. And there'll be hot tea, and fish and chips from Frankie's. We'll be in and out of the water all day long, just like dozens of other kids all along the beach. Back then I thought that all seas must be the same. I recall my amazement when I swam in the Mediterranean for the first time.

The best trips took us further. We'd drive north, up the Great North Road and across the Great Northern Coalfield, where pitheads still filled the landscape and men in their thousands still worked underground. We headed to what lay beyond: the beaches and sea villages of Northumberland; Craster, Embleton, Beadnell. These were wild and lovely places: long, pale beaches with rolling dunes behind; the Farne Islands stretching towards the horizon; the ruined castle of Dunstanburgh on its rocky black headland; Bamburgh Castle, high above its village and its beach; Lindisfarne Castle like a mirage way out on its long, low island; distant lighthouses. Everything was on a greater scale: a sea so wide you could see the curve of the earth upon it; the Cheviot Hills rising darkly above the land behind; families scattered sparsely across the great sweeps of sand. Flights of puffins dashed over us, terns danced above the waves, oystercatchers picked at the shore, gannets plunged from on high.

And there were seals, and sometimes dolphins and porpoises, that rolled in the water's surge.

Mam sat in a deckchair unwrapping our picnic while we played war games in the dunes with Dad. On the days I recall, the younger children were now with us: Barbara, who so quickly disappeared, then Mary and Margaret. We lit driftwood fires. We built castles from damp sand and from the weird objects thrown up by the sea. We played in the rock pools, turning stones to find crabs below. And we swam and swam, then took the long drive home again, sleeping and dreaming as we headed back towards Tyneside's light.

As I grew older I left family trips behind. And Dad died, so the trips were no longer possible anyway. But I still went there with my friends. We took the slow bus from Newcastle, or we hitchhiked in pairs. Sometimes we took tents and pitched them at the small duneside site in Beadnell or at Waren Mill beyond Bamburgh. Sometimes we slept in bus shelters or under fishing boats or in soft hollows in the dunes. We took loaves of bread and tins of spam and hunks of cheese. We had bonfires and beach parties. We swam in the shallow waters of Beadnell

Bay while the sun went down over the Cheviots and the sea and sky glowed pink and gold. I fell in love for the first time on Beadnell Beach – with an eighteen-year-old art student. I was fifteen. She must have been humouring me, but we sat by the embers deep into the night. We watched the rays of Longstone Lighthouse sweeping across the sea, the land, the sea again. We talked about the beauty of the moon, gasped in wonder at the stars and at this world, and I gazed at her as the light passed over, and imagined she must be some lovely creature from the sea itself.

I still go there as often as I can, to walk the beaches in that intensely clear air and light. I wade in the water (I don't swim – I understand now how stunningly cold the water is!). I sometimes go there to write, and even when I'm not writing, the words are somehow always there, part of the geography of my imagination.

Stupor Beach, the village in the story, isn't a real place. It exists in a fictional Northumberland – it's a little like Boulmer or Newton or Alnmouth. The girl who tells the tale lives in a version of the wooden shacks that still exist in the dunes around those places. They're beautiful, much-loved rickety creations, built decades ago as holiday homes by long-gone pitmen.

Annie loves the place where she lives. She knows that somehow her true identity comes from the sea. **99**

half a creature from the sea

My mother says that all things can be turned to tales. When she said it first I thought she meant tales like fish tails, but I was wrong. She meant tales like this, tales that are stories. But this tale of mine is very like a fish tail too.

This is about me and my mum, and where we come from. And it's about the man who came one sunlit day and took the picture that hangs on the wall by my bed and shows the truth of me. His name was Benn. So this little tale of mine is some of his tale, too.

I'm Annie Lumsden and I live with my mum in a

house above the jetsam line on Stupor Beach. I'm thirteen years old and growing fast. I have hair that drifts like seaweed when I swim. I have eyes that shine like rock pools. My ears are like scallop shells. The ripples on my skin are like the ripples on the sand when the tide has turned back again. At night I gleam and glow like the sea beneath the stars and moon. Thoughts dart and dance inside like little minnows in the shallows. They race and flash like mackerel further out. My wonderings roll in the deep like seals. Dreams dive each night into the dark like dolphins do, and break out happy and free into the morning light. These are the things I know about myself and that I see when I look in the rock pools at myself. They are the things that I see when I look at the picture the man from America give to me before he went away.

Our house is a shack and is wooden, white and salty. We have a room each at the back with a bed each and a cupboard each and a chair each. We have a kitchen just like everybody has and a bathroom just like everybody has. From the kitchen window we can see the village past the dunes – the steeple of St Mungo's Church, the flag on top of Stupor Primary School, the chimney pot on the Slippery Eel. At the front of the shack is the room with the big wide window that looks out across the rocks and rock pools and the turning sea towards the rocky islands. There are many tales about the islands. Saints lived on one of them long ago. Another of them has an ancient castle on a rock. It's said that mermaids used to live out there, and sing sailors to their doom. We are in the north. It is very beautiful. They say it's cold here, especially the water, but I know nothing else, so it isn't cold to me. Nor to Mum, who loves this place too. She was brought up in the city, but ever since she was a girl she knew her happiness would be found by the sea.

We have a sandy garden with a rickety fence and in the garden are patterns of seashells, and rocks that Mum has painted with lovely faces. Mum sells models made from shells – sailing ships and mermaids' thrones and fancy cottages – in The Lyttle Gyfte Shoppe next to the Slippery Eel. She sells her painted rocks there, too. When I was little I thought that these rocks were the faces of sisters and brothers and friends that had been washed up by the sea for me. This made Mum laugh.

"No, my darling, they are simply rocks."

Then she lifted one of the rocks to her face and showed how all things, even rocks that have lain for ever on an ordinary beach, can be made to turn to tales.

"Hello," she whispered to this rock, which bore the face of a sweet dark-haired little boy on it.

"Hello," it whispered back in such a soft, sweet voice.

"What is your name?" Mum said.

"My name is Septimus Samuel Swift," replied the rock, and Mum held it close to her lips and let it look at me as it told its tale of being the seventh son of a seventh son and of travelling with pirates to Madagascar and fighting with sea monsters in the Sea of Japan.

"Was that you that spoke the words?" I asked.

She winked and smiled.

"How could you think such a thing?" she said.

And she stroked my hair and set off singing a sea shanty, the kind she sings on folk nights in the Slippery Eel.

She finds tales everywhere − in grains of sand she picks up from the garden, in puffs of smoke that drift out from the chimneys of the village, in fragments of smooth timber or glass in the jetsam. She will ask them, "Where did you come from? How did you get here?" And they will answer her in voices very like her own, but with new lilts and squeaks and splashes in them that show they are their own. Mum is good with tales.

Sometimes she visits Stupor Primary School and tells them to the young ones. I used to sit with the children and listen. The teachers there, Mrs Marr and Miss Malone, were always so happy to see me again. "How are you getting on?" they asked, while the children giggled and whispered, "She's dafter than ever."

Long ago, they tried me at Stupor Primary School. It didn't work. I couldn't learn. Words in books stayed stuck to the page like barnacles. They wouldn't turn themselves to sound and sense for me. Numbers clung to their books like limpets. They wouldn't add, subtract or multiply for me. The children mocked and laughed. The teachers were gentle and kind but soon they started to shake their heads and turn away from me. They asked Mum to come in for a chat. I'd been assessed, they said. Stupor Church of England Primary School couldn't give me what I needed. There was another school in another place where there were other children like me. I stood at the window that day while they talked at my back. I looked across the fields behind the school towards the hidden city where that other place would be. It broke my heart to think that I must spend my days so distant from my mum and from the sea. "It's for the best," said Mrs Marr. That was a momentous moment, the moment of my first fall. My legs went weak beneath me and I tumbled to the floor and the whole world went watery and dark, and wild watery voices sang sweetly in my brain and called me to them. I came out of it to find Mum weeping over me and shaking me and screaming my name like I had drifted a million miles away, and the teacher yelling for help into the phone.

I reached up and caught Mum's falling tears.

"It's all right," I whispered sweetly to her. "It was lovely, Mum."

And it was. And I wanted it to happen again. And soon it did. And did again.

There followed months of trips to hospitals and visits to doctors and many, many tries to go past my strangeness and to find the secrets and the truth in me. There were lights shone deep into my eyes, blood sucked out of me, wires fixed to me, questions asked of me. There were stares and glares and pondering and wondering, and medicines and needles, and much talk coming out of many flapping mouths, and much black writing written on much white paper. I was wired wrong. The chemicals that flowed in me were wrong. My brain was an electric storm. There had been damage from disease, from a bang on the head, damage at my birth. It ended with a single doctor, Dr John, in a single room with Mum and me.

"There is something wrong with Annie," said Dr John.

"Something?" asked my mum.

"Yes," said Dr John. He scratched his head. "Something. But we don't know what the something is so we haven't got a name for it."

And we were silent. And I was very pleased. And Mum hugged me.

And Dr John said, "All of us are mysteries, even to us white-coated doctors. And some of us are a bit more of a puzzle than the rest of us."

He smiled into my eyes. He winked.

"You're a good girl, Annie Lumsden," he said.

"She is," said Mum.

"What's the thing," said Dr John, "that you like best in the whole wide world?"

And I answered, "My mum is that thing. That, and splashing and swimming like the fishes in the sea."

"Then that's good," he said. "For unlike most of us, you have the things you love close by you. And you have them there on little Stupor Beach. Be happy. Go home."

So we went home.

A teacher, Miss McLintock, came each Tuesday. I stayed daft.

We went back to Dr John each six weeks or so. I stayed a puzzle.

And we walked on the beach, sat in the sandy garden. Mum painted her rocks and glued her shells, and told her tales and sang her shanties. I swam and swam, and we were happy.

"I sometimes think," I said one day, "I should have been a fish."

"A fish?"

"Aye. Sometimes I dream I've got fins and a tail."

"Goodness gracious!" said Mum.

She jumped up and lifted my T-shirt and looked at my spine.

"What's there?" I said.

She kissed me.

"Nowt, my little minnow," she said.

She looked again.

"Thank goodness for that," she said.

I fell many, many times. It happened in the salty shack, in the sandy garden, on the sandy beach. My legs would lose their strength and I would tumble, and the whole of everything would turn watery, and it was like I really turned from Annie Lumsden into something else – to a fish or a seal or a dolphin. And when the world turned back into sand and rocks and shacks and gardens, I would find Mum sitting close by, watching over me, waiting for me to return, and she'd smile and say, "Where've you been, my little swimmer?" I'd tell her I'd been far away beneath the sea to places of coral and shells and beautifully coloured fish, and she'd smile and smile to hear the words loosened from my tongue as I told my travelling tales. At first, Mum was scared that I would fall and lose myself when I was in the water, and that I would drown and be taken from her, but we came to know that it did not, and would never, happen, for in the water I am truly as I am – Annie Lumsden, seal girl, fish girl, dolphin girl, the girl who cannot drown.

Then there came the sunlit day, the day of Benn. I lay on the warm sand at Mum's side. My body and brain were reforming themselves after a fall. Every time it happened, it was like being born again, like coming out from dark and lovely water and crawling into the world like a little new thing. She was gently stroking my seaweed hair, and we were lost in wonder at the puzzle of myself and the mystery of everything that is and ever was and ever will be. I gazed at her and asked, "Mum, tell me where I come from."

And she started to tell me a tale I knew so well, ever since I was a little one.

"Once," she said, "when I was walking by the sea, I saw a fisherman."

It was the old familiar tale. A man was fishing on the beach, casting his line far out into the water. A handsome man, in green waterproofs and green wellies. A hard-working man from far down south, taking a break at Stupor Beach. Mum passed by. They got to talking. He said he loved the wildness of the north. They got to drinking and dancing in the Slippery Eel. He listened to Mum singing her shanties. He called her a wild northern lass. He wasn't a bad man, not really, just a bit careless and a bit feckless. He stayed a while then quickly went away. He was searched for and never was found. Charles, his name was, or he said it was. To tell the truth, he wouldn't have made a decent daddy. It was better like this, just Mum and me.

But that day I put my finger to her lips.

"No," I told her. "Not that old one. I know that one."

"But it's true."

"Tell me something with a better truth in it, something that works out the puzzle of me."

"Turn you into a tale?"

"Aye. Turn me to a tale."

She winked.

"I didn't want to tell you this," she said. "Will you keep it secret?"

"Aye," I said.

She leant over and looked at my back and stroked my spine.

"Nowt there," she said. "But maybe it's time to tell the truth at last."

And I lay there on the sand beneath the sun, and the sea rolled and turned close by, and seagulls cried, and the breeze lifted tiny grains of sand and scattered them on me. And Mum's fingers moved on me and she breathed and sighed and her voice started to flow over me and into me as sweet as any song, and it found in me a different Annie Lumsden; an Annie Lumsden that fitted with my fallings, my dreams, my body and the sea.

"I was swimming," she murmured. "It was summer, morning, very early – milky white sky, not a breath of wind, water like glass. Most of the world was deep asleep. Not a soul to be seen but a man in the dunes with a dog a quarter of a mile away. Nowt on the sea except a single dinghy slipping northwards. Gannets high, high up and little terns darting back and forth into the water for fish, and nervy oystercatchers by the rock pools. The tide had turned, and it went back nearly soundless, just a gentle lovely hissing as it drained away; and all around, the secrets of the sea were given up – the rocks, the pools, the weeds, the darting creatures and the crawling and the scuttling creatures, the million grains of sand. And as I swam I was drawn backwards and outwards towards the islands, and further from the line of jetsam and my things. Rocks began appearing all around. A great field of seaweed was exposed near by, with stems as thick as children's arms and long brown rubbery leaves."

"Were you young?"

"Fourteen years younger than I am today. A young woman, and strong, with strong, smooth swimming muscles on my shoulders. My things were high up on the beach beyond the jetsam – a red plastic bag, a green towel laid out. I remember as I swam and dived and drifted that I felt stunned, almost hypnotised. I kept trying to look back to the red and green, to remind myself that the solid world was the world I'd come from and that I must swim back again."

She smiled at me.

"You know that feeling?"

I smiled.

"You know I know that feeling."

"And as I drifted I felt the first touch on me."

"The touch?"

"A gentle tender touch. At first I told myself it was the shifting of the seaweed, or the flicker of a little fish fin. But then it came again, like something touching, deliberately touching. Something moved beneath. It moved right under me. A flickering swimming thing, slow and smooth. And it was gone. Then I was suddenly cold, and tiredness and hunger were in me. I stayed calm. I swam breaststroke slowly for the shore. I knelt in the wet sand there and told myself that I'd been wrong, I'd been deceived. I looked back. The sea was empty. I started to walk up the slope of wet sand towards my things. A bird screamed. I looked back again. A little tern hung dancing in the air close behind me, beak pointing down towards the water. It screamed again, then wheeled away as the man appeared from the brown-leaved weed."

"The man?" I whispered.

"He was slender, but with great shoulders on him. Hair slick like weed. Skin smooth and bright like sealskin. He crouched at the water's edge, poised between the land and sea. He cupped his hands and drank the sea. He raised his eyes towards the low milky sun and lowered them again. I could not, dared not, move. I saw the fin folded along his back."

"The fin?"

"I saw his webbed fingers, his webbed toes. His eyes were huge and dark and shining. He laughed, as if the moment brought him great joy. He cupped his hands again and poured water over himself. Then he raised his eyes and looked at me, and after a moment of great stillness in us both, he left the sea and came to me."

"You ran away?"

"There seemed no threat in him, no danger. I looked along the beach. The man with his dog in the dunes was a world away. The man with the fin came out. He knelt a yard away from me."

"Did he speak?"

"There was a sound from him, a splashing sound, like water rather than air was moving in his throat."

"What was he?"

"A mystery. A secret of the sea. He was very beautiful. I saw in his eyes he thought I was beautiful too."

I looked into my mother's eyes. What did I see there? The delight of memories or the delight of her imaginings?

"He was my father?" I whispered.

Her eyes were limpid pools.

"That was the first day," she said. "We moved no closer to each other. We did not touch. I saw the water drying on him, leaving salt on his beautiful skin. When he saw this, he lowered himself into the field of weed again and he was gone. But he came back again on other early milky mornings when the sea was calm. The last day he came, he stayed an hour with me. He came onto the land. We stayed in the shade beneath the rocks. I poured water from the rock pools over him. He was very beautiful, and his liquid voice was very beautiful."

"He was my father?"

"I touched his fin, his webs, his seaweed hair that day. I remember them still against my fingers. That last day we had to hurry back to the water. Despite the rock-pool water, his skin was drying out, his voice was coarse, his eyes were suddenly touched with dread. We ran back to the water. He sighed as he lowered himself into the water. We looked at each other, he from within the sea, I from without. He reached out of the sea to me. His hand was dripping wet, and in it was a shell – this shell."

She opened her palm. In it was a seashell.

"Then he swam away."

I took the shell from her. It was as ordinary as any seashell, as beautiful as any seashell.

"I'll cut the story short," she said. "Nine months later you were born."

"And it's true?"

"And yes, it's—"

We heard a click. We turned. A man was standing close by. He held a camera to his face. He lowered it.

"Forgive me," he said.

He moved towards us.

"But you were so lovely, the two of you there. It was just like the girl had been washed up by the sea."

We said nothing, were still lost in the tale that Mum had told.

"Name's Benn," he said. "I'm passing through.

Staying at your Slippery Eel. Came to take pictures of your islands."

He asked to be forgiven again. He took our silence for coldness, a desire to be left alone. He bowed, continued on his way.

"Please," said Mum.

He paused, looked back at us.

"We have few pictures of ourselves," she said. "Could we have the one you've taken today?"

He grinned, and we came back fully into the world, and Mum asked him into our sandy garden for tea.

He told us of his travels, of faraway cities and mountains and seas. He said he loved the feeling of moving through the world, light and free, moving through other people's stories. Sometimes, he said, when he got his photographs home they were like images from dreams and legends. He laughed with delight at Stupor Bay. He swept his hands towards the sea and the islands.

"Who'd've guessed a place like this was waiting for me."

We said we'd hardly ever moved from this place, and for the first time, as I looked at Benn, I found myself thinking that one day we might move away.

He told us about America, and the kids called Maggie and Jason.

"You got the perfect gifts for them," he said.

He bought a rock painted with the face of a grinning angel and the seashell model of a mermaid.

He sipped his tea and ate his scone. He took more photographs of us and of the shack and the islands.

"I always take home tales as well," he said.

He winked at Mum.

"You look like you might know a tale or two."

That night Mum sang shanties in the Slippery Eel. I sat with Benn and drank lemonade and nibbled crisps. Between the songs he told me of all the seas he'd seen around the world. He dipped the tip of his finger into his beer.

"An atom of the water in this," he said, "was one day in the Sea of Japan." He dipped his finger again. "And an atom of this was in the Bay of Bengal. All seas flow into each other." He licked his finger, laughed. "And into us."

I swigged my lemonade. I felt the Baltic Sea and the Yellow Sea and the Persian Gulf pour through me. Rain pattered on the window at our backs. Mum's voice danced around the music of a flute. We joined in with the choruses. We tapped the rhythms on the table. Benn drank and told me of his home and his family so many miles away.

"I'm happy when I'm there," he said. "But then I travel, and I find so many places to be happy in."

Mum's singing ended and she sat between me and Benn, and her voice was edged with laughter. At closing time we stood outside. The rain had stopped, the clouds had dispersed, the moon was out. The sea thundered on the shore.

"I'll do those pics tonight," he said. "Use night time as a dark room."

He touched Mum's face. He told her she was beautiful. I turned away. They whispered. I think they kissed.

The man with the fin surfaced in my dreams. I spoke the watery words for "dad". He spoke the airy words for "daughter". We swam together to southern seas of coloured fish and coral, to northern seas of icebergs and whales. We swam all night from sea to sea to sea to sea, and when I woke, the sun was up and there were already voices in the garden.

"Come and see," said Mum when I appeared at the door.

Her eyes were wide and shining.

"Come and see," said Benn.

I walked barefoot through the sand. There were photographs scattered on the garden table. Mum held another photograph against her breast.

"You ever see one of these things develop?" said Benn.

I shook my head.

"At first the things in them are seen like secret things, through liquid – like secret creatures glimpsed beneath the sea. They're seen by a strange pale light that shines just like a moon." He narrowed his eyes, gazed at me, smiled. "These are the secrets I glimpsed last night, Annie Lumsden."

Then he stepped away from us, faced the islands, left us alone.

I sifted through the photos on the table: Mum and me, the garden, the shack, the islands. Mum still held the other to her breast.

"Look, Annie," she said.

She bit her lip as she tilted the photograph over at last and let me see.

162

There we were, Mum and me at the water's edge. Like Benn said, it was like I was something washed up by the sea, like Mum was reaching out to help me up, to help me to be born. I saw how seaweedy my hair truly was, how sealy my skin was. Then I looked away, looked back again, but it was true. A fin was growing at my back. Narrow, pale, half formed, like it was just half grown, but it was a fin.

Mum touched me there now, below my neck, between my shoulders. She traced the line of my spine. I touched where she touched, but we touched only me.

"Nothing there?" I whispered.

"Nothing there."

I traced the same line on the photograph. I looked at Benn, straight and tall, facing the islands and the sea.

"Could Benn...?" I started.

"How could you think such a thing?" said Mum.

I looked at her.

"So the tale was true?" I said.

She smiled into my eyes.

"Aye. The tale was true."

And I pushed the photograph into her hand, and ran away from her and ran past Benn, and ran into the waves and didn't stop until I'd plunged down deep and burst back up again and swum and felt the joy of the fin quivering at my back, supporting me, helping me forward.

I looked back, saw Mum and Benn at the water's edge, hand in hand.

"You saw the truth!" I yelled.

"And the truth can set you free!" Benn answered back.

He went away soon afterwards. He said he had a boxer to see in London and maybe an actress in Milan, and there was a war he needed to attend to in the Far East, and... He shrugged. Must seem a shapeless, aimless life to folk like us, he said.

"You get yourself to the States one day," he said to me. "You go and see my Maggie."

I gulped.

"I will," I said, and as I said it I believed it.

"Good. And you can be sure she'll know your tale by then."

We waited with him for a taxi outside the Slippery Eel. He had his painted rock and his shell mermaid. He held Mum tight and kissed her.

I held the shell that Mum had given me.

"Can I...?" I said to her.

She smiled and nodded.

"It's for you," I said to Benn. "And then for Maggie."

He held it to his ear.

"I hear the roaring of the sea. I hear the whisper of its secrets. I hear the silence of its depths." He winked. "I know it's very precious, Annie. I'll keep it safe."

And he kissed me on the brow. Then the taxi came, and the man from America left Stupor Bay.

Afterwards things were never quite the same. Things that'd seemed fixed and hard and hopeless started to shift. Words stopped being barnacles. Numbers were no longer limpets. I started to feel as free on land as I did in the sea. I fell less and less. Mrs McLintock started talking about trying me in a school again. Was it to do with Mum's tales and Benn's photograph? One day I dared to tell Doctor John about the man with the fin. He laughed and laughed. I dared to show him Benn's picture and he laughed again. Then he went quiet.

"Sometimes," he said, "the best way to understand how to be human is to understand our strangeness."

He asked to look at my back. He peeped down beneath the back of my collar.

"Nothing there?" I said.

"Yes. There is an astonishing thing there. A mystery. And sometimes the biggest mystery of all is how a mystery might help to solve another mystery." Then he laughed again. "Pick the sense out of that!" he said.

He smiled.

"Come back in a year's time, Annie Lumsden," he said.

And, of course, it was all to do with simple growing up, with being thirteen, heading for fourteen and beyond. And it was to do with having a mum who thought there was nothing strange in loving a daughter who might be half a creature from the sea.

"The library was a couple of streets away from home: a small branch library, the kind of place we all take for granted, the kind of place that wrong-headed people say has outlived its time. It was close to Felling Square and the Victoria Jubilee pub, where folk gathered around the piano in a side room to sing old songs and tell old tales. And it was just across the street from a patch of grass where I played football as a boy. On one side of the road, as I ran around with Peter, Kev, Colin and Tex, I imagined being a famous footballer. On the other, I dreamed of being a published author. I'd often go into the library at dusk, when we couldn't see the ball any more. As my footballing dreams receded and my writerly dreams increased, I'd go in wearing Levi's and Ben Sherman instead of muddy jeans and battered football boots. I remember reading John Wyndham, Irving Stone, Charles

Williams, Morris West. I thought I looked very modern and sophisticated when I took books from the Recommended New Novels section, though I often felt rather confused. I recall the exact moment I drew Hemingway's short-story collection, *The First Forty-Nine Stories*, from a shelf. I felt a shock of recognition as I opened it and began to read. I'd always known that I wanted to be a writer, and suddenly I had an idea of what kind of writer I wanted to be. This strange serendipitous mixture of discovery and recognition would be repeated in that building as I grew older – the first reading of D. H. Lawrence, for instance, or Stevie Smith.

For most of my teenage years I was fascinated by the paranormal. I loved the library's Religion and Philosophy section, skimming past the books about worthy saints and famous thinkers and seeking the barmier books, to plunder them for information about ghosts and spirits, clairvoyance, spontaneous combustion, levitation, spirit writing, human vanishings – and poltergeists. It was said that the most disturbing books about such matters, too dangerous to be allowed freely into the world, were locked away in a secret room over the hill in the central library in Gateshead. One I especially hungered for became legendary to me: *The Projection of the Astral Body* by Carrington and Muldoon. I never found it. I was also a fan of Hammer horror films, of TV's *The Twilight Zone* and of Dennis Wheatley's weird and terrifying novels, such as *The Devil Rides Out* and *The Ka of Gifford Hillary*. I loved *The Third Eye* by T. Lobsang Rampa. It told of Lobsang's boyhood in the monasteries and mountains of Tibet, his initiation into ancient mysteries, the operation on his skull that opened up his powers of clairvoyance. I dreamed of being him. I walked through the streets of Felling trying to feel possessed by him. Then it turned out that Lobsang was a hoaxer. He was Cyril Hoskin, a plumber's son from Devon, and he'd never stepped foot outside the British Isles. How disgraceful! But it didn't matter to me. Wasn't that what writers were supposed to do – make things up, make lies seem like truth, create new versions of themselves? I read a lot about Buddhism, chanted the Upanishads to myself, practised yoga, stood on my head beside my bed, breathed *Om Om Om*, tried to meditate. I spent night after night attempting to travel in the astral plane, just like Lobsang did. No success. If only I'd been able to get my hands on that book by Carrington and Muldoon...

The world was striving to be new. All across Tyneside, the old dark terraced streets were being torn down. Estates in bright new brick and pebbledash, like Leam Lane Estate in this story, were spreading out across the open spaces. New tower blocks rose all over the landscape. Politicians talked about a world of white-hot technology; we were about to send a man to the moon; *Tomorrow's World* on the BBC told us about cures for cancer, driverless cars, paper pants, self-cleaning clothes, giant carrots, robots, laser beams, jetpacks. What a future was to come!

But the past, and ancient superstitions and religious beliefs, kept reasserting themselves. St Patrick's Church was packed with people of all ages. I was an altar boy until I was about fifteen, serving at Masses and weddings and funerals. Like most of my friends, I continued to take Communion and go to confession. Every year a plane full of St Patrick's parishioners flew to Lourdes in France with the priest to see the miracles and healings, and to pray to Our Lady to be healed themselves. Many of my relatives – my grandma, my Uncle Maurice, my Auntie Anne – went on these trips. They came home, their eyes shining, carrying Our Lady-shaped bottles of holy water that we used along with medicines to treat coughs and colds, and much more serious diseases. And there were plaster statues and prayer cards, and garish plastic grottos with lights that flashed around Our Lady and the kneeling St Bernadette.

Tales and rumours showed how difficult it was for some folk to adjust to the new world. They kept ponies in their brand-new dining rooms and chickens on their balconies. Old women read each other's tea leaves in Dragone's. There were tales of weeping statues. Superstitions abounded: don't walk under ladders, don't cross on the stairs, never open an umbrella indoors, don't spill salt, always leave a house through the same door by which you entered... There were tales of ghosts and hauntings in the brightly lit brick and pebbledashed homes. As in the story of Joe Quinn and his poltergeist, a film crew did try to record the ghosts that walked at night and terrified a family in a brand-new house on Leam Lane Estate.

And, of course, despite the hopes inspired by some of the speakers on *Tomorrow's World*, death and sickness didn't go away. Despite modern medicine and surgery, Lourdes water and prayer, I lost my dad to cancer when I was fifteen. And just like Davie, the narrator of the story, I lost a sister, too. Barbara was only a year old when she died; I was seven. "

joe quinn's poltergeist

So, I'm in Holly Hill Park with Geordie Craggs. We're watching the lasses play tennis when Joe Quinn saunters through the gate.

"Pretend we've not seen," I say.

No good. He heads straight for us. He's got a packet of coconut mushrooms and he's holding them out.

Stupid Geordie takes one. He even says ta.

"Have another," says Joe. "Gan on. I've got tons."

Maria Caldwell jumps high and grunts, and smashes the ball straight into the fence.

"Prefer a Midget Gem?" says Joe to me. "I've got some of them and all."

"No," I mutter.

"Nowt wrong with being friendly," he says.

"I'll have one," says Geordie, and Joe smiles and sits down on the grass close by.

It's the middle of the afternoon, the middle of the holidays, and hot as hell. The air's shimmering and you can feel the heat rising from the earth. Josephine Minto wipes her forehead with a towel, swigs from a bottle of lemonade, or something, and gets ready to serve. She looks over to check I'm still watching. She's the best – it's obvious. She'll win easily. The yellow ball's a blur as it flashes over the net. Maria doesn't even see it. I want to cheer, but I don't.

"I've got a poltergeist," says Joe as Josephine gets ready to serve again.

"A what?" says Geordie.

"Poltergeist."

I spit. Typical Joe bliddy Quinn.

"What's one of them?" asks Geordie.

"Kind of ghost," says Joe. "Davie'll know. Davie?"

I say nothing.

"There was stuff flying all over the house the other

night," Joe goes on. "Cups and plates and stuff."

"Stuff flying?" says Geordie.

"That's what they do, poltergeists. They send everything barmy."

Geordie's mouth dropped open.

"There's a window smashed and all, and a door's hangin' off its hinges."

"Hell's teeth."

"Aye," says Joe. "Me mam says it's a sign of disturbance in the spirit world. Or the house has entered some kind of vortex or something."

"Vortex," says Geordie.

"Geordie, man," I mutter.

"I knaa," says Joe. "Hard to believe, eh? Mebbe you should come and see for yoursels?"

"Could we?" says Geordie.

"That is if you're not too scared."

"Course we're not, are we, Davie? When should we come?"

"It starts happenin' round about teatime. So come for tea. Come today. I'll tell me mam to put some extra chips on, eh?"

Geordie's all wide-eyed.

"Aye," he says. "Alreet, Joe."

Joe gets up and walks away.

"Flying cups!" says Geordie.

I sigh. Stupid Geordie. Joe turns round and lobs a few Midget Gems at us. Geordie catches none of them and starts picking them out of the grass. Josephine squeals and yells, "Game and first set to Miss Minto!"

"Broken windows!" Geordie gasps. "Do you think we'll really see it?"

"Aye," I say. "We'll see it's just daft Joe Quinn and his even dafter mother."

"Worth having a look though, eh? You've said yourself that the world's a weird place."

"But I didn't mean Joe Quinn, and I didn't mean bliddy poltergeists."

He jams a few gems into his mouth.

"At least we'll get some chips."

Joe Quinn. What a dreamer. Take his dad, for instance. If he wasn't a hit man in Arizona, he was robbing banks in China; he'd stashed away a million quid in Chile for Joe's future; he'd send flight tickets for Joe when he was eighteen and they'd live the lives of outlaws. Turned out he was in Durham Prison for beating a bloke half to death on Newcastle Quayside one Friday night.

"Aye," said Joe when we found out. "But it took half a dozen coppers to bring him in, and he only done it because the bloke impugned me mother."

"Impugned?" I said.

"That's the word. And there's no way me dad could let that happen to me mam."

The mother. She was another one. She'd been on tours with the Rolling Stones; she'd danced for the King of Thailand; she'd dined with Nikita Khrushchev.

"So what you doing on Leam Lane Estate?" I said.

"It's just till I get some education under me belt. And till me dad gets out. Then she says the world's our oyster."

Joe Quinn. He was the one who laughed when my sister died. He was the one who asked what the blubbing was for. I don't think he even remembers. It was years ago. To him it was just nowt. And now it's poltergeists. Hell's teeth.

Anyway, we go. We wait till Josephine's got game, set and match. She looks at me and I look at her, and we both hesitate, and I wonder, should I tell Geordie to go to Joe's himself? But I don't, and we head off. No need to tell our mams. Mine'll think I'm at Geordie's, his'll think he's at mine. We pass the new priest, Father Kelly, as we leave the park. He's standing under a cherry tree, in his long black robe, smoking. He waves at us. We wave back.

We walk down The Drive. We're parched, so we stop at Wiffen's and buy some pop.

"We're bliddy daft," I say. "It's a wild goose chase."

"Flying plates, man!" says Geordie. "Smashed windows!"

He starts on about the ghost they had at Wilfie Mack's house a couple of years back, the one where the telly reporter and the cameraman stayed all night to watch for it.

"And they saw absolutely nowt," I say.

"Aye, but they said they definitely felt something. And there was that weird shadow. Remember, Davie?"

I shrug.

"And look what happened to Wilfie just two weeks later."

"Aye," I say finally and shudder, despite the baking heat.

We reach the estate and turn into Sullivan Street. Lots of the front doors are wide open. Some of them have got stripy plastic curtains dangling, to keep the flies out. A gang of half-naked kids are playing football further down the street. Their ball comes bouncing at us and they scream at us to kick it back. I do, and back it flies in a dead straight line.

No sign of anybody at Joe's. The curtains are closed at the front and the door's shut. We head down the side of the house. The back garden's baked mud and clay, hard as stone. It's dead quiet. Then suddenly the back door's wide open and Joe's there, grinning. Mrs Quinn's behind him with her arms crossed.

"Hello, boys," she says. "Why don't you step inside?"

The kitchen table's set. There's orange squash, tomato sauce and a big pile of bread and butter.

"Joe said you'd like some chips," she says.

She slides cut potatoes into boiling fat.

"Sit down," she says. "Could be a while."

"That's right," says Joe. "Doesn't just come to order."

She laughs, and tousles his hair.

"Do your mams know you're here?" she says.

"No," we tell her.

She shakes the chips.

"You're the one whose sister died, aren't you?" she says to me.

I flinch.

"Aye," I say.

"Any sign of her since?"

"What?"

She smiles.

"Never mind," she says. "Look. That's the broken window Joe told you about."

It's the narrow pane at the top of the kitchen window. I imagine a knife flying through it, or a fork.

"I should put Sellotape or something over it," she says. "But it's nice to have a bit of breeze in this heat. Joe, show them the plates, son."

He opens the drawer in the table, and takes out some broken bits of cups and plates, and puts them in front of us.

"Ever seen owt like that?" he asks. He holds up a jagged bit in wonder.

"They were ordinary proper plates," he says, "and then…"

There's a record player on the kitchen bench. His mam drops a record onto the turntable. A voice and a guitar start wailing.

"You won't have heard this," she tells us. "They're underground, from California."

She starts dancing, swinging her arms around her head and her hair falls back and forward over her shoulders. She's got her eyes closed, as if she's in a dream. I can't help watching. She's not like any other mams I know. A slice of bread and butter flies over her head and slaps onto the kitchen wall. Geordie gasps and curses and looks at me, but nobody else says anything. It's like Joe and his mother haven't seen.

Soon the chips are done.

Mrs Quinn tips them into a bowl, leans over the table and puts them onto our plates.

"Tuck in," she says.

I make a butty, a layer of chips and tomato sauce between two slices of bread. Lovely. Then another slice of bread and butter flies across the room.

Geordie bursts out laughing.

"That was you!" he says to Joe.

Joe just shakes his head and goes on eating. His mam leans over us. Her hair is yellow as corn. I can feel her breath on me.

"Maybe you have to believe that," she says to Geordie. "But Davie, I think you're different. What did you see? How do you explain it?"

There's no way to answer. I take another bite of my

butty. Geordie's sniggering at my side. Mrs Quinn rests her hand on my head.

"Just be quiet for a moment," she says to me. "Relax and try to feel what is happening in this place. Feel what Joe and I feel, even on a sunny afternoon in an ordinary house on an ordinary estate. There is a disturbance. We are passing through some kind of vortex. Can you feel it, Davie?"

I can feel that Geordie wants to get away but I can't move.

Mrs Quinn moves her hand over my scalp and I go dizzy.

"Just imagine," she murmurs, "what it is like at night, when the chairs are shifting and the doors are banging and…"

Geordie snorts.

There's a dog howling somewhere. There's the sound of something breaking upstairs.

Mrs Quinn takes her hand away. She stares at the ceiling.

"Did you sense something?" she says softly.

I don't know how to answer.

"You did," she says. "I know it. Only special people can. We are surrounded by strange forces."

Geordie snorts again. He stuffs some chips into his mouth.

"Howay, Davie," he says. "Time to go."

"You're a churchgoer, aren't you, Davie?" says Mrs Quinn. "Yes, I know you are. You understand things like this, don't you? Things beyond our ken."

"Ken who?" mutters Geordie.

"And you have your priests," Mrs Quinn goes on. "Maybe you could talk of this to your priest. Maybe he could come and rid us of our poltergeist and bring this house some peace. Maybe he'll feel it's his duty."

I get up. A few chips bounce off the opposite wall.

She holds my arm a moment. She breathes into my ear.

"You'll ask him, will you, Davie? Just for me?"

I try to imagine telling all this to Father O'Mahoney. I see him rolling his eyes at such nonsense, telling me to go for a good long run or to say ten Hail Marys and a Glory Be.

"Aye," I mutter.

We head for the door.

"Duck!" yells Joe.

A plate or something crashes into the wall.

"It's getting worse!" he cries.

"Begone!" shouts Mrs Quinn. "Begone, ye demon poltergeist!"

I run with Geordie past the footballing kids. He's laughing his head off. I'm trembling in fright.

I dream that night, of course I do. There's flying chips and bread and butter and knives and forks, and Geordie's howling like a dog. Josephine's hitting a tennis ball again and again over my head. Mam wakes me in the morning and I jump as if she's a ghost come up from Hell to get me.

I ask her straight away, like it's part of the dream, "Did she ever come back, Mam?"

"What on earth's the matter with you?" she says. She strokes my head gently. "And did who ever come back?"

"Barbara," I say.

"Barbara?"

"Yes."

"Oh, son. What kind of dream were you having?"

"She couldn't ... could she?"

"No."

"Could she?"

Mam goes still.

"There was just the one time…"

She looks away. She touches her cheek with her fingertip the way she does.

"What time?" I whisper.

"I felt her touch me, son, on my shoulder. A couple of weeks after…"

I wait. I watch.

"I heard her whispering, 'I'm all right, Mammy. Don't worry, Mammy, I'm all right.'"

"Did you see her?"

"No. And it was just the once. Maybe it was just a… But it felt like her, son. It made me feel… I didn't feel so desolate." She sighs. "I didn't tell you. I didn't want to upset you."

Then her eyes are shining as she smiles.

"Look at that sun," she says. "What a summer we're having, eh?"

"Aye."

"You'll be seeing Geordie, eh?"

"Aye."

She smiles again.

"She'll always love us, won't she?" she says. "And we'll always love her."

She leans down to kiss my cheek.

"Come on, then," she says. "Up and out and off you go. Have fun."

"Did you believe it, mam?"

"That she came back for a moment? I felt her and heard her so I suppose I have to. Come on. Up and out. The day's already flying by."

I head for Geordie's but I keep scanning the streets for Josephine. I pass by the park and listen for the pop and thump of racquets and balls. When I turn the corner by the Co-op I bump right into Father Kelly in his long black gown. He's the new young priest, straight from Ireland. He's leaning against the wall of the shop like he's been bliddy lying in wait for me. He laughs and takes a deep drag of his cigarette.

"Having a quick fag, Davie," he says. "Getting up me strength to pay a visit to Mrs Malone."

"Oh," I say.

"She'd test the faith of St bliddy Francis himself," he says. He makes a quick sign of the cross. "'Scuse the French. Off to Geordie's, are you?"

"Yes, Father."

"Good lad. Make the most of it." He holds out his cigarette. "Want a drag or two?"

186

I don't move. He laughs again.

"I know some of you boys get started early."

He smokes then flicks the cigarette away. I want to move on but I can't. It seems like he's the same.

"You know her?" he says. "The Missus Malone?"

"A bit, Father."

"They say she's lapsed," he tells me. "They say other things."

He lights another cigarette.

"You've heard?" he asks.

"Dunno, Father."

"Best not to. These things are sent to test us."

He shields his eyes from the sun's glare and looks around. I still can't move.

"Father," I say.

"Yes?"

"I think I'm starting to believe in things I shouldn't."

"Protestantism?" he says.

"No, Father."

"Atheism?"

"No, Father."

I hear kids laughing in the park.

"It's never Sunderland!" he exclaims.

"No, Father."

"Well, that all seems pretty safe. Your seat in Heaven is assured."

He moves his hand through the air in blessing.

"Things like ghosts," I blurt out. "Things like that."

"Jesus, ye'd be at home in Ireland, lad."

"Poltergeists."

"They're the best, eh? Flinging stuff here, there and everywhere."

"So they're real?"

"Real? What's real? The air's real. Can you see it? God's real. Can you see him? And the Devil. Or mebbe God and the Devil is all of this. You and me and that tree over there, and those birds above and the wall of the bliddy Co-op." He sighs. "That's heresy, though. Forget I said it."

I catch the scent of wine or something on his breath. Maybe altar wine from this morning's Mass.

"Poltergeists," he says. "Now I'd like to see one of those boys in action."

"Would you?" I say.

"Who wouldn't?"

He takes a deep drag on his cigarette, then drops it suddenly, stamps it out, and heads off to Mrs Malone's.

★   ★   ★

Geordie wants to play football and we kick around for a bit in his front street, but I'm hopeless. I can't help it. I'm drawn back to Joe's. Can't think about anything else. I tell him I think we should go again.

"Did you not see?" Geordie says. "It was Joe chucking all the stuff around. It's just Joe bliddy Quinn being Joe bliddy Quinn. And she's letting him."

"There was something," I say.

"So now you're sticking up for him when you're the one who always says he's just a freak."

"I'm not sticking up for him! It's nothing to do with him. It's—"

He snorts.

"Oh, I impugn you!" he mocks. "I am so sorry. We are surrounded by strange forces!"

He chips the ball into the air, knees it, heads it then lashes it into the front garden wall.

He leaps high and punches the air.

"Goaaaaal!" he yells. "Right into the top corner of the vortex!"

Then he turns to me.

"You won't catch me in that damn loony bin again," he says.

I turn away.

"Begone!" he yells, and he screeches like a demon.

I go up onto the top fields and lie there, and the long grass waves above my eyes. The sun's bright, the sky's blue, the larks are singing wild. Sometimes a thin cloud drifts by. I sit up and look down at everything: the town, its square, its streets, its new estates, its steeples and parks. Hear the drone of traffic and engines. The dinning of caulkers in the shipyards on the river far below. Kids squealing somewhere. I'm sure I can hear the pop of tennis balls. I see a lad and his lass walk through the grass a hundred yards away then lie down in it together.

The heat comes from the earth and from the sky. The distant sea's dark blue. Is this everything, all this stuff around me? Is this where everything happens? I think of Barbara, the way she used to giggle and wave as I arrived home from school. I think of Josephine Minto, her eyes, her hair, the way her legs move as she leaps, the way Barbara would have turned out if she'd not died. I think of Joe Quinn's poltergeist. I think of God. I watch the shadows getting longer down in the pale streets of Leam Lane. Somebody cries in joy or pain, and after an age I get up and move on. My body moves but I feel like I'm not part of it. What am I? Body, brain, soul, or all of these? Infant, boy, man, or all those things together? Or nothing, just nothing at all?

"Davie!" yells somebody, some kid playing with other kids on the playing fields. I wave but don't know who it is.

"Davie!" he yells again, and keeps on yelling as I walk on, "Davie, Davie Davie!" till the word means nowt; is just a sound, just part of all the sounds around me and inside me. *Davie, Davie, Davie…*

Time's flying and it's already darkening as I enter Sullivan Street again. I don't go to the house. I play football with the half-naked skinny kids till we can hardly see the ball and the lights in the houses are being switched on. It must be late. Mothers start calling and one by one the kids begin to disappear. I smell food cooking. There're songs and laughter. I watch Joe's house. Did a curtain move? Did I hear something breaking? Then the screaming starts. High-pitched, incomprehensible. It must be Mrs Quinn. I realize there's someone at my shoulder, a woman, and other women and men gathering in the gloom, and knots of kids. Then there's the sound of breaking glass.

"It's a bliddy madhouse," someone mutters.

"And wait till the bliddy bloke gets out," another says.

A little girl starts crying.

Then Joe's outside with us, hurrying from the house. There's a dark patch on his brow that must be blood. He comes straight to me.

"Davie!" he gasps. "Come and see!"

I step back.

"Come on!" he says. "It's like it's getting wilder just for you!"

"What do you mean, for me?"

"I knew you must be here. It's like you bring more energy or something. It's like—"

Behind him there's a crash, another splintering of glass. He tugs my arm. I break free, turn and run from Sullivan Street. I hear him calling my name and laughing as I go. Thrown stones skitter and skip around my feet.

I meet Father Kelly in the street again, two days later. This time he's stepping out of the Columba Club, and this time there's beer on his breath. He's still in his black robes in this August heat. A wooden crucifix dangles from his throat.

He laughs.

"We meet again," he says. "Mebbe the good Lord has a plan for us."

He lights a cigarette.

"Missus Malone and I had a grand little meet," he says.

"That's good, Father."

"Aye. She's a one, eh? And how's all that believing stuff you were on about?"

"The same, Father."

"Don't think too much. That's probably the answer." He winks. "Or have a pint or two."

"I've got a poltergeist, Father," I say.

"Have you now?"

"Yes, Father."

"There's a thing. And where might you be keeping this poltergeist?"

"In Sullivan Street, Father."

He smiles. He pats my shoulder.

"Such lives you lads lead," he says.

"Will you come and see it, Father?"

"Let's see. I have to get the host to Mollie Carr.

There's Maurice Gadd that's had the stroke. Catechism catch-up for a husband that's decided to convert. And those wild McCracken bairns! They need to know the truth about the fires of Hell… But I'm sure I can fit in a poltergeist or three."

"It usually starts late afternoon."

He tousles my hair.

"Late afternoon. Sullivan Street. I'll see you there."

He winks and taps his nose.

"And we'll not be mentioning this to the Father O'Mahoney, will we, Davie?"

"No, Father."

"No indeed."

I join in with a great football match on the high field. There's dozens of us, from little kids to teenagers, rushing back and forward on the green. Must be twenty, twenty-five a side. We run, we yell, do long sliding tackles, leap high to try to head the flying ball. I take a shot that swerves just past the post. Another wallops into Billy Campbell's belly. I have a little run, beat one man, then two, rush on, tumble, jump up again. I lose myself. I'm not me – I'm a proper player. I'm at Wembley, at St James's Park, and all the others are too. We struggle for our teams. One side leads and then the other, then the first fights back again. In dashing through the field and playing with the ball we change ourselves, we change the world. Our muscles ache, our hearts thump, our lungs are fit to burst. We laugh and groan and cheer and yell.

"YEEESS! YEEEESSSSSS! OH YES!"

And afterwards I walk with Geordie through the light. In the sky above the sea there's something sparkling. The larks sing high over our heads. A butterfly lands on Geordie's collar. I gently touch it free and we watch it fly away. He tells me that he heard Josephine asking about me, and that he sees why I say she's beautiful. I tell him I'm trying to sort out the poltergeist.

"Sort it out?"

"What it is. Why it's there."

"It's him. It's her. That's all."

"Father Kelly is going to look."

"To look and then to say it's all a load of crap."

"We'll see."

I hurry home and grab some bread and cheese, and hurry out again.

"No time to stop?" says Mam.

I shake my head.

"Places to go," she sighs. "People to see. A life to live."

I hesitate a second, catch her eye.

"OK?" she whispers.

"Aye. OK."

"We quiver on the edge of an immensity," says Father Kelly. We've encountered each other on the road down to Leam Lane. "It is outside us and within. I knew it as a boy, looking at the sky, looking at the starsh, looking at myshelf." His voice is slipping. "I knew it looking out upon the ocean from the hillsh of Kerry." He lights a cigarette. "Don't get into theshe," he says. He takes a little silver flask from his robe and sips from it. "Don't get into drink," he says. His hand is shaking as he points across the earth, the sea, the sky. "I shee it here as you do. I know you shee how it all quakes and shines and trembles, Davie. I know you hear how it hums and shings."

We walk on. We come to Sullivan Street.

"And don't get into God," he whispers, as if he's speaking to himself. "Don't get into none of that."

★   ★   ★

We are unexpected, of course. Mrs Quinn is lying on a battered sun lounger in the back garden with her skirt pulled up to her thighs. Underground music drifts from the house. Joe is nowhere to be seen.

"I brought a priest," I say unnecessarily.

"Did you now?" says Mrs Quinn.

She regards the man at my side, his long black gown, black sandals, crucifix, bare white calves.

"My name ish Father Kelly," he says.

"Rosemary Quinn," she says.

"Davie told me of your dishturbance."

"Did he now? Can I get you a cup of tea? Or there may be a bottle or two of beer around." She stands up. She tugs the straps of her sundress back up onto her shoulders. "So have you come to calm it?"

He shrugs.

"It was not part of my training, Mrs Quinn, but there ish maybe something that I…"

"Joe!" calls Mrs Quinn. "Joe! Davie's here with the priest to see the poltergeist!"

A cup flies down from an open upstairs window and bounces in the grass.

"OK!" yells Joe. "I'm coming down."

Inside the kitchen, fragments of broken crockery lie

against the skirting boards. There's a new little jagged hole in one of the windows. Strips of wallpaper are curling from the walls. Joe comes downstairs with an orange Elastoplast on his brow.

"And look at this," he says.

He lifts up a chair and shows that one of its legs has been ripped off.

"Just came down one morning and there it was like this," he says.

His mother stares at the priest.

"What is doing this?" she says. "What are these strange forces?"

She holds out a bottle of beer and a glass to him. He pours carefully. He drinks. She stands close, leans up to him.

"Is it God?" she whispers. She widens her eyes. "Or is it that Devil, Father?"

A knife clatters against the wall. The priest flinches. He looks at Joe, at me. He drinks. There's a sound of something shattering upstairs.

We all stand silent, we listen and watch. A dog howls. The sun is sinking over the estate. I am poised to be terrified, to be illuminated, for the forces to work again. For a while nothing more happens. There's just stillness, silence and the immensity within and outside us. We all sigh.

"You must be hungry, Father," says Mrs Quinn. "I'll put some chips on, shall I?"

"Aye," he says, "I have had a day without much nourishment in it."

"And you lads," she says. "Why don't you go outside, enjoy the last rays of the sun. And give that poor mutt a drink."

We do. We perch on the edge of the sun lounger.

"Is it you?" I say.

"Course it's not. In fact, according to me dad, it's him."

"What?"

"We went to see him in jail on Sunday. What a bliddy nightmare place. He said he'd been focusing his thoughts on the house, making things move by the power of his will."

"What? Why?"

Joe holds out a packet of cigarettes to me. I don't take one. He lights one for himself and blows the smoke across my face.

"I think he's mebbe trying to harm us," he says. "He's coming up with all these tales of what me mother's doing while he's inside. I think he's goin' bliddy mad, Davie. You should see how wild his eyes are now. You should see how scared the officers are of him. He's turnin' to a bliddy monster! How's Josephine?"

"Eh?"

"You shagged her yet?"

A clod of earth flies up from the ground and over our heads.

"That was you!" I cry.

"No, it wasn't. Have you, eh?"

I'm about to go for him but his mother's at the door. The chips are done. We go inside and sit at the little Formica table. Father Kelly's into the second bottle of beer. The air is golden through the broken window. The chips, the ketchup and the bread are all delicious. My mug of tea trembles as I lift it. It tilts and tea splashes down onto the table top. Mrs Quinn puts her hand over mine.

"You OK, Davie?" she says.

"Aye."

Father Kelly smiles.

"The boy – like all boys – ish prey to great forces, great hungers, great emotionsh."

He chews his chips. He swigs his beer. He doesn't

flinch as a plate spins from the table to the floor. He leans forward and speaks in hushed tones, as if to communicate with nobody but himself.

"In Ireland," he says, "such things were known, before the dead hand of the Church took us in its dreadful grip."

He laughs. He stands up and flings his plate with its last few chips against the kitchen wall.

"Forgive me, Mrs Quinn," he says. "I will pay for the damage, of course."

"Oh, no need, Father."

He laughs again, loudly. He picks up his glass and flings that against the wall too.

"Another beer, perhaps?" says Mrs Quinn. "You boys…"

Joe takes my arm and leads me out. He shuts the door. We start fighting straight away. We punch each other, grab each other's throats, shove each other's heads onto the ground. We struggle and kick and roll and grunt. At last I get him properly down and I straddle him. Blood from my nose drips down onto him.

"I'll effing kill you, Quinn," I say.

"Why's that, then?" he snarls.

"Because you don't know bliddy why, that's why!"

"What a load of bliddy crap! Go on, then. Do it! Ha!" His face twists into a sneer. "You haven't got the bliddy guts."

I spit on him. He spits upwards at me. Saliva and snot and blood dangle and drop in the air between us. We struggle on, but in the end it all disgusts me and I roll away, groaning and cursing at the sky.

Joe gets up onto the sun lounger. He lights a cigarette.

A full moon's already shining in the sky. There are moths already flying. Bats already flicker in the white late light. We say nowt for ages.

"It drives you mad," I say at last.

"What does?" answers Joe.

"The bliddy moon."

"Bliddy thing!" He shakes his fist at it. "Bliddy stupid round thing shining in the sky!"

I watch it shining down on him.

"You ever want to kill everything?" he says.

"Aye."

"Really?"

"Aye. Every bliddy thing that lives and that has ever lived."

"And God?"

"Aye, him. Pummel him to bliddy dust."

"Aye! Ha! Aye!"

I look at him through the moonlight. His eyes are glittering like mine must be. His face is shining. His heart is bursting like mine, and his mind is yearning and his soul is soaring. We know we're just the same. And in the weird mix of silver light and dark between us, things begin to rise. Just little things – broken stems of weeds, tiny twigs, fallen flowers, scraps of paper, fragments of dust and bits of stone. They rise and hang there, shining where the moonlight touches them, as if it is the light that holds them suspended. They shift and slowly spin as the air moves past them. It only lasts a few short seconds then they fall again and there's only emptiness where they once were, and the possibility that things like them might rise again.

Joe breathes smoke into the moonlight.

"Was that you?" he says.

But there's no way to answer, we both know that.

The darkness darkens and the moonlight brightens. I know it's time to move but I don't, not until the priest comes out again.

"Still here, Davie?" he asks.

"Aye, Father."

"So let's go off together, eh?"

203

"Aye, Father."

He laughs.

"You have a splendid poltergeist, Joe Quinn," he says.

Joe laughs too. Upstairs, beyond the open window, something breaks.

"Thanks, Father," says Joe.

Inside, Mrs Quinn is singing.

I walk with the priest out of Leam Lane. We take the road between the dark fields and the town. We hear laughter, sudden cries, the hooting of an owl, the beating of the engines at the heart of everything.

"There is no God," says Father Kelly.

"I know that, Father."

"There is no Heaven to go to. And no Hell."

"I know that, Father."

"There's only us, and this."

"I know that, Father."

"But what an usness, and a thisness." He laughs at himself. "I couldn't have said such words an hour or two ago."

We separate at The Drive and go our different ways. I walk beneath dense trees. Nervous birds flutter in the nests above my head. I feel the thinness of me, the littleness of me, and the vastness and the weirdness of me. I become the darkness all around, I become the night. Tomorrow I will be a different Davie, and I will be the day. Suddenly I know the poltergeist is me. It is in me. It is me in fury at Joe Quinn, me in love with Josephine, me in hatred of the non-existent God; it is me in dread and bliddy grief, it is me in wonder at this place, this earth, this moon, this night. I know the poltergeist is all of us, raging and wanting to scream and to fight and to start flinging stuff; to smash and to break. It is all of us wanting to be still, to be quiet, to be in love, to be at peace.

I walk onward, begin to disappear, to truly be the dark.

And as I move through the black shadows cast by the dense overhanging shrubs of Sycamore Grove, I know that this should be the moment when I feel the gentle touch on my shoulder, and hear the longed-for whisper in my ear.

Of course they do not come.

Her touch will only come in dreams.

The whisper will be heard in stories that I'll come to tell.

She will be given endless life in memories and in words.

I walk on below the streetlights towards the square, towards my home.

Tomorrow I'll play football with Geordie and the lads on the high fields.

Soon I will kiss Josephine Minto beneath the cherry tree in Holly Hill Park.

Father Kelly will return to Ireland, where he will be unfrocked.

Mr Quinn will kill a cellmate and will stay in jail.

Joe Quinn's poltergeist will disappear.

And there will be other occurrences, an immensity of them, and the world and all that's in it will continue to hum and sing, to shake and shine, to hold us in its darkness and its light.

"By the time I was nineteen, I was at university. I'd grown my hair, I wore jeans and cheesecloth shirts, I listened to Pink Floyd and Leonard Cohen, and read Ginsberg and Dostoyevsky. I lived on a student grant – a very generous one, because my mother was a widow raising the family on her own. At the end of my first year I got a summer job in Swan Hunter's shipyard on the Tyne, and used the money from that to hitchhike away for a month in Greece with my girlfriend, Rhona. We met hundreds of others like ourselves: young, free, educated Western Europeans who roamed across the continent, who believed in love and peace. We slept on beaches, drank retsina, ate souvlaki, lay in the sun, swam in the warm Mediterranean sea.

When my dad had been nineteen, in 1942, the Second World War had already been going for three years. Both his education and his working life stopped. He was enlisted into the signals corp, taken away from the streets of Tyneside for military training in Glasgow. Then he was sent to the jungles of Burma to fight the Japanese. He wouldn't get home again until 1946. He married in 1948, and then we children began to come into the world.

He didn't talk much about his experiences of war and I don't remember asking him much about it. Maybe he encouraged me to think that as the days of war were gone, and it had all happened in a different age, I should keep on looking forward, moving forward. He believed in education, in progress. Like most men of his generation my father wanted his children to create a new and better world.

When I was growing up, the evidence of war was all around. There were ration books in Grandma's cupboard, and stifling gas masks that we used to wear to pretend we were monsters. I had a pair of trousers made from the blackout curtains that had once hung at my grandmother's window as the German bombers droned overhead. There was an abandoned gun emplacement beyond the playing fields, where mighty cannon had pointed towards the North Sea. On beautiful Northumbrian beaches, rows of huge concrete cubes stood below the dunes, designed to impede invasion from the sea. They're still there, all these years later, sinking inch by inch into the earth. So are the little pillboxes with horizontal slits for machine gunners. We used all these sites for our childhood games, and they infected our play. We played "Die the Best", shrieking with pain, flinging ourselves across the dunes, tottering in death agonies as the invaders came in. In the gardens, streets and fields we played "Bomb Berlin", Germans versus English, English versus Japanese. We yelled out, *Achtung! Schnell! Banzai!* and *Die, you rat!* and ran with our arms spread wide like spitfire's wings, calling out "Ratatatatat!"

In the adult world, deadlier games were played. Nuclear arsenals multiplied. Bombs were tested. Nervous and paranoid fingers hovered close to the button that could bring destruction to us all. The Iron Curtain was up. Bombs were raining down on Vietnam. Many thought that war had not really ended: that the peace in which we grew up was just a breathing space; that the worst was yet to come.

This is a story about the post-war world. The traumas of Eastern Europe are brought to Felling in the person of an East German boy, Klaus Vogel. The heroes of the story are the outsiders, Klaus Vogel and Mr Eustace. I never knew any East German kids, but there were quite a number of Poles growing up among us – their families had escaped the invading Nazis just before the war. It was only later that I began to understand the deadly perils these families had lived through.

I knew about conchies – conscientious objectors – and how they were treated with contempt. Sometimes my friends and I wondered, what if war came back again? Would we join up? Would we fight, or would we be conchies? Would we be different from our fathers?

My dad died when I was fifteen and he was just forty-three. As a nineteen-year-old hitchhiking across Europe, I started to understand what he and men like him had gone through, what the whole world had gone through. I started to understand how privileged I was to grow up in a world without war, to be able to go to university, to grow my hair, to swim in the Med.

I set this story in the autumn, in what always seemed to be one of the darkest parts of Felling, beyond Watermill Lane, not too far from the graveyard at Heworth. There, trees hung heavy and dark over the pavements and verges. We often walked under them to play football on the broad playing field by Swards Road. It was best at dusk, as the stars came out above and frost began to glitter on the grass. **99**

Klaus Vogel & the bad lads

We'd been together for years. We called ourselves the Bad Lads, but it was just a joke. We were mischief-makers, pests and scamps. We never caused proper trouble – not till that autumn, anyway; round about the time we were turning thirteen; round about the time Klaus Vogel came.

The regulars were me; Tonto McKenna from Stivvey Court; Dan Digby; and the Spark twins, Fred and Frank. We all came from Felling and we all went to St John's. Then there was Joe Gillespie. He was a year or so older than the rest of us, and kept himself a bit aloof, but he was the leader, and he was great. His hair was long and curled over his collar. He wore faded Levi's, Chelsea boots, Ben Sherman shirts. He had a girlfriend, Teresa Doyle. He used to walk hand in hand with her through Holly Hill Park. I used to dream about being just like Joe – flicking my hair back with my hand, winking at girls, putting my arm round one of the lads after a specially good stunt, saying, "We done really good, didn't we? We're really bad, aren't we? Ha ha ha!"

All of us, not just me, wanted to be a bit like Joe in those days.

Most days, after school, we took a ball onto the playing field at Swards Road and put two jumpers down for a goal. We played keep-up and penalties, practised diving headers, swerves and traps. We played matches with tiny teams and a single goal, but we still got carried away by it all, just like when we were eight or nine. We called each other Bestie, Pelé, Yashin, and commentated on the moves: "He's beaten one man; he's beaten two! Can he do it? *Yeees!* Oh no! Oh, what a save by the black-clad Russian!" We punched the air when we scored a goal and waved at the invisible roaring crowd. Our voices echoed across the playing field and over the rooftops. Our breath rose in plumes as the air chilled and the evening came on.

We felt ecstatic, transfigured. Then after a while one of us would see Joe coming out from among the houses, and we'd come back down to the real world.

Joe usually had a trick or two of his own lined up, but he always made a point of asking what we fancied doing next.

Tonto might say, "We could play knocky nine door in Balaclava Street."

Or Frank might go, "Jump through the hedges in Coldwell Park Drive?"

But we'd all just groan at things like that. They were little kids' tricks, and we'd done them tons of times before. Sometimes there were new ideas, like the night we howled like ghosts through Mrs Minto's letter box, or when we phoned the police and said an escaped lunatic was chopping up Miss O'Sullivan in her front garden, or when we tied a length of string at head height right across Dunelm Terrace. But usually the best plans turned out to be Joe's. It was his idea, for instance, to put the broken bottles under Mr Tatlock's car tyres, and to dig up the leeks in Albert Finch's allotment. We went along with Joe, but by the time that autumn came, some of his plans were starting to trouble us all.

One evening, when the sky was glowing red over St Patrick's steeple, and when it was obvious that none of us had anything new to suggest, Joe rubbed his hands together and grinned. He had a rolled-up newspaper stuck into his jeans pocket.

"It's a cold night, lads," he said. "How about a bit of a blaze to warm us up?"

"A blaze?" said Tonto.

"Aye." Joe winked. He rattled a box of matches. "Follow me."

He led us up Swards Road and across The Drive and into the narrow lane behind Sycamore Grove. We stopped in the near darkness under a great overgrown privet hedge. Joe told us to be quiet and to gather close.

"Just look at the state of this," he whispered.

He put his hand up into the foliage and shook it. Dust and litter and old dead leaves fell out of it. I scratched at something crawling in my hair.

"Would *your* dads let *your* hedge get into a mess like this?" he said.

"No," we answered.

"No. It's just like he is. Crazy and stupid and wild."

"Like who?" whispered Frank.

"Like him inside!" said Joe. "Like Useless Eustace!"

Mr Eustace. He lived in the house beyond the hedge. No family, hardly any pals. He'd been a teacher for a while but he'd given up. Now he spent most of his time stuck inside writing poems, reading books, listening to weird music.

"We're gonna burn it down," said Joe.

"Eh?" I said.

"The hedge. Burn it down, teach him a lesson."

The hedge loomed above us against the darkening sky.

"Why?"

Joe sighed. "Cos it's a mess and cos we're the Bad Lads. And he deserves it."

He unrolled the newspaper and started shoving pages into the hedge. He handed pages to us as well. "Stuff them low down," he said, "so it'll catch better."

I held back. I imagined the roar of the flames, the belching smoke. "I don't think we should," I found myself saying.

The other lads watched as Joe grabbed my collar and glared into my eyes.

"You think too much," he whispered. "You're a Bad Lad. So *be* a Bad Lad."

He finished shoving the paper in. He got the matches out. "Anyway," he said, "he was a bloody conchie, wasn't he?"

"That was ages back. He was only doing what he believed in."

"He was a coward and a conchie. And like me dad says, once a conchie..."

"Don't do it, Joe."

"You gonna be a conchie too?" he said. "Are you?" He looked at all of us. "Are *any* of you going to be conchies?"

"No," we said.

"Good lads." He put his arm round my shoulder. "Blame me," he whispered. "I'm the leader. You're only following instructions. So do it."

I hated myself, but I shoved my bit of crumpled paper into the hedge with the rest of them.

Conchie. The story came from before any of us were born. Mr Eustace wouldn't fight in the Second World War. He was against all war; he couldn't attack his fellow man. He was a conscientious objector. When my dad and the other lads' dads went off to risk their lives fighting the Germans and the Japanese, Mr Eustace was sent to jail, then let out to work on a farm in Durham.

He'd suffered then; he'd suffered since. My dad said he'd been a decent bloke, but turning conchie had ruined his life. He'd never find peace. He should have left this place and started a new life somewhere else, but he never did.

Joe lit a match and held it to the paper. Flames flickered. They started rising fast. Tonto was already backing away down the lane; Fred and Frank were giggling; Dan had disappeared. I cursed. For a moment, I couldn't move. Then we were all away, running hunched over through the shadows, and the hedge was roaring behind us. By the time we were back at Swards Road, there was a great orange glow over Sycamore Grove, and smoke was belching up towards the stars.

"Now that," said Joe, "is what I call a proper Bad Lads stunt!"

And no matter what we thought inside, all of us shivered with the thrill of it.

Next morning I went back to the lane. It was black and soaking wet from the ash and the hosepipes. The hedge was just a few black twisted stems. Mr Eustace was in the garden talking to a policeman. He kept shrugging, shaking his head. He caught my eye and I wanted to yell out, "You're useless! What did you expect? You should have started a new life somewhere else!"

Joe was nowhere in sight but Fred and Frank were grinning from further down the lane. Neighbours were out, muttering and whispering. None of them suspected anything, of course. They knew us. We were Felling lads. There was no badness in us. Not really.

That was the week Klaus Vogel arrived. He was a scrawny little kid from East Germany. The tale was that his dad was a famous singer who'd been hauled off to a prison camp somewhere in Russia. The mother had disappeared – shot, more than likely, people said. The kid had been smuggled out in the boot of a car. Nobody knew the full truth, said my dad, not when it had happened so far away and in countries like that. Just be happy we lived in a place like this where we could go about as we pleased.

Klaus stayed in the priest's house next to St Patrick's and joined our school, St John's. He didn't have a word of English, but he was bright and he learnt fast. Within a few days he could speak a few English words in a weird Geordie–German accent. Soon he was even writing a few words in English.

We looked at his book one break.

"How the hell do you *do* it?" asked Dan.

Klaus raised his hands. He didn't know how to explain. "I just…" he began, and he scribbled hard and fast. "Like so," he said.

We saw jagged English words mingled with what had to be German.

"What is it?" said Tonto.

"Is story of my *vater*. My father. It must be…" Klaus frowned into the air, seeking the word.

"Must be *told*," I said.

"*Danke*. Thank you." He nodded and his eyes widened. "It must be told. *Ja!* Aye!"

And we all laughed at the way he used the Tyneside word.

After school Klaus talked with his feet. Overhead kicks, sudden body swerves, curling free kicks: the kind of football we could only dream of. He was tiny, clever, tough. We gasped in admiration. When he played, he lost himself in the game, and all his troubles seemed to fall away.

"What'll we call you?" asked Frank.

Klaus frowned. "Klaus Vogel," he said.

"No. Your football name. I'm Pelé. You are…"

Klaus pondered. He glanced around, as if to check who was listening. "Müller," he murmured. "*Ja!* Gerd Müller!"

Then he grinned, twisted, dodged a tackle, swerved the ball into the corner of the invisible net and waved to the invisible crowd. All the lads yelled, "Yeah! Well done, Müller!"

The first time Klaus Vogel met Joe was a few weeks after he'd arrived. Since the hedge-burning, things had gone quiet. Joe spent most of his time with Teresa Doyle. We'd seen him a couple of times, leaning against a fence on Swards Road watching us play, but he hadn't come across. Now here he was, strolling onto the field in the icy November dusk. I moved to Klaus's side.

"He's called Joe," I whispered. "He's OK."

"So this is the famous Klaus Vogel," said Joe.

Klaus shrugged. Joe smiled.

"And your dad's the famous singer, eh? The *op-era* singer."

"Aye."

"Giz a song, then."

"What?" said Klaus.

"He must've taught you, eh? And we like a bit of op-era here, don't we, lads? Go on, giz a song." Joe demonstrated. He opened his mouth wide and stretched his hand out like he was singing to an audience. "Go on. You're in a free country now, you know. Sing up!"

Klaus stared at him. I wanted to say, "Don't do it," but Klaus had stepped away, closer to Joe. He took a deep breath and started to sing. His voice rang out across the field. It was weird, like the music that drifted from Mr Eustace's house. We heard the loveliness in it. How could he *do* such things?

But Joe was bent over, struggling with laughter, and then he was waving his hands to bring Klaus to a halt.

Klaus stopped, stared again. "You do not like?" he asked.

Joe wiped the tears of laughter from his eyes. "Aye, aye," he said. "It's brilliant, son."

Then Joe opened his own mouth and started singing, a wobbly high-pitched imitation of Klaus. He looked at us and we all started to laugh with him.

"Mebbe we're just not ready for it, eh, lads?"

"Mebbe we're not," muttered Frank, turning his eyes away.

Klaus looked at us too. Then he just shrugged again. "So. I will go home," he said.

"No," said Joe. "You can't."

"Can't?"

"We can't let you." He grinned. He winked. "We got to initiate him, haven't we, lads? We got to make him one of the Bad Lads." He showed his teeth like he was a great beast, then he smiled. "'Specially when you consider where he comes from, eh?"

"What you mean?" asked Klaus.

"From *Germany*," said Joe. "Not so long ago we'd have been wanting to kill you. You'd've been wanting to kill us."

He raised his hand like he had a gun in it and pointed it at Klaus. He pulled an imaginary trigger. Then he smiled. "It's nowt, son," he said. "Just some carry-on. What'll it be, lads? Knocky nine door in Balaclava Street? Jumping through hedges in Coldwell Park Drive?"

"The hedges," I said. I put my hand on Klaus's

shoulder. "It's OK," I whispered. "We're just messing about. And it's on your way home."

So Klaus came with us. We cut through the lanes to Coldwell Park Drive and slipped into the gardens behind, then Joe led us and we charged over the back lawns and through the hedges while dogs howled and people yelled at us to cut it out. We streamed out, giggling, onto Felling Bank. Joe held us in a quick huddle and said it was just like the old days. He put his arm round Klaus.

"Ha!" he said. "You're a proper Bad Lad now, Herr Vogel. You're one of us!"

Then we started running our separate ways through the shadows.

Klaus caught my arm. "Why?" he said.

"Why what?"

"Why we do *that*? Why we do what Joe says?"

"It's not like that," I said. I paused. "It's..." But my voice felt all caught up inside me, like it couldn't find words.

"Is *what*?" said Klaus.

He held me like he really wanted to understand. But I had no answers. Klaus shrugged his shoulders, shook his head, walked away.

★   ★   ★

Klaus kept away from the Bad Lads for a while. He scribbled in his book, writing his story. He sang out loud in music lessons. He dazzled everyone with his football skills during games. There were rumours that the body of his mother had turned up. The whole school prayed for the liberation of East Germany, for the conversion of Russia, for Klaus Vogel and his family.

One day after school I came upon him walking under the trees on Watermill Lane. He walked quickly, swinging his arms, singing softly.

"Klaus!" I said. "What you doing?"

"I am being free!" he said. "My father said that one day I would walk as a free man. I would walk and sing and show the world that I am free. So I do it. Look!"

He strode in circles, swinging his arms again.

"Do I look like I am free?" he said.

"Yes," I laughed. "Of course you do."

He laughed too. "Ha! As I walk I think of him in his cell. I think of her."

"They would be proud of you," I said.

"Would they?"

"Yes."

He laughed again, a bitter laugh. "And as I walk

I think of my friends here," he said. "I think of you;
I think of Joe."

"Of Joe?"

"*Ja!* Him!"

"You think too much, Klaus. Come and play
football, will you? Come and be Gerd Müller."

And he sighed and shrugged. OK.

It was getting dark. Frost already glistened on the field.
The stars were like a field of vivid frost above. Klaus
played with more brilliance and passion than ever. We
watched him in wonder. He ran with the ball at his
feet; he flicked it into the goal; he leapt with joy; he
danced to the crowd.

Then Joe was there, his footsteps crackling across
the grass. He had a small rucksack on his back.

"Herr Vogel," he said. "Nice to see you again."

He stepped closer and put his arm round Klaus's
shoulder. "Sorry to hear about…" He held up his hand,
as if to restrain his own words. "Our thoughts are with
you, son."

He turned to the rest of us. "Now, lads. It's a fine
night for a Bad Lads stunt."

You could tell it was almost over with us and Joe.

We gathered around him reluctantly; our smiles were forced when he told us he had the perfect trick. But he was tall and strong. He smelt of aftershave; he wore a black Ben Sherman, black jeans, black Chelsea boots. We hadn't broken free of him. He drew us into a huddle. He smiled and told us we'd always been the Bad Lads and we'd keep on being the Bad Lads, wouldn't we?

No one said no. No one objected when he told us to follow. I think I hesitated for a moment, but Klaus came to my side and whispered, "You will not go? But you must. We must all follow our leader, mustn't we?"

And Klaus stepped ahead, and I followed.

Joe led us to The Drive, towards the lane behind Sycamore Grove.

"Not again," I sighed.

"It's like me dad says," said Joe. "He should've been drove out years back." He turned to Klaus. "It's local stuff, son. Probably your lot had better ways of dealing with the Eustaces than we ever had."

Klaus just shrugged.

"Anyway, lads. It's just a bit of fun this time." He opened his rucksack, took out a box of eggs. "Here, one each. Hit a window for a hundred points."

A couple of the lads giggled. They took their eggs. Joe held the box out to me. I hesitated. Klaus took one and looked at me. So I took an egg and held it in my hand.

Joe smiled and patted Klaus's shoulder. "Good Bad Lad, Herr Vogel," he murmured.

Klaus laughed his bitter laugh again. *"Nein,"* he said. "I am not a good Bad Lad. I am Klaus Vogel."

He stepped towards Joe.

"No, Klaus," I muttered. I tried to hold him back but he stepped right up to Joe.

"I do not like you," he said. "I do not like the things you make others do."

"Oh! You *do not like*?" said Joe.

"Nein."

Joe laughed. He mocked the word – *"Nein! Nein! Nein!"* – as he stamped the earth and gave a Nazi salute. He grabbed Klaus by the collar, but Klaus didn't recoil.

"You could crush me in a moment," he said. "But I am not ... *ängstlich*."

"Frightened," I said.

"Ja! I am not frightened. *Ich bin frei!"*

"Ha! *Frei. Frei.*"

"He is free," I said. And in that moment, I knew that he *was* free, despite his father's imprisonment, despite his mother's death, despite Joe's fist gripping his collar. He had said no. He was free.

Joe snarled and drew his fist back. I found myself reaching out. I caught the fist in mid-air.

"No," I said. "You can't do that."

"What?"

"I said no!"

Joe thumped us both that night, in the lane behind Mr Eustace's house. We fought back, but he was tall and strong and there was little we could do against his savagery. Tonto and the others had disappeared. Afterwards I walked home with Klaus through the frosty starlit night. We were sore and we had blood on our faces, but soon we were swinging our arms.

"Do I look like I am free?" I said.

Klaus laughed. *"Ja!* Yes! Aye!"

And he began to sing and I tried to join in.

A couple of days later he came with me to Mr Eustace's house. I knocked at the door and Mr Eustace opened it.

"I burned down your hedge," I said.

He peered at me. "Did you now?" he said.

I chewed my lips. Music was playing. Beyond Mr Eustace the hallway was lined with books.

"I'm sorry," I said. "I was wrong."

"Yes, you were."

I felt so clumsy, so stupid.

"This is Klaus Vogel," I said. "He is a writer, a footballer, a singer."

"Then he is a civilized man. Perhaps you can learn from him."

I nodded. I was about to turn and lead Klaus away, but Mr Eustace said, "Why don't you come inside?"

We followed him in. There were books everywhere. In the living room was an open notebook on a desk with an uncapped fountain pen lying upon it. The writing in the book was in the shape of poetry.

Mr Eustace stood at the window and indicated the ruined hedge outside. "Is that how you wish the world to be?" he asked me.

"No," I answered.

"No."

He made us tea. There were fig rolls and little cakes. He spoke a few words to Klaus in German, and Klaus gasped with pleasure. Then Mr Eustace put another record on. Opera. High sweet voices flowing together and filling the house with their sound.

"Mozart!" said Klaus.

"Yes."

Klaus joined in. His voice rang out. Mr Eustace closed his eyes and smiled.

Me as a kid on the new council estate

also by David Almond